Men's Intrusion, Women's Embodiment

Research on violence against women tends to focus on topics such as sexual assault and intimate partner violence, arguably to the detriment of investigating men's violence and intrusion in women's everyday lives. The reality and possibility of the routine intrusions women experience from men in public space – from unwanted comments, to flashing, following and frottage – are frequently unaddressed in research, as well as in theoretical and policy-based responses to violence against women. Often at their height during women's adolescence, such practices are commonly dismissed as trivial, relatively harmless expressions of free speech too subjective to be legislated against.

Based on original empirical research, this book is the first of its kind to conduct a feminist phenomenological analysis of the experience for women of men's stranger intrusions in public spaces. It suggests that intrusion from unknown men is a fundamental factor in how women understand and enact their embodied selfhood.

This book is essential reading for academics and students involved in the study of violence against women, feminist philosophy, applied sociology, feminist criminology and gender studies.

F. Vera-Gray is a Research Fellow in the Law School at Durham University, UK, interested in drawing together feminist phenomenological conceptual approaches and empirical research on violence against women and girls.

Routledge Research in Gender and Society

Men's Intrusion, Women's Embodiment

A critical analysis of street harassment

F. Vera-Gray

Routledge
Taylor & Francis Group

LONDON AND NEW YORK

First published 2017
by Routledge

2 Park Square, Milton Park, Abingdon, Oxfordshire OX14 4RN
711 Third Avenue, New York, NY 10017

Routledge is an imprint of the Taylor & Francis Group, an informa business

First issued in paperback 2018

British Library Cataloguing in Publication Data
A catalogue record for this book is available from the British Library

Library of Congress Cataloging in Publication Data
Names: Vera-Gray, F., author.
Title: Men's intrusion, women's embodiment : a critical analysis of street
harassment / F. Vera-Gray.
Description: New York : Routledge, 2016. | Series: Routledge research in
gender and society
Identifiers: LCCN 2016004645| ISBN 9781138951594 (hardback) |
ISBN 9781315668109 (e-book)
Subjects: LCSH: Sexual harassment of women. | Public safety. | Public
spaces–Social aspects.
Classification: LCC HQ1237 .V467 2016 | DDC 305.42–dc23
LC record available at http://lccn.loc.gov/2016004645

ISBN: 978-1-138-95159-4 (hbk)
ISBN: 978-1-138-36032-7 (pbk)

Typeset in Times New Roman
by Wearset Ltd, Boldon, Tyne and Wear

For my brother,
who would argue with everything in here.

I miss you.

Contents

Illustrations

Figures

Tables

Foreword

There is little more exciting and rewarding than participating in the process of a young feminist scholar pursuing their ideas and dreams. For Fiona Vera-Gray this was to connect two passions: philosophy and sexual violence. She was one of the first graduates of the Child and Woman Abuse Studies Unit's MA at London Metropolitan University: the kind of student that you feel privileged to have in a class, who thinks clearly and fast, draws on practice based knowledge and pushes everyone to further insights and clarifications. I still use the concept she developed in her MA dissertation: describing Rape Crisis Centres as a location for a Whole Place Self. This encapsulates a philosophical approach which positions women as more than what they have endured and survived: that their past, present and potential futures are not determined, albeit changed, by violence and abuse. It is this radical feminist perspective, that women's lives and selves are changed in complex ways by coping with the threat and reality of violence, which formed the foundation of the PhD on which this book is based.

It was a pleasure to supervise her, to travel the process of refining a question and methodological approach, data collection and analysis with a woman who seeks to go deeper, to explore issues in new and revealing ways. One of the specific pleasures has been the ways in which Fiona has drawn on and developed concepts from my work and thinking, some of which I have neglected to write up for publication, but have become key ideas I use in teaching.

The core concept in my PhD was that sexual violence (now probably expressed as men's violence against women) was a continuum, that there was a connection between the mundane everyday intimate intrusions most women and girls experience and the forms of abuse which are considered crimes and worthy of legal intervention. One aspect of the continuum explored in *Surviving Sexual Violence* was the links between sexual harassment, sexual assault and rape. This book takes that analysis much further, and in the process creates a new concept – men's intrusions in public space. By centring women's accounts as the fulcrum for analysis it becomes clear that some intrusions are not sexual or sexualised, and are difficult to name as harassment. Nonetheless women know that something is happening in the interaction that draws on, and attempts to reproduce, gender power relations: men feel entitled to women's attention and this permits them to intrude on our being in the world. We learn this early in our lives, along-side the threat and reality of men's violence.

We have become used to commentary on how women change their behaviour in order to control what can seem like an unavoidable risk, but women's calcula-tions and actions are more complex than mere self-limitation. I have termed the thinking processes, decision making and embodied watchfulness that women employ 'safety work'. It is work because it occupies time, requires energy and effort – all of which could be used for more rewarding activities. As this book demonstrates safety work can become an automatic reflex, especially when in public space alone as a woman: so automatic that we no longer notice the strat-egies that we use in our attempts to limit or avoid intrusions. The feminist research process of this research encouraged women to notice, to make visible what had been hidden, revealing a creative and varied set of strategies and that some women on some days choose to explicitly challenge the limitations.

For women who have experienced violence and abuse there is an additional layer of 'violence work': the time and energy they invest in making sense of what happened and what it means, dealing with an aftermath that spans a life-time. One of the reasons I dislike the concepts of 'recovery' and 'healing' is that they underplay the ways in which one's life and sense of self are changed, and continue to be changed, by the legacies of violence and abuse. There is no 'return to normal', no way to rub out the many consequences of having had control over your body and mind wrested away. One of the poignant things many survivors say is that their abuser rarely pays a price but they feel that they have a life sentence: sentenced to doing violence work as the resonances and implications shift over the time and sometimes space. What this book reveals is that women with histories of abuse often have to do both either simultaneously or in sequence as they explore their responses to everyday intrusions. They understand the concept of the continuum through their lived experiences.

The innovative use of Simone de Beauvoir as a theoretical lodestone adds an important new layer of theory to perspectives on violence against women, and some of the findings in the chapters that follow will intrigue and possibly even surprise readers. This book is, in multiple ways, an important contribution to feminist scholarship on violence, abuse and to understanding what we need to change in order to achieve women's liberation.

Liz Kelly
January 2016

He came up to me and was like my mate wants to lick you out.
It just makes you feel like you're doing something wrong.

Preface

This book will not be an easy read. Threaded through the text is a poetic transcript shaped from the words of the 50 women who participated in a research project on men's stranger intrusions in public space.

This transcript was created through extracting every particular intrusive encounter that women recalled in the research conversations, and every time women gave a general comment about the way they responded. The list of both particular encounters and general responses was then randomised and the poem constructed through interlacing men's practices and women's responses. The words of the women participating were not edited or altered in any way – each sentence in the poem is verbatim and every specific encounter and general response is represented.

The resulting piece is a hybrid poem in 50 voices. It is difficult, overwhelming, shocking, never-ending, repetitive, exhausting – capturing some of the phenomenological texture of being a woman in public. This representation can only ever be partial; I make no claims for a universalised experience. What I wanted was a way to connect women's voices across their commonalities without collapsing the ways in which every particular woman experiences men's violence differently based on social and personal locations and histories. A way of recreating for the reader something of the way the experience is lived; that sudden feeling of being pulled outside of yourself, without wanting, without warning. Interrupted, disrupted. Intrusion.

To the reader who has never had these experiences I ask you to bear witness. To the routine and the shocking. The repetition, exhaustion. To the seemingly never-ending mundaneness of it all.

And to those who've had many, in the past and the present, I hope you find some validation here, as I did throughout this process.

For what we experience is not trivial and how we respond is not accidental.

You need to find a version of the world you can be in.

Acknowledgements

My unbounded gratitude and respect for every woman who spoke to me about her experiences of men's intrusion – both formally and in passing. I hope I've done justice to what you shared.

My thanks and admiration to the women who shared this journey with me, Ava, Jo, Karin and Maria in particular. Without you I wouldn't have developed as much, or laughed as hard.

Thanks to Jonathan Webber and the participants at the Beauvoir workshop of the Rethinking Existentialism project at Cardiff University, in November 2015. You had perfect timing. To Stevi Jackson and Susan J. Brison, both of whom read and helped with earlier versions, to Heidi and Emily at Routledge for their guidance and support, and to Nicole Westmarland for making it happen.

To Holly, Liz and Maddy, all of whom have inspired me for years. Thank you for your work, your comments and your kindness. I feel lucky to have you in my life.

And finally for the patience and care of the people I love on both sides of the world, and the one in my home. Thank you.

He started talking to me more like saying oh where are you going?
My thing has been to physically remove myself, not to confront.
He followed me literally all the way home.
I just don't see them, my eyes glaze over.

He was shouting at me and whistling at me saying sexy thing
and all of this
and I was 13.

He got off and he called me a tranny and a minger.
I don't know yeah I try to brush it off.
He's definitely having a wank, he's definitely doing it. In Morrisons.
I built up such a barrier.
He just had his hand there on my chest.
It's easier just to get off.
He snapped a picture and then walked back out,
he didn't run, he just walked back out
really casual as if he'd just strolled in.
And then he pointed out to me his massive erection.
I'll tuck my hair into my hat.
I had this big long fringe and he made some comment
about that must get in the way
when you're giving blowjobs.
He leaned over and asked if he could take my photograph.
I try not to sit next to a man.

He bit my neck and he had his hand on my left breast
and he squeezed my breast really hard.
He hit me.

A couple of guys as I was walking were like hey babe.
I'll wear jeans just because it's safer.
Oi bitch, oi slag, get your tits out you slag.
I always walk with purpose.
The other guy waiting there goes oh cheer up love.
I want to talk back but you're taking that risk.
Oi you come over here, sit on my face.
His trousers around his ankles
just jerking off.

                              He slapped me across the face.
                              He said can I come on your tits.
             He was pushing the gate trying to get through and screaming.
                         It's easier to pretend I don't hear anything.

1 Introduction

The knowledge base that has been built since the explosion in feminist consciousness-raising, research, theory and practice on violence against women during feminism's second-wave, illustrates vast contributions to the project of defining the world from women's phenomenological position. The urgency of developing frameworks that could be translated into the language of law and policy however, has resulted in an increasing disconnection from the initial calls to articulate women's everyday experience. The reality and possibility of the routine intrusions women experience from men in public space, from the ubiquitous 'smile or cheer up' to flashing, following and frottage, remain mostly unaddressed in current research as well as in theoretical and policy-based responses to violence against women and girls. Often at their height during women's adolescence, such practices are frequently dismissed as harmless expressions of free speech, too subjective to be legislated against: the claim one woman's harassment may be another woman's compliment. At worst such experiences are understood as a part of what psychologist Richard Lazarus (1984) has termed 'daily hassles', low-level stressful experiences that irrespective of their potential for negative health and adaptive impacts, are an unavoidable part of life.

It is remarkable then, that in the face of such trivialisation, men's stranger intrusions on women in public have become a point of mobilisation for modern feminist movements; unifying feminist perspectives that may diverge in discussions of pornography or prostitution. Responding to the existence of significant legal barriers to prosecution globally,[1] social media has been harnessed as a tool to share experiences of what is commonly termed 'street harassment' as well as to support and validate women's experiential realities. Established by Emily May in 2005, the non-profit Hollaback! movement currently has chapters in 84 cities and 31 countries, whilst another American based site 'Stop Street Harassment' has developed as a resource hub for research and prevention work on street harassment, as well as an online blog space (Kearl, 2010). In 2012, a website and Twitter account created in England to record experiences of 'everyday sexism' quickly went global, spreading to over 15 countries and collecting more than 50,000 entries within just 18 months (Bates, 2014). In India, the 2011 publication of a study on women's safety and freedom in Mumbai's public spaces has begun a movement of women 'loitering' as a political and social statement across several Indian cities (Phadke, Khan & Khan, 2011). Alongside this, the accessibility of the internet in public space has been seized upon to provide an avenue for immediate active response to intrusion whilst avoiding the potential for escalation perceived in responding to the perpetrator. As such, smartphone applications have been developed to map harassment, including in India (Fightback)[2], Egypt (Harassmap)[3] and worldwide through Hollaback!'s iPhone application.[4]

The popularity of online spaces to record this particular form of men's violence when not used as frequently for other forms, may stem in part from contextual factors inherent in the encounter itself. It may be that such experiences singularly lend themselves to online sharing due to their occurrence in public space – thus bearing a public nature – and to some of the same reasons problematising effective legislation: the inability to conclusively identify the perpetrator or the difficulty in validating one's own experience. Despite the increase in visibility of men's intrusion, due in no small part to this rise of online sharing, there are still large gaps in knowledge on the more mundane examples of men's intrusive practices, their frequency, content and, importantly, *meaning*. The spread of community-based activism has helped direct attention to the existence of an international problem in need of both an expanding evidence base and new perspectives for understanding the experiential realities for women of both victimisation and survival. This book answers such a call, carving a space where the experience of men's intrusion is not discounted due to its regularity, nor the impact denied due to the multiple and complex ways women habituate ourselves to it. At its core is an analysis of 50 women's accounts of their experiences, both those given on reflection and those recorded on the street, alongside the development of a theoretical framework that participates in the current reclamation of unique philosophical insights of Simone de Beauvoir, drawing together phenomenological analysis and empirical social research.

Bringing back Beauvoir

One of the central claims here is that Simone de Beauvoir's work to develop what Sara Heinämaa (2003) terms 'a phenomenology of sexual difference' offers unexplored conceptual tools for speaking about connections and commonality, without collapsing the diverse ways in which women live men's violence based on social and personal histories. Beauvoir can be drawn on to help us build theory across forms of violence against women and girls, linking questions of agency and autonomy to a context of structural power relations, and reconnecting feminist research on men's violence to what is routine in women's lives. Her unique development of the concepts of situation and ambiguity offers a compelling philosophical frame through which to explore the impact of men's violence on women's sense of self. Mobilising her conceptualisation of the self as a situated freedom expressing the ambiguity of existence, enables a balancing of complexity, difference and commonality in a similar way to one of the foundational frames used in current studies of violence against women: Liz Kelly's (1988) continuum of sexual violence. Despite acknowledgement of the importance of *The Second Sex* for the feminist movement in France and, following the English translation, across both America and England, Beauvoir's philosophical contributions have traditionally been subsumed under that of Jean-Paul Sartre's, and her insights on women largely relegated to feminism's history. A resurgence in Beauvoirian scholarship in the past 30 years, however, seeks to reclaim her unique philosophical contribution, a contribution Beauvoir herself repeatedly denied.[5] Margaret A. Simons has written extensively on the problematic positioning Beauvoir herself made of her work, most often claiming her writing as simply exercises in Sartrean ontology (see Simons, 2010). Simons argues that on closer examination – and particularly in light of her posthumously published texts – Beauvoir's insights are startlingly original and that her work deserves its own position in the philosophical canon.[6] It is in her development of – and departures from – her colleagues that Beauvoir has considerable potential for feminist research, theory and practice on issues of violence against women and girls. Her notable departures here are from Sartre in her vision of the self as situated freedom and her development of a Merleau-Pontian view of the self as an embodied body-subject, the 'bodily-self'.

Parallel to this renewed interest in Beauvoir, there is what has been described as a 'chronic need in contemporary feminist debates to theorise responsible female agency' (Stavro, 2000: 133), particularly in regards to women's embodied agency. Shelly Budgeon (2003) critiques the way in which analyses of female embodiment often figure women as passive objects of representation rather than subjects acting on, in and through the body. Abigail Bray and Claire Colebrook (1998) advance a similar critique in their argument for a positive feminist ethics, foregrounding how the Cartesian mind/body dualism haunts much corporeal feminism. For Budgeon, Bray and Colebrook, approaches that focus on the body as a site of representation – and that posit such representation as a negation of materiality – hide the ways in which we live our bodies as an ambiguous blend of both, situated within a whole series of events, connections and contexts. Such a claim is comparable to the binary set up in the early 1990s between 'victim' and 'power' feminism, where the former was criticised as constructing women as lacking agency (Wolf, 1993; Paglia, 1994; Roiphe, 1994) and the latter as failing to acknowledge the complex and problematic relationship between feminists and power (Kelly, Burton & Regan, 1996). This tension is growing again in some modern feminist debates where the focus for some feminists on the contexts in which women are making choices is held by others as negating women's ability to choose. Such contestations demonstrate the need to find an accessible conceptualisation of women's agency that can also hold the multifaceted and complex ways in which structural oppression impacts, conflicts, points to and limits choice and action.

It is here that revisiting Beauvoir's work offers particular possibilities for mobilising what Lois McNay (2004) terms a 'reworked phenomenology' – moving away from the idea of a pure phenomenology with its assumed universality and

belief in a detached observer. Beauvoir develops a form of feminist phenomenology, an expression of individual experience mobilised for the social and political purpose of taking stock of women's situation under patriarchy – articulating
rather than abstracting from shared social and material realities. Her work provides a framework for theorising corporeality that foregrounds the temporality of
human 'being' and 'becoming', alongside refusing to resolve the tensions of
living experience.[7] This ability to maintain ambiguity is central to Beauvoir's
unique contribution and creates an interesting space for work on modalities of
female embodiment,[8] though much corporeal feminist analysis has instead built
on the work of male philosophers such as Gilles Deleuze (1994) and Maurice
Merleau-Ponty (2002).[9] Focusing particularly on the development given in the
second volume of *The Second Sex*, Beauvoir's insights into the self as a situated
body-subject offer a useful philosophical paradigm for exploring women's living
experience of Kelly's (1988) continuum of sexual violence. Despite this, her text
can be dismissed as too impenetrable in its language and too dated in its representations of the lives of women. The former criticism is a result both of Beauvoir's philosophical training, meaning she employed language and concepts
rooted in particular linguistic histories, and, for English readers, an effect of the
many recorded problems with original translation of the text.[10] Whilst the desire
to translate philosophical concepts into accessible language (and a lived experience) led Beauvoir and many of her colleagues to write fictive philosophy,[11] *The
Second Sex* remains a dense and thoroughly philosophical text. The second criticism, that the situation Beauvoir was outlining is no longer representative of the
lives of women in the twenty-first century, is sadly too optimistic when applied
to routine experiences of men's violence. It is true that in the post-war years
when Beauvoir was writing, the situation of many women was remarkably different; this has not happened by chance but rather by the over 50 years of committed feminist activism and political reform, some of which was ushered in by
the publication of her book. Her discussions of the situations of the mother or
the housewife may not resonate with feminism's fourth wave, and her examination of the circumstances limiting women's freedom may have deepened with
the benefit of Crenshaw's (1989) work on intersectionality, however there is a
key meeting point between the situation Beauvoir was outlining and that of
many of the 50 women who participated in this research project: the impact of
men's stranger intrusions on women in public.

> If they wander the streets, they are stared at, accosted. I know some girls,
> far from shy, who get no enjoyment strolling through Paris alone because,
> incessantly bothered, they are incessantly on their guard: all their pleasure is
> ruined.
>
> (Beauvoir, 2011: 358)

The resonance of this with the closing comments of one of this project's participants, 20-year-old Lucy,[12] shows that in terms of the living experience of
men's intrusion, little has changed in the intervening years.

One of my friends the other day said, 'I love walking home through [city] at night.' I had to walk back from work because a friend couldn't give me a lift, at one o'clock in the morning. And he was like, 'oh that's fine. It's nice to look at the river.' And it might be nice to look at the river if I wasn't pet- rified the whole time. I'm not going to stop and look at the river because I need to get back quickly so I don't get raped.

(Lucy)

Men's intrusive practices as a context situating women's freedom remains, and yet it is a context rarely examined. Over half a century later and there is a notable lack of evidence on the range and extent of men's intrusion in public. Women's stories are shared online and with each other at a rate never seen before, but still there is a gap in being able to articulate what experiencing this range of intrusive practices feels like – its phenomenological texture.

The problem of naming

Currently, empirical studies on the range of men's intrusion experienced by women in public spaces, its prevalence, manifestations and harms, and the mean- ings it holds for both the men who practice it and the women who experience it, is a small body of work. The existing literature is cross-disciplinary, from socio- logical and legal studies exploring frequencies and remedies, to psychological perspectives examining impact and harm. Feminist approaches to the phenom- enon are varied, but all argue that far from being insignificant, the experience of intrusion from unknown men in public is a routine manifestation of the contin- uum of sexual violence (Kelly, 1988), and plays a substantial role in generating and regenerating Connell's (2002) 'gender orders'; the historically constructed patterns of power relations between women and men. Across this body of liter- ature there is a gap in detailed explorations from an explicitly philosophical standpoint, with Sandra Lee Bartky's (1990) brief exploration of the experience of catcalls and whistles in her philosophical essay on psychological oppression a notable exception. The sparse academic treatment is acknowledged by many writers working in this area (Kissling, 1991; Bowman, 1993; Tuerkheimer, 1997), seen as the result of how trivialisation and commonality combine to render the experience invisible as a social problem.[13] In addition, the difficulty of naming deserves a central space in discussions of the relative silence given the expansion in the knowledge base on other forms of men's violence against women.

The lack of agreement on what constitutes the phenomenon, the harm it causes and how to define it renders comparison between studies complicated and also presents problems for survey methodologies. Separating particular intrusive practices into distinct categories does not represent the ways in which these prac- tices are lived and risks normalising practices that are excluded from question construction. Combined with this, the mechanisms of minimisation meet with definitional and experiential ambiguity around 'what counts', to render precise measurement difficult. Studies focused on women's experiences of 'street harassment', for example may miss experiences women do not define as harassing or that occur in off-street public places such as public transport, public buildings such as libraries, or – an area with growing recognition – the public space of the internet. As Beauvoir's 'inessential Other', women's experience does not appear 'as the source of an authoritative general expression of the world' (Smith, 1987: 51), thus social phenomena that are experienced by women in different ways than men struggle for articulation. Evidence for this claim is found in the contradictory language often used in reference to forms of violence overwhelming targeted at women. Where the same event is experienced differently by men and women, existing discursive framings mean that women are obliged to acknowledge the meanings men attach to the experience as well as to describe it from a women's phenomenological standpoint.[14] There are also difficulties in how the qualifier 'unwanted' is common across different studies in this area. This presents an unasked question about what counts as unwanted or unwelcome in a gender order where many women are socialised to expect and even to desire evaluative sexual attention from unknown men. The assumptions underlying the use of the terms 'unwanted' or 'unwelcome' are that intrusive practices that are not experienced in this way are unproblematic or at least do not 'count'. It moves focus away from the practices of men, who in practicing intrusion are unaware of whether particular practices are wanted by individual women. Their motivations are left unexamined, as is the possibility of negative impact for the women who may experience such intrusions as wanted or desired. It also decontextualises how women make sense of men's intrusion based on both wider social messages and previous histories of intrusion and men's violence. From this follows a further question about what or who is being missed in the prevalence literature, and what they would reveal of the range and extent of men's intrusion. When 'unwanted' excludes the experiences of women who experience particular practices – such as verbal intrusions or the gaze – as complimentary, the ability to explore if there is a difference in practice or impact for experiences that are lived as desired is closed off.

Counting the continuum

With an understanding of how the terminology used has a powerful impact on who responds and whether they see their experiences reflected in the questions asked, several prominent studies have attempted to measure the frequency with which women and girls experience intrusion from unknown men in public space. All, notably, are based in the Global North. Carol Brooks Gardner's 1995 study, based on extensive research including in-depth interviews with nearly 500 women and men, is still cited as one of the most influential. With a methodology that did not rely solely on survey research, combined with her broad category of 'public space harassment', Gardner finds the phenomenon extremely common: all of the 293 women in her study reported experiencing some form of public harassment, and all but nine regarded it as 'troublesome'. This high prevalence finding was replicated in an American study based on a nationally representative telephone survey of 612 adult women conducted in 2000. The poll found almost 87 per cent of women in America between the ages of 18 and 64 had experienced some form of harassment on the street by an unknown man at some time in their life (see Oxygen/Markle Pulse, 2000). Canadian findings correlate with this American data. A large survey of 1,990 Canadian women conducted in 1992 was used as the basis for Lenton, Smith, Fox and Morra's (1999) study on what they termed 'public harassment'. The study critiques previous feminist analyses based on 'personal experience, case studies, and in-depth interviews' such as Gardner (1995), Kelly (1988), Stanko (1990) and Wise and Stanley (1987) – authors most concerned with representing women's lived experiences – by claiming that these studies are devalued through their lack of generalisability. This illustrates the motivations of many attempts to measure the practice, as seeking evidence in order to feed into legal and policy frameworks rather than to accurately reflect the experience of such encounters.

Nearly 81 per cent of the women surveyed in the Lenton *et al.* (1999) study reported having been stared at in a way that made them feel uncomfortable one or more times since the age of 16; 28 per cent had experienced 'indecent exposure'; and over 22 per cent indicated that they had experienced 'other' types of unwanted harassment. Only 9 per cent of women surveyed reported that they could not remember experiencing any form of unwanted attention from a man in public. MacMillan, Nierobisz and Welsh (2000) analysed telephone interviews of a national sample of 12,300 Canadian women, aged 18 years and over living in 10 provinces. The study remains one of the largest samples to date focused solely on this phenomenon, and it attempted to measure the impact of stranger harassment on perceived safety. The vast majority (85 per cent) of the women surveyed had experienced 'male stranger harassment in public' and those experiences had a significant and detrimental impact on perceived safety in public. The study thus substantially backs up the claim that experiences of 'street harassment' may explain the 'crime paradox' – where research has consistently found that women fear violence in public spaces more than men yet their risk of victimisation by strangers, at least as measured by crime statistics, is far lower (see for example Warr, 1984). The authors make a strong case for the inclusion of what they term 'stranger harassment' in research on sexual harassment, identifying that the conditions normally considered key in facilitating sexual harassment, being sociocultural, institutional and traditional gender role socialisation, may need to expand to include criminological concerns such as opportunity and guardianship. The study, however, does not include experiences of non-sexualised intrusions, such as interruptions, insults or comments on women's demeanour.

Moving to a cultural context closer to that lived in by most of the participants in this study, a poll conducted by the End Violence Against Women Coalition (EVAW, 2012) continues this labelling of the experience as unwanted and also the framing of sexual harassment. It asked women who live in London about their experiences of unwanted contact or attention of a sexual nature in public spaces and on public transport over the last year, giving the examples of wolf-whistling, sexual comments, staring and exposure. The findings drawn from 523 women, demonstrate the impact of generational differences: 41 per cent of women aged 18–34 had experienced unwanted sexual attention in public spaces compared to 21 per cent of all women surveyed. They also found high levels of unwanted sexual attention on public transport, particularly for women aged 18–24 (with 31 per cent reporting experiences), reflecting both generational differences in terms of what is lived as 'harassment' and also perhaps who is more likely to regularly use public transportation. These findings sit alongside that of one of the only other England specific surveys (Crawford, Jones, Woodhouse & Young, 1990), which found that approximately 40 per cent of women in Islington, North London, reported having been harassed (defined as being stared at, approached, followed or spoken to) during the survey year. The findings of women's experiences over the past 12 months measured by these English studies are thus expectedly lower than the North American studies measuring women's experiences since the age of 16. In addition, the difference in cultural contexts may also impact on findings, contexts that are operating to set Goffman's (1990) unspoken rules of engagement between people in public places, or Connell's (2002) gender relations.

In 2014, the European Union Agency for Fundamental Rights (FRA) published the results of an EU-wide survey of violence against women, based on interviews with 42,000 women across the 28 member states of the European Union (FRA, 2014). It is difficult to draw directly from this survey for the phenomenon under investigation here, as sexual and physical violence was separated out from behaviours such as 'inappropriate staring' or 'unwelcome touching, hugging or kissing', with information on the setting of the act given for the former but not the latter.[15] Broadly, however, the survey found that almost a quarter (22 per cent) of the women surveyed had experienced physical or sexual violence from a non-partner, with 31 per cent of this physical violence being perpetrated by a stranger and 23 per cent being sexual violence perpetrated by a stranger. For this non-partner violence, 20 per cent occurred in public environments, such as out in the street, a car park or other public area. In addition, the survey asked specific questions about sexual harassment, finding just over half (*n*=21,180) of the women surveyed had experienced sexual harassment at least once in their life. In most cases since they were 15 years old, the perpetrator was an unknown person (68 per cent), with the most common forms being indecent exposure (83 per cent of women experiencing indecent exposure indicating the perpetrator was unknown) and cyber-harassment (73 per cent indicating an unknown perpetrator). Questions about the location of sexual harassment were not asked and, in addition, the framings used were again those of only measuring intrusions experienced as unwelcome or offensive. The findings on cyber-harassment are particularly interesting as the rise of Internet accessibility has meant that it is a rapidly growing public space arena for men to practice intrusion – again suggesting it may be time to review the labels applied to the phenomenon; to fully consider the benefits and limitations of the terminology of 'street harassment'.

Men's stranger intrusion: a phenomenological framing

There are limitations with the most commonly used framing of 'street harassment', though it must be noted even this term is not used consistently. The different practices included across the literature evidences how little work has been done to ask women themselves how they define their experiences.[16] It is rare for an explicit, self-reflective examination to be conducted explaining an authors' choice of terminology, its benefits and limitations, and recognition of any impact this may have had on their findings. Within the legal literature, which dominates attempts to define the practices, there is a reliance on binaries, either something is 'street harassment' or it is not. Liz Kelly's (1988) concept of a continuum, however, enables the maintenance of the ways in which experiences of the routine and mundane operations of the gender order can be lived as ambiguous, defined differently both between women and also by the same woman across different contexts. This reveals a tension between providing a framework that can be used and understood by individuals as reflecting lived realities, and providing one that can be operationalised easily in legal and policy contexts. It may be that this tension cannot be reconciled. My project here is to begin a conversation on the framings used for the former. Appealing to the notion of the phenomenological epoché and the bracketing of experience (Husserl, 2001) this suggests that attempts to 'bracket' the dominant narrative of 'street harassment' requires careful negotiation of terminology to enable wider stories which may not fit into categories of harassment, both those seen as too trivial and too criminal to be categorised in this way. Michelle N. McKenzie-Mohr and Suzanne Lafrance (2011) use the term 'dominant narratives' to capture how the wider stories on social phenomena readily available for use as explanatory frameworks can operate to silence experiences that are understood to 'not count' within the framework provided. Drawing from the experiences of participants here, the street was not the most frequent arena for women to experience the practices under the banner of 'street harassment', and emotional responses ranged through complimented, insulted, harassed, intimidated, confused, annoyed and terrified – often moving across these states within the same encounter. Though it can be argued that terminology of 'street' is to be understood as an abbreviation for any public place rather than a definitive location,[17] it does mark a separation between physical and non-physical public space. Given the growing evidence of women's experiences of men's intrusion online, such separation hampers opportunities to explore the overlaps and differences, as well as the cumulative impact on women of intrusion by unknown men in public.[18]

What was needed in the formative parts of this study was to develop tools, including language, to enable the disclosure of a socially hidden issue whilst avoiding a presupposition of frequency, which can be read in framings such as 'commonplace intrusions' (Kelly, 1988) or 'everyday sexism' (Bates, 2014). The search was for a framing to enable a joint exploration of both the ordinary and extraordinary practices evidencing men's entitlement to act on women, as well as help to connect criminal forms of violence against women such as rape to the more routine interruptions of women in public space; allowing for experiences that may not feel harassing yet still impacted on how women lived their bodily-self. In addition to this, there is a uniqueness to the experience of men's stranger intrusion on women (lived, as will be seen, as connected to other forms of violence against women), that is uncaptured by frames that do not include the perpetrator or target. Street or stranger harassment (see Fairchild, 2007, 2010) diverts focus to the location or relationship and risks decontextualising the experience, removing who is the actor (and why), who is acted upon (and why) and how the meanings for both are located within a wider system of structural gender inequality. Such terminology also risks excluding experiential realities that do not fit the sexual harassment framework – from which the label of street harassment was drawn – such as the impact of anticipation, or intrusions that are not 'sexual' in nature. Laura Beth Nielsen's (2004) use of the term 'offensive public speech', does something similar. Such an approach enables Nielsen to capture a wide range of practices including sexually suggestive speech, race related speech and even begging, putting practices on a broader continuum, which illuminates points of intersection with race and gender. There is a significant obstacle, however, in focusing only on 'sexually suggestive speech', speech that can be directed from women to men, in that such a frame loses the ways in which the practice is located within the wider framework of structural gender inequality and thus has particular meanings when directed from men to women – meanings which are compounded by intersecting inequalities of race and class.

Given these limitations, we may find opportunities in a return to how such practices were conceptualized in early work on violence against women – as intrusions (see Stanko, 1985, 1990, Kelly, 1988). Intrusion is used here to refer to deliberate act of putting oneself into a place or situation where one is uninvited, with disruptive effect ('Intrusion', 2001). Following such a definition, there is no need to evidence a desire to harm or disrupt the target, the focus is on the deliberateness of the practice, whilst 'uninvited' shifts from 'unwanted' as a qualifier that affirms the power of the target to choose who is able to enter their physical and emotional space. It foregrounds the actions of the perpetrator, rather than their intentions or the target's response, allowing for a broader range of practices to be addressed. Intrusion as a verb also more closely fits the phenomenological experience where one's inner world is entered into rather than solely acted on. Shifting terminology from 'street harassment' to 'intrusion' thus assists in coming closer to the experience as it is lived; intrusion not only onto but, crucially, into women's experience of their bodily-self. Keeping the perpetrator within the frame is also important, given the particularities of intrusion when directed from men to women – particularities which are uncovered by the current study. Critical masculinities theorists including Malcolm Cowburn and Keith Pringle (2000), have suggested the use of 'male' can work to hide how men's violence is the result of men's practices, not their biological 'maleness'. As such I use men's stranger intrusions to denote those specifically carried out by unknown men, and men's intrusion to refer to the broader range of relationships women may have with men who use intrusive practices. In this way I move from 'street harassment' to 'men's stranger intrusions on women in public space'.

Such a move has limitations. Naming practices such as rape as a form of men's intrusion risks losing what is gained from naming such actions as violence: the power not just for legislative redress but also acknowledgement of harm. It is not my intention to undermine or trivialise, though it is also important to note that terminology carrying particular connotations, such as 'violence' with its intimations of physical attack and outward aggression, can work to silence experiences that are more diffuse than this. One frame need not replace the other; rather, open discussions about terminology assist in expanding the vocabulary we have to speak of women's living experience. There is also the difficulty of introducing a new term when 'street harassment' as a concept is the more understandable – exemplified in the necessary inclusion of 'street harassment' in the title of this book. Sally Engle Merry's work on translating human rights concepts across borders offers an interesting response here. For Merry, '[i]t is the unfamiliarity of these ideas that make them effective in breaking old modes of thought' (2006: 178), arguing that in order for new concepts (or new language for old concepts) to effect practical change they must be seen as familiar but never fully indigenised. Such positioning is also found in the work of Audre Lorde, who declared the importance of returning to our concepts, of testing, revising and reforming them in new contexts to test their efficacy and potential for change. For Lorde, 'there are no new ideas still waiting in the wings to save us ... only old and forgotten ones, new combinations, extrapolations and recognitions from within ourselves, along with the renewed courage to try them out' (Lorde, 1986: 35). It is in this spirit, of adventure and possibility, that men's stranger intrusions on women in public is introduced. A framing that sits closer to the epistemological basis of this study; born of the connections between phenomenology and feminist empirical research on violence against women.

Chapter overview

This book is divided into eight chapters, beginning with this introduction. Each chapter builds on the theoretical work of the chapter before, and as such you may find it most useful to read the book as a narrative rather than approaching each chapter as self-contained. However even the most well-meaning of readers may wish to cut to specific parts of interest and as such what follows is a brief preview of what can be found in each chapter.

The challenge of researching the ordinary is reflected in the links between the principles and practice of a feminist research methodology, and the ontological concerns of existential-phenomenology. Chapter 2 develops these connections in building a feminist phenomenological approach to violence against women and girls. Such an approach heralds the importance, and difficulty, of researching the ordinary, and as such this chapter outlines the development of particular research tools and processes designed to help uncover aspects of participants' existence that were so routine as to become hidden.

Where living experience and the continuum of sexual violence were key loc-ators for the design of the research methodology, the work of Simone de Beau-voir and Maurice Merleau-Ponty on situation, embodiment, habit, and freedom, provided the lens through which analysis was conducted. Chapter 3 explores these core concepts, laying the theoretical foundations for understanding the phenomenological impact of men's intrusion.

Chapters 4 and 5 present the empirical findings of the study. Chapter 4 presents the most common practices reported by participants, categorised into: ordinary interruptions, verbal intrusions, and the gaze (including 'creepshots'). Chapter 5 looks to those that were experienced less routinely and that through this were often more memorable: physical intrusions (including rape), flashing and public masturbation, and following, as well as outlining how intrusions were experienced by participants as interconnected, often framed in relation to the imminent potentiality of rape.

Chapter 6 investigates in more detail how men's intrusive practices came to be experienced in the way they were, turning first to an examination of participants' early experiences of intrusion, in both childhood and adolescence, before begin-ning an exploration of how men's intrusion starts to become incorporated into habituated modes of women's embodiment. This is further developed in Chapter 7, highlighting disparities in projected impact and frequency as well as conceptual-izing the impact of men's stranger intrusion on women in public in terms of devel-oping both external awareness and an external perspective on the bodily-self. This culminates in a particular mode of embodiment marked by bodily alienation.

Chapter 8 concludes in addressing the possibilities for restoration from this alienated modality of embodiment, tracing the resistance in women's stories and finding their attempts to transform the habitual attitudes taken towards the body. It outlines possibilities for feminist campaigning and policy reform as well as suggesting ways in which further research could be developed to continue build-ing our understanding of the interplay between men's practices and women's embodied selfhood. The chapter ends in pointing to how the struggle to inhabit the body directly in the world requires the adoption of new habits – a conscious process of disruption – for those who want to reclaim an experience of the body as the self and the world as our own.

A note on terminology and translations

Throughout the book, references made to *The Second Sex* are for the new English version (Beauvoir, 2011), translated by Constance Borde and Sheila Malovany-Chevallier.[19] This is in recognition of the severe problems with the original English translation by Howard Parshley, outlined in detail by Margaret A. Simons (1983) and Toril Moi (2002) and also addressed in part through this book. In addition, it is important in this introduction to note that the term 'woman' is employed in its Beauvoirian sense as a category, not used to imply one set of circumstances applicable to all as a mysterious essential 'quality' of womanhood, though Simone de Beauvoir has often been wrongfully critiqued as suggesting just this. Relating the phenomenological experience for women of men's stranger intrusion requires recognition of how this experience is lived in complex and contradictory ways. As such, this project was not conducted in order to generalise from the findings of the 50 women who participated. This book aligns with Iris Marion Young's (2005) belief that the concept of gender is a tool for theorising structures more than subjects, whilst using Beauvoir's theory of ambiguity to complicate such a clear division. For Young, gender is

> a particular form of the social positioning of lived bodies in relation to one another within historically and socially specific institutions and processes that have material effects on the environment in which people act and reproduce relations of power and privilege among them.
>
> (2005: 22)

Without signifying a singular situation for all however, we must also avoid 'the masculine trap of wanting to enclose us in our differences' (Beauvoir interviewed in Simons, 1999: 18). Drawing from Sartre's later philosophy Young (2005) responds to this challenge through building a conceptualization of 'woman' as a series not a group; a series that despite the individual variation in each woman's experience, opportunities, and possibilities, has 'a unity that can be described and made intelligible ... specific to a particular social formation during a particular epoch' (2005: 29). 'Woman' is thus used to acknowledge the existence of an always incomplete series of social, shared, embodied realities, exploring the commonalities between and differences amongst a particular set of women, participating in this research at a given moment in time.

Notes

1 DLA Piper & Thomson Reuters Foundation for Hollaback! (2014) have developed a highly useful resource containing relevant laws related to street harassment in 36 jurisdictions: Argentina, Australia, Belgium, Canada, Colombia, Croatia, Czech Republic, England, France, Germany, India, Ireland, Israel, Italy, Mexico, Nepal, New Zealand, Peru, Poland, South Africa, Turkey, and 15 states in the United States of America.

2 Based in India, the Fightback application includes a panic button that uses location services such as GPS (Global Positioning System), SMS (Short Message Service), email and Facebook to alert others if a woman feels in danger. See www.fightback-mobile.com/.

3 Harassmap is an application created for women in Egypt which uses a SMS system to anonymously and immediately report incidents of sexual harassment. See http://harassmap.org/.

4 Hollaback! launched their iPhone application in 2010. The app, which is available worldwide, enables women to quickly post a story to the Hollaback! website and enter their location either through GPS or manually. The location is recorded on a publically available map and women are contacted via email to ask for more details.

5 For more on Beauvoir's denial of her philosophical contribution see Simons (1990, 2010); Le Doeuff (1989); Kruks (1990); Fullbrook and Fullbrook (1993); Gothlin (2001); Heinämaa (1999); and Moi (1999, 2008).

6 Simons is supported in this endeavour by writers including Michèle Le Doeuff (1989, 1997), Sonia Kruks (1987, 1990, 1992, 2005a, 2005b) and Toril Moi (1992, 1999, 2008).

7 I use the terms 'living body' and 'living experience' instead of the conventional 'lived', to further emphasise our temporality as well as the role of our active processes in creating the body and experience as we live it. This will be further fleshed out in Chapter 3.

8 The terminology of 'modes' and 'modalities' employed in relation to embodiment here are not used to represent set and stable categories of experience but rather are employed with the acknowledgment that our temporality and agency create modes that shift across situations and contexts – Beauvoir's 'becoming'. Their use refers to the ways in which we take up and experience our embodiment. The fact that we are embodied is part of our *facticity*, the intractable conditions of human being. We can choose the attitudes we take towards the material facts of our embodiment – for example alteration, modification or destruction of the body – and we can also experience our embodiment in different modes – for example mediated, alienated, directly. We cannot, however, choose to not be embodied. The highlighting of the shifting nature of modes of embodiment also appears in Gail Weiss' (1999) claim that embodiment

> suggests an experience that is constantly in the making, that is continually being constituted and reconstituted from one moment to the next. To talk about modes of embodiment therefore, is not to invoke a set of Kantian categories, absolute and inviolable, but rather, to talk about modes that are themselves continually changing in significance and appearance over time.
>
> (43)

9 See for example the work on female embodiment from Iris Marion Young (2005) and Gail Weiss (1999).

10 The acknowledged problems with the original English translation are addressed in more detail in Chapter 3.

11 Seen in her most popular fictional works *L'Invitee*, translated to English as *She Came to Stay* (Beauvoir, 1999) and *Les Mandarins*, translated as *The Mandarins* (Beauvoir, 1982).

12 All participants were given the opportunity to name themselves and as such names used may be pseudonyms.

13 Such trivialisation is productively challenged through the inclusion of men's intrusion on women in public in work detailing the range and extent of violence against women, making the practice visible. See Westmarland (2015) for a recent example of this.

14 It is well known to feminists how language limits how accurately we can describe the world from women's phenomenological position (Cameron, 1998; Spender, 1985, West, 1987). Women by necessity use terms such as 'sexual violence' or 'sexual harassment', which defines the experience both from the perpetrator's perspective (sexual), and their own (violence/harassment) rather than come from a label solely referring to the experience from a woman's standpoint such as, for example, 'sexist violence', as the latter would struggle for recognition. This possible reframing is also not without its own limitations. What we lose in moving to 'sexist violence' may be the ways in which sex or 'the sexual' is used as the tool of violence – something that is contained within the term 'sexual violence'.

15 Even where location questions were asked, data was not analysed in terms of the number/percentage of women who had experienced stranger intrusion in public spaces. Though one can reasonably assume a large proportion of unknown perpetrators offend in public spaces, strangers can also occupy home or work settings and similarly partners or known men can perpetrate in public spaces such as shopping centres or public transport.

16 Recently activists such as Holly Kearl (2010) have made steps towards filling the gap in identifying women's definitions born of experiential knowledge. In asking women how they define street harassment, Kearl (2010) gives examples of definitions which pull on the concepts of intrusion, disrespect and intimidation and states the most commonly used words in responses were 'unwanted', 'sexual', 'uncomfortable', 'touch' and 'threat'. It is important to note, however, that despite her intent to examine the definitions of 'ordinary' women, when none of her published responses from the women she surveyed included feeling 'harassed' Kearl follows the dominant framing and names the experience as street harassment.

17 Cynthia Bowman (1993) acknowledges this, stating in a footnote that

> (a)lthough the street is in fact one very common venue, I use the word 'street' here simply as an abbreviation for any public place; this type of harassment takes place in many other venues, such as buses, trains, taxis, bus stations, and the like
>
> (n. 7, 25)

18 The overlaps in impact are gaining recognition. In 2016, Hollaback! launched a new project 'Heartmob' aiming to be the first ever platform seeking to combat online harassment. Given that Hollaback! is an international movement against street harassment, the parallels in experiences of intrusion between online and offline public spaces, and the parallel needs for support and action to challenge, are evident in this initiative.

19 Toril Moi (2010) has also signalled problems with the Borde and Malovany-Chevallier translation, however at the time of writing it is the best possible version of Beauvoir's text in English (see Daigle, 2013 for an evaluation).

References

Bates, L. (2014) *Everyday Sexism*, Simon and Schuster.

Bartky, S. L. (1990) *Femininity and Domination*, Routledge.

Beauvoir, S. d. (1982) *The Mandarins*, Friedman, L. M. (transl.), Penguin.

Beauvoir, S. d. (1999) *She Came to Stay*, Senhouse, R. & Moys, Y. (transl.), W. W. Norton.

Beauvoir, S. d. (2011) *The Second Sex*, Borde, C. & Malovany-Chevallier, S. (transl.), Vintage.

Bowman, C. (1993) 'Street Harassment and the Informal Ghettoization of Women', *Harvard Law Review*, 106 (3), pp. 517–580.

Bray, A., & Colebrook, C. (1998) 'The Haunted Flesh: Corporeal Feminism and the Politics of (Dis)embodiment', *Signs*, 24 (1), pp. 35–67.

Budgeon, S. (2003) 'Identity as an Embodied Event', *Body & Society*, 9 (1), pp. 35–55.

Cameron, D. (1998) *The Feminist Critique of Language: A Reader*, Psychology Press.

Connell, R. W. (2002) *Gender*, Polity Press.

Cowburn, M., & Pringle, K. (2000) 'Pornography and Men's Practices', *Journal of Sexual Aggression*, 6 (1), pp. 52–66.

Crawford, A., Jones, T., Woodhouse, T., & Young, J. (1990) *The Second Islington Crime Survey*. Centre for Criminology, Middlesex Polytechnic.

Crenshaw, K. (1989) 'Demarginalizing the Intersection of Race and Sex: A Black Feminist Critique of Antidiscrimination Doctrine, Feminist Theory and Antiracist Politics', *The University of Chicago Legal Forum*, pp. 139–167.

Daigle, C. (2013) 'The Impact of the New Translation of The Second Sex', *The Journal of Speculative Philosophy*, 27(3), pp. 336–347.

Deleuze, G. (1994) *Difference and Repetition*, Columbia University Press.

DLA Piper and Thomson Reuters Foundation for Hollaback! (2014) *Street Harassment: Know Your Rights*, www.ihollaback.org/wp-content/uploads/2014/10/Street-Harassment-Know-Your-Rights.pdf [accessed 22 November 2015].

EVAW (End Violence Against Women Coalition) (2012) *4 in 10 Young Women in London Sexually Harassed Over Last Year*, www.endviolenceagainstwomen.org.uk/news/20/4-in-10-young-women-in-london-sexually-harassed-over-last-year [accessed 13 May 2012].

Fairchild, K. (2007) *Everyday Stranger Harassment: Frequency and Consequences*. PhD thesis. New Brunswick: Rutgers, State University of New Jersey.

Fairchild, K. (2010) 'Context Effects on Women's Perceptions of Stranger Harassment', *Sexuality and Culture*, pp. 191–216.

Fanon, F. (2008) *Black Skins, White Masks*, Philcox, R. (transl.), Grove Press.

FRA (2014) *Violence Against Women: An EU-Wide Survey Main Results*, European Union Agency for Fundamental Rights, http://fra.europa.eu/sites/default/files/fra-2014-vaw-surveymain-results_en.pdf, [accessed 2 March 2014].

Fullbrook, E., & Fullbrook, K. (1993) *Simone de Beauvoir and Jean-Paul Sartre: The Remaking of a Twentieth-Century Legend*, Harvester.

Gardner, C. B. (1995) *Passing By: Gender and Public Harassment*, University of California Press.

Garko, M. G. (1999) 'Existential Phenomenology and Feminist Research', *Psychology of Women Quarterly*, 23 (1), pp. 167–175.

Goffman, E. (1990) *The Presentation of Self in Everyday Life*, Penguin.

Gothlin, E. (2001) 'Simone de Beauvoir's Existential Phenomenology and Philosophy of History in Le Deuxieme Sexe', in O'Brien, W., & Embree, L. (eds), *The Existential Phenomenology of Simone de Beauvoir* (Vol. 43), Springer, pp. 41–51.

Heinämaa, S. (1999) 'Simone de Beauvoir's Phenomenology of Sexual Difference', *Hypatia*, 14 (4), pp. 114–132.

Heinämaa, S. (2003). *Toward a Phenomenology of Sexual Difference: Husserl, Merleau-Ponty, Beauvoir*, Rowman & Littlefield.

Husserl, E. (1960) *Cartesian Meditations*, Cairns, D. (transl.), M. Nijhoff.

Husserl, E. (2001) *Logical Investigations* (Vol. 1). Findlay, N. J. (transl.), Psychology Press.

'Intrusion' (2001) in Pearsall, J. (ed.), *The New Oxford English Dictionary*, Oxford University Press.

Kearl, H. (2010) *Stop Street Harassment: Making Public Places Safe and Welcoming for Women*, Praeger.

Kelly, L. (1988) *Surviving Sexual Violence*, Polity Press.

Kelly, L. (1996) 'Weasel Words: Paedophiles and the Cycle of Abuse', *Trouble and Strife*, 33, www.troubleandstrife.org/articles/issue-33/weasel-words-paedophiles-and-the-cycle-ofabuse/ [accessed 1 February 2014].

Kelly, L., Burton, S., & Regan, L. (1996) 'Beyond Victim or Survivor: Sexual Violence, Identity and Feminist Theory and Practice', in Adkins, L., & Merchant, V. (eds), *Sexualizing the Social: Power and the Organization of Sexuality* (47), Macmillan, pp. 77–101.

Kissling, E. A. (1991) 'Street Harassment: The Language of Sexual Terrorism', Discourse &Society, 2 (4), pp. 451–460.

Kruks, S. (1987) 'Simone de Beauvoir and the Limits to Freedom', *Social Text: Theory/Culture/Ideology*, 17, pp. 111–122.

Kruks, S. (1990) *Situation and Human Existence: Freedom, Subjectivity, and Society*, Unwin Hyman.

Kruks, S. (1992) 'Gender and Subjectivity: Simone de Beauvoir and Contemporary Feminism', *Signs*, 18 (1), pp. 89–110.

Kruks, S. (2005a) 'Beauvoir's Time/Our Time: The Renaissance in Simone de Beauvoir Studies', *Feminist Studies*, 31 (2), pp. 286–309.

Kruks, S. (2005b) 'Simone de Beauvoir and the Politics of Privilege', *Hypatia*, 20 (1), pp. 178–205.

Lazarus, R. S., & Folkman, S. (1984) *Stress, Appraisal, and Coping*, Springer.

Le Doeuff, M. (1989) *Hipparchia's Choice: An Essay Concerning Women, Philosophy, Etc.*, Selous, T. (transl.), Blackwell.

Le Doeuff, M. (1997) 'Simone de Beauvoir and Existentialism', in McBride, W. L., *Sartre's French Contemporaries and Enduring Influences*, Routledge, pp. 199–212.

Lenton, R., Smith, M. D., Fox, J., & Morra, N. (1999) 'Sexual Harassment in Public Places: Experiences of Canadian Women', *Canadian Review of Sociology*, 36 (4), pp. 517–540.

Lorde, A. (1986) *Our Dead Behind Us: Poems*, New York: W. W. Norton.

Macmillan, R., Nierobisz, A., & Welsh, S. (2000) 'Experiencing the Streets: Harassment and Perceptions of Safety Among Women', *Journal of Research in Crime and Delinquency*, 37 (3), pp. 306–322.

McKenzie-Mohr, S., & Lafrance, M. N. (2011) 'Telling Stories Without the Words: "Tightrope Talk" in Women's Accounts of Coming to Live Well after Rape or Depression', *Feminism & Psychology*, 21 (1), pp. 49–73.

McLeod, E. (1982) *Working Women: Prostitution Now*, Croom Helm.

McNay, L. (2004) 'Agency and Experience: Gender as a Lived Relation', *The Sociological Review*, 52 (2), pp. 173–190.

Merleau-Ponty, M. (2002) *Phenomenology of Perception*, Smith, C. (transl.), Routledge.

Merry, S. E. (2006) *Human Rights and Gender Violence: Translating International Law into Local Justice*, University of Chicago.

Moi, T. (1992) 'Ambiguity and Alienation in The Second Sex', *Boundary*, 19 (2), pp. 96–112.

Moi, T. (1999) *What is a Woman? And Other Essays*, Oxford University Press.

Moi, T. (2002) 'While We Wait: The English Translation of The Second Sex', *Signs*, 27 (4), pp. 1005–1035.

Moi, T. (2008) *Simone de Beauvoir: The Making of an Intellectual Woman*, Oxford University Press.

Moi, T. (2010) 'The Adulteress Wife: Review of a New Edition of The Second Sex', *The London Review of Books*, 32, pp. 3–6.

Nielsen, L. B. (2004) *License to Harass: Law, Hierarchy, and Offensive Public Speech*, Princeton University Press.

Oxygen/Markle Pulse (2000) 'Oxygen/Markle Pulse Poll Finds: Harassment of Women on the Street Is Rampant; 87% of American Women Report Being Harassed on the Street By a Male Stranger', *The Free Library*, PR Newswire Association LLC, www.thefreelibrary.com/Oxygen%2fMarkle+Pulse+Poll+Finds%3a+Harassment+of+Women+on+the+Street+Is...-a062870396 [accessed 5 June 2013].

Paglia, C. (1994) *Vamps & Tramps: New Essays*, Random House

Phadke, S., Khan, S., & Ranade, S. (2011). *Why Loiter?: Women and Risk on Mumbai Streets*, Penguin Books India.

Roiphe, K. (1994) *The Morning After: Sex, Fear and Feminism*, Hamish Hamilton.

Simons, M. A. (1983) 'The Silencing of Simone de Beauvoir Guess What's Missing from The Second Sex', *Women's Studies International Forum*, 6 (5), pp. 559–564.

Simons, M. A. (1990) 'Sexism and the Philosophical Cannon: On Reading Beauvoir's Second Sex', *Journal of the History of Ideas*, 51, pp. 487–504.

Simons, M. A. (1999) *Beauvoir and The Second Sex: Feminism, Race and the Origins of Existentialism*, Rowman & Littlefield.

Simons, M. A. (ed.) (2010) *Feminist Interpretations of Simone de Beauvoir*, Penn State Press.

Smith, D. E. (1987) *The Everyday World as Problematic: A Feminist Sociology*, University of Toronto Press.

Spender, D. (1985) *Man Made Language* (2nd ed.), Routledge & Kegan Paul.

Stanko, E. (1985) *Intimate Intrusions: Women's Experience of Male Violence*, Unwin Hyman.

Stanko, E. (1990) *Everyday Violence: How Women and Men Experience Sexual and Physical Danger*, Pandora.

Stavro, E. (2000) 'Re-Reading The Second Sex Theorizing the Situation', *Feminist Theory*, 1 (2), pp. 131–150.

Tuerkheimer, D. (1997) 'Street Harassment as Sexual Subordination: The Phenomenology of Gender-Specific Harm', *Wisconsin Women's Law Journal*, 12, pp. 167–206.

Warr, M. (1984) 'Fear of Victimization: Why are Women and the Elderly More Afraid?', *Social Science Quarterly*, 65, pp. 681–702.

Weiss, G. (1999) *Body Images: Embodiment as Intercorporeality*, Routledge.

West, R. L. (1987) 'The Difference in Women's Hedonic Lives: A Phenomenological Critique of Feminist Legal Theory', *Wisconsin Women's Law Journal*, 3 (81), pp. 81–145.

Westmarland, N. (2015) *Violence Against Women: Criminological Perspectives on Men's Violences*, Routledge.

Wise, S., & Stanley, L. (1987) *Georgie Porgie: Sexual Harassment in Everyday Life*, Pandora.

Wolf, N. (1993) *Fire with Fire: The New Female Power and How it Will Change the 21st Century*, Chatto & Windus.

Young, I. M. (2005) *On Female Body Experience: 'Throwing Like a Girl' and Other Essays*, Oxford University Press.

He physically had his junk hanging out the side of his shorts.
I can walk around with blinkers on
He asked if he could sit by me again.
I'll always be listening to music.
He said well I would just like to talk to you.
I walk a little different now and I do different things with my face
He was looking at me in a way that was just like,
you are just a piece of meat
and I'm loving the show.

He stayed leaning into me,
was rubbing his crotch against me
and he had an erection.
I used to carry a Stanley knife.

They just started shouting at me every day.
I would never now get onto a bus and sit by the window.
And then he put my finger in his mouth.
I always check men and I watch their behaviour.
He leaned across me and pinned me back and tried to take off my skirt.
You have to have your shutters down.

He came up very close to me, like inches away from me,
and said something like
loving the stockings girlie.
He was constantly leaning over and being like where are you going
and what are you doing
and is this a holiday
and have you got a boyfriend.
He seemed to be slowing down as if he wanted me to pass him.
He didn't say anything, he just attacked me.
He walked past us and went oh my god, lesbians.
You live in this bubble all of the time.
He turned to me and he says you look very beautiful.
I've even taken my phone out sometimes and pretended to talk to someone.
Someone shouted across the street at me 'nice, ah, mammary glands.'

I won't make eye contact or anything, I don't want to give them the chance

And this guy came up to me and basically tried to have sex with me
outside the shop, when I was 14,
dragged me around the corner and started trying to pull the coat off.
And he kept, he kept saying

                              there's no need to be frightened of me.

2 The importance of the ordinary

Everyday practices and the living experiences of women are at the heart of the continuum of sexual violence, a phenomenological frame for understanding men's violence against women. One of the key discoveries in Liz Kelly's *Surviving Sexual Violence* (1988) was the extent and range of the forms of sexual violence participants had experienced, leading to Kelly conceptualising their experiences as located on a continuum. Such a theorisation marked a shift in thinking, from a focus on individual manifestations of men's violence against women as discrete categories to the recognition of the commonality and connections between different forms. To do this, Kelly drew on the dual meanings of the term 'continuum' to replicate the complexity of the relationships women have to experiences of sexual violence, both those they have experienced themselves and those that have been experienced by other women. Her conceptualisation is not about hierarchy. With the key exception of violence that results in death she holds that: 'the degree of impact cannot be simplistically inferred from the form a woman experiences or its place within the continuum' (Kelly, 1988: 76). The continuum of sexual violence is instead about the living experience of sexual violence, and the ways in which it connects contextually to particular meanings for individual women. How to uncover this individual meaning whilst holding possibilities for overlaps and difference, becomes the theoretical and methodological challenge. This position resonates with one of the core tenets of the phenomenological tradition drawn on by Simone de Beauvoir; namely that phenomena have meaning in their being meaningful to some *one*. Subjective meaning is made through relation, relating instances of violence to each other, the wider social context in which we operate, and to the way in which we understand our possibilities and enact our projects. Kelly's work can thus be drawn together with both Beauvoir and some of the theoretical underpinnings of feminist standpoint epistemology to begin sketching an outline for a feminist phenomenological approach to violence against women and girls.

The continuum of men's intrusive practices

The concept of the continuum of sexual violence talks to what is lived by women as an experiential continuum of men's intrusive practices. The concept of a continuum assists in moving outside of a crime framework whereby practices are separated and a hierarchy is created. Such hierarchal positioning risks losing how the quieter forms of intrusion, those experienced by women as a restriction in freedom, rely on the possibilities and realities of the louder, criminal forms, to have the particular impact they do. Such a consideration reveals an underlying tension: the desire to collate similarities alongside holding both the ambiguity of, and particularities between/within, different experiences of men's intrusion. Examining the experience of men's intrusion in detail unearths the interdependency of individual practices, problematising their separation into clear and concise categories. This connects to Maurice Merleau-Ponty's (2002) development of Husserl's (1960) concept of 'horizons' whereby all experience is understood as horizontal – linked internally to all other experiences – and also to Liz Kelly's (1988) continuum of sexual violence. Kelly's conceptualisation demonstrated how the splitting of men's intrusive practices into the distinct groupings often necessary for analysis, can disrupt attempts to reflect the meanings such practices have in individual women's lives. For Beauvoir this splitting matters as '[i]t is within the whole context of a situation that leaves her few outlets that these singularities take on their importance' (Beauvoir, 2011: 357). Building on the work of Kelly and others, critical masculinities theorists Malcolm Cowburn and Keith Pringle suggest that the ways in which different patriarchal processes generate and are generated by what they term 'men's oppressive practices' intersect with each other in a series of social locations – 'to the extent that any one of those 'locations' can only be fully appreciated when it is seen in the context of the others' (Cowburn & Pringle, 2000: 59). The importance of understanding men's intrusive practices in relation to each other is thus a key part of any attempt to understand the way they operate and the place they occupy in women's lives.

Relationship then, to ourselves, others and the world, is central in a phenomenological approach to understanding violence against women and girls. Reviewing Merleau-Ponty's *Phenomenology of Perception*, Simone de Beauvoir signalled the importance of relationship for living experience, stating that '[i]t is impossible to define an object apart from the subject by whom and for whom it is the object' (translated in Heinämaa, 2003: 75). Such a conceptualisation of the interrelation and interdependency between subject and object provides interesting possibilities for feminist work on women's objectification, suggesting the importance of bringing the ways men enact their embodied subjectivity more clearly into the frame. It highlights the difficulties in understanding the mechanisms of men's structural power without investigating what the relations between and amongst women and men reveal of our relationship to our bodily-self. This notion of relationship helps to unearth how experiences of men's stranger intrusion in public spaces are lived; understood and experienced by women in relation to personal and collective histories of men's violence. The continuum can assist here in capturing the connections between different forms of violence against women, as well as a woman's own individual experiences of these different forms. The concept of a continuum of men's intrusive practices exists not only between categories but, crucially, within them. In this way such a concept helps mirror the ways in which women make sense of experiences of men's violence, relating an individual experience to both what has come before, for us and others, and what may follow.

The concept of a continuum also facilitates an exploration of men's routine intrusive practices as a manifestation of men's power, and the ways in which they are lived by women as extensions of men's criminal intrusion such as sexual assault or rape. In building her conceptual framework, Kelly introduced the term 'commonplace intrusions', bringing into language the daily intrusions women experience in public space. Using the example of the seemingly innocent 'cheer up love', Kelly explored the meanings behind this remark: 'the expectation that women should be paying attention to and gratifying men, rather than preoccupied with their own thoughts and concerns' (1988: 106). This meaning links to that of other forms of sexual violence, where the underlying attitude of men's entitlement to women's bodies and minds is expressed. Critics of Kelly have pointed to this approach as prioritising individual subjectivity (Price, 2005), resulting in difficulties in codifying acts legally and developing a general analysis of women's subjugation. There is a tension here; indeed, the difficulty in fitting the complexities of the ways in which violence against women is experienced into a legal framework has resulted in research and policy focus on those behaviours that can readily be identified as criminal such as sexual assault or intimate partner violence involving physical violence (Kelly, 2012). Price's critique however does not allow room for the possibility that Kelly's intention may not have been to develop theory to inform a legal framework, but rather to articulate women's experiential realities. Revisiting the continuum over two decades later, Kelly (2012) argues that the focus on criminal behaviour in the years since the concept was developed has meant that the gaps she initially uncovered have yet to be closed. Kelly claims researchers have lost interest in the fabric of women's lives and that '[t]he everyday, routine intimate intrusions which were so key to the continuum have dropped off many agendas' (Kelly, 2012: xviii). Such a claim gives insight to her initial purpose. The continuum provides a phenomenological conceptualisation of men's violence against women and girls where the experiential links between different episodes of men's violence are maintained, in contrast to the imposition of the discrete categories favoured by policy and legal framings. Instead of aiming for a general analysis, *Surviving Sexual Violence* is located alongside Stanley and Wise (1983) in not making claims for one true social reality 'out there' to be uncovered, but rather heralding the importance of attempting to articulate the experience of men's violence against women as it is lived. This lived or living reality is a necessarily situated, embodied reality that, far from being subjective and thus less valid than 'objective' understandings, is the only access to reality we can ever truly achieve. Such positioning provides the starting point for a feminist phenomenology of men's violence against women.

Towards a feminist phenomenology of violence against women and girls

The relative silence in research and policy on the more ordinary practices of men's intrusion is particularly interesting not only given the steep rise in knowledge on other forms of violence against women, but how the knowledge base itself grew from calls to focus on the everyday. During the 1970s key feminist texts began to raise the issue of men's violence against women both in its criminal and mundane manifestations. Susan Brownmiller (1975) theorised rape as a tool of social control and Germaine Greer (1971) used the concept of 'petty rapes' to describe the ways in which the everyday and the presumed rare 'sledgehammer' (Stanko, 1985) experiences of men's intrusion were connected. During the late 1980s and early 1990s in England, feminist research and activism combined to substantially build the knowledge base, with a number of leading contributors pointing to the importance of recognising the ordinary forms of men's violence and highlighting the danger in relegating such practices to a set of aberrant behaviours from a deviant minority of men (Hanmer & Saunders, 1984; Kelly, 1988; Stanko, 1985; Wise & Stanley, 1987). The necessary focus on policy, combined with the limits of survey methodology,[1] has led to a steep rise in knowledge about forms of violence against women that can readily be identified as criminal, such as sexual assault or intimate partner violence, to the detriment of investigating men's violence and intrusion in women's everyday lives.

Adopting a feminist phenomenological perspective on men's violence against women and girls creates possibilities to address this imbalance. A phenomenological approach has the potential to assist a feminist reframing of what becomes in a medical model a syndrome/disorder or through a legal framework as acceptable/unacceptable extensions of the same act. Both legal and medical frameworks focus on a clear distinction between normal and abnormal behaviours, with behaviours classed as the latter thus falling into the realm of legal sanctions and medical interventions. Feminist critiques focusing on violence as routine in women's lives, argue that: '[w]hat becomes lost ... in this commonsensical separation between "aberrant" and "typical" male behaviour is a woman-defined understanding of what is threatening, of what women consider to be potentially violent' (Stanko, 1985: 10). For Kelly, this separation results in limited definitions of sexual violence, which in turn benefit men through distinguishing a small group of 'deviant' men from the 'normal' majority, with the consequence of creating 'a group of men who we can justify thinking and talking about as other' (Kelly, 1996: 1). The concern, that a phenomenological frame can help address, is that narratives of medical and criminal frameworks have achieved 'master status' (Frank, 1995) for understanding violence against women and girls. Such status directs attention away from the complexities of women's living experiences of men's violence, experiences that may be lived as connected, and that commonly are not the subject of medical or legal redress. In a legal framework, the distinction between acceptable and aberrant practices is often based on a standard of reasonableness. Such a standard has been effectively argued by interdisciplinary feminists as invariably located in the perspective of a reasonable (white) man, and as such is unable to accommodate gender and race specific harms (see Collins, 2000; Crenshaw, 1989; Harris, 1990; Heben, 1994–95; West, 1987). Similarly, feminist theorists have critiqued the trauma discourse of violence against women for the assumed neutral basis for measurement of what are or are not 'normal' responses and behaviours (Brown, 1995; Burstow, 1992; Herman, 1992; Smith, 1990). A phenomenological approach offers possibilities for feminists wanting to explore the impacts of men's violence in terms of what it means for women's everyday living experience, meanings that may sit outside of the available dominant frameworks.[2]

What is needed is a systematic analysis of what is often taken as purely personal experience (French, Teays, & Purdy, 1998), an approach that foregrounds the importance of analysing ordinary experiences and practices in attempts to understand the mechanisms of gender inequality. Drawing from the phenomenological tradition can help such an endeavour. Deriving from the Greek *phainomenon* (appearance) and *logos* (reason or word), phenomenology was founded by Edmund Husserl at the turn of the nineteenth century. Husserl (1960) held that the world of immediate or lived experience takes precedence over the objectified and abstract world of the natural sciences, as it is that which makes itself first known to consciousness. What came to be known as existential-phenomenology was developed by Martin Heidegger, Husserl's student. Where Husserl had seen the task of phenomenology to be the description of the lived world from the viewpoint of a detached observer (using the phenomenological epoché, where experience is bracketed and things are examined 'as they are'), Heidegger claimed the observer cannot, in actuality, separate their self from the world, and that Husserl's prioritising of 'lived experience' still supported a false dichotomy between the world as we live it and the world as it is. Consequently, for what came to be known as existential-phenomenology, the modalities of conscious experience are also the ways one is in the world, a shift from the 'lived-world' to the concrete experience of being-in-the-world, or 'being there': Heidegger's (1996) concept of *Dasein*. Crucially 'in' here refers to an inextricable *entanglement with* the world; human beings are not 'in' the world as water is 'in' a glass. We cannot know our world outside of ourselves in it, and similarly we cannot know ourselves outside of existing in the world. In this way existential-phenomenology departs from Husserl in the claim that our material reality, Stanley and Wise's 'doing' of everyday life (1993), is our only point of access; human reality is necessarily situated. Any claim to reality or knowledge is at the same time always the expression of a particular standpoint; a perspective originating in our embodiment.

To understand the possibilities of a feminist phenomenology then, there is a need to acknowledge both what is feminist in phenomenology and what is phenomenological in feminism. Sara Heinämaa (2006) neatly captures this in explaining how the twofold relationship between feminist and phenomenological inquiries works to strengthen both perspectives.

On the one hand phenomenology offers methodological and conceptual tools for the development of a philosophical alternative to contemporary feminist naturalism and constructionism. On the other hand, contemporary feminism challenges the idea of a sexually neutral subjective, and this poses the question of whether the transcendental self described by the phenomenologists is of one type or of two (or several).

(Heinämaa, 2006: 503)

Here is where we can see the uniqueness of the feminist phenomenological perspective, distinct from phenomenology in its pure sense through the acknowledgment, with Heidegger, of the impossibility of assuming a position on the world of detached observer. The subsequent recognition follows that instead of a generalisable independence from the material facts (the world 'as it is'), phenomenological description can only seek to describe the commonalities that spring from singular situated existence.[3] Husserl's assertion that we must 'go back to the things in themselves' (2001: 168) can be used in this approach to refer to the return to existence as we live it, without the according claim that this living experience expresses a form of universal truth. This position is found in feminist critiques of a purely phenomenological approach to research, grounded in the ability of the researcher to bracket off their own assumptions and come to the research free from hypotheses or preconceptions. It appears in Donna Haraway's (1988) paper on the science question in feminism, where Haraway argues for the recognition of 'situated knowledges' in which the researcher asserts all knowledge as partial and never universal. Elizabeth Grosz goes further, suggesting that the concept of 'knowledge' itself is embedded in a patriarchal history and that one of the tasks of feminism is to conduct a 'structural reorganisation of positions of knowing, their effects on the kinds of object known, *and* our pregiven ways of knowing them' (Grosz, 1993: 207, emphasis in original). Feminist sociologists Liz Stanley and Sue Wise, proponents of the call to examine the 'personal, the everyday and what we experience – women's lived experience' (Stanley & Wise, 1983: 146), also question alongside existential-phenomenology the notion of an impartial observer in social research – a question responded to in part through the interdisciplinary range of feminist scholars whose work is often grouped under the heading of feminist standpoint epistemology (see Haraway, 1988; Harding, 1991; Hartsock, 1983; Collins, 2000; Smith, 1987; Weeks, 1998).

Though charged with coming from an essentialist position on 'women's knowledge' (see Mason, 2002), many standpoint theorists advocate for feminist standpoints – plural but related (see Hartsock, 2006). For Hartsock, the key is that feminist standpoints are the result of a conscious process of moving from unmediated experience to understanding experience as set in the historical context of social relations within which an individual is located – a notion we see indebted to Beauvoir's work on situation, more fully detailed in the following chapter. This notion of continual process in achieving feminist standpoints links to the existential-phenomenological concept of a 'project'. Kathi Weeks argues it is in this sense that the notion of a feminist standpoint is employed; 'a standpoint is a project, not an inheritance; it is achieved, not given' (Weeks, 1998: 136). Standing in for being part of a collective engagement with political projects is therefore what 'separates a standpoint from a survey of what individual women might report, and allows standpoints to become technical devices that can allow for the creation of better accounts of the world' (Hartsock, 2006: 180). This idea of 'better' accounts has been challenged by Lois McNay (2004), suggesting that such claims reassert rather than undo dichotomies of objectivity and subjectivity through granting 'experience' the epistemological privilege previously given to objectivity – an argument similar to that directed by Heidegger (1996) against Husserl's prioritising of lived experience. Identifying similarities between feminist standpoint theory and the concept of embodied subjectivity found in Merleau-Ponty, together with Beauvoir's work on ambiguity, helps to respond to such a charge.[4] The primacy of perception for Merleau-Ponty is the view that as the body-subject, I am situated by a material body that forms my unique point of view on the world. This view is inescapable, it is foundational to how we experience our world and create meaning. We thus do not 'have' a body like we have a house; similar to Heidegger's description of the particular 'in' with which we are 'in' the world, we are inextricably entangled with our bodies and our world to the point that our existence is only made possible through this entanglement. We are, and can only ever know ourselves as and through, our bodily-self. Beauvoir built on this conceptualisation in her work on situation, as well as in her notion of the self as in a perpetual mode of 'becoming'. For both approaches, feminist standpoint epistemology and a Beauvoirian exploration of situated subjectivity, experiential realities are held as the source of knowledge claims. It is the careful exhumation of these realities, that guide the methodological decisions of a feminist phenomenological project.

Feminist phenomenological methodologies: principles

The epistemological basis of a feminist phenomenological methodology is best explained through appeal to Rosi Braidotti's (1993) concept of 'transdisciplinarity', referring to the crossing of disciplinary boundaries without concern for the vertical distinctions around which they have been organised. Sketching the links between existential-phenomenology and feminist research methodologies, Michael Garko (1999) points to five points of similarity: everyday experience or the 'life-world'; illumination of concealed phenomena; intentional consciousness; the relationship between subject/object; and suspending the taken for granted. In drawing the principles underlying such an approach, however, it is important to recognise that there is no single, definable feminist research methodology – a point we would want to be true of a feminist phenomenological approach – rather there are multiple methodologies that can be employed for a feminist purpose. For Kelly, Burton and Regan (1994: 46) '[w]hat makes research "feminist" is not the methods as such, but the framework within which they are located, and the particular ways in which they are deployed'. The lack of a single definition encourages a flexible research practice that creates opportunities for raising new questions or discovering innovative research techniques in an attempt to excavate and examine the structures creating and maintaining women's inequality. In this sense, feminist research is a form of praxis, seeking to enable new understandings to address aspects of women's oppression and which can then be used as a resource in the creation of social change. In recognising marginalised experience, it problematises hierarchies of power that privilege one way of knowing over another (again reminiscent of Heidegger's critique of Husserl), questioning not only what we know but how, and importantly who or what is defining and defined by it. The illumination of such hierarchies of power, and recognition of the importance of women's voices in understanding women's living experience, is also an important entry point for Beauvoir who attends to the importance of recognising the position and role of the questioner and using this to resist making claims for a totalising system.[5]

> ... [I]t is no doubt impossible to approach any human problem without partiality: even the way of asking the questions, of adopting perspectives, presupposes hierarchies of interests; all characteristics comprise values; every so-called objective description is set against an ethical background. Instead of trying to conceal those principles that are more or less explicitly implied, we would be better off stating them from the start.
>
> (Beauvoir, 2011: 16)

Despite the usefulness of phenomenology in illuminating normative assumptions, feminist perspectives aim to also keep the researcher visible in the frame of the research; an interested and subjective actor (Stanley & Wise, 1993), who guides the research process and both construes and claims findings. Following this, my own role as researcher, asking questions, interpreting responses and making decisions throughout the writing process of omission and inclusion, is the frame through which all findings are situated. The intention here is to create what Stanley and Wise (1990) term 'accountable knowledge', where the situation giving rise to a project's findings is made visible, including the situated reasoning process of the researcher.

There is thus a clear theoretical resonance, and yet phenomenological studies in and through violence against women are rare and sit within the small body of work developing a philosophical perspective on violence against women, work that to date has been centred solely on rape or domestic violence (see Brison, 2002; Cahill, 2001; Davhana-Maselesele, 2011; Denzin, 1984; Mui, 2005; Pineau, 1989; and Du Toit, 2009). A phenomenology of violence against women suggests that it is not only the experience of the forms more commonly covered by legal regulation and media attention that are worthy of philosophical analysis, but also those commonly dismissed as trivial because of their very everydayness. Such an approach enables us to balance some of the tension found in attempts to theorise women's agency as lived in the current gender order, reaching beyond the continuum of cause and effect or the binary of subject/object. It meets a growing demand for conceptual work on men's violence against women grounded in empirical research and encourages us to refocus on the consequences of men's intrusion for how women live and experience our bodily-selves. The ordinary becomes important, the routine a revelation, and attention is directed to examining the everydayness and everynightness of our living experience (Smith, 1987).

Feminist phenomenological methodologies: practice

The holding of embodied, living experience as the basis of our knowledge claims signals the importance of examining the concrete details of our existence. If, in everyday life, we are actively engaged in a taken-for-granted experience of the world, examining this experience is difficult – by definition it appears as being 'just the way it is'. Feminist and critical race theorists have challenged this 'taken-for-grantedness' by pointing out how the everyday world can only be taken for granted if one is entitled to do so. Heidegger's critique of Husserl's phenomenological epoché suggests that part of our phenomenological task should be to unpick and describe this taken-for-grantedness itself: not in order to separate the world as it habitually presents itself to us from the world 'as it is', but rather to uncover the role of habituation in our experience of our world. To operationalise this within an empirical study on men's violence against women, a methodological approach is needed to enable participants to speak of aspects in their living experience that, due to their very basis as part of women's situation, are absorbed into the background becoming unremarkable and, through this, unspoken. In a cultural context where rape and/or intimate partner violence form the plots of Hollywood movies and bestseller novels, and media representations focus on the exceptional and sensational instances of violence, there is a risk that ordinary encounters are lost. The concern here is that the focus on fear may override attention centring on practices that impact women's freedom. Recalling the notion of 'dominant narratives' (McKenzie-Mohr & Lafrance, 2011) and the discussion detailing some of the limitations of the harassment framework in the previous chapter, the stories available to understand and speak of experiences in public space are mainly framed in a binary of either compliment (sexual) or threat (harassment). Such narratives hide the ways in which encounters may be experienced as both, as well as discount experiences, such as 'cheer up', that do not fit into either framing. In addition, throughout participant accounts the mechanisms of normalisation combined with definitional and experiential ambiguity around 'what counts', to render precise measurement difficult. The 'experience of following' exemplifies this where, unless the intrusion escalated, participants here felt uncertain of whether their perception of being followed was accurate. The impact of habituated responses, which will be covered in more detail later, may also mean that women's successful resistance is lost in attempts to measure frequency.

The methodological task is how to combat such framings in the research process, widening out the stories that can be told and/or unearthing those that cannot. To combat the force of the habitual, the research design aimed to first assist in participants becoming more aware of men's intrusion and their responses through an initial conversation, and then to invite participants to examine new experiences in light of this heightened awareness through recording them as they happened over a period of two weeks to two months in research notebooks that acted as prompts in the follow-up conversations. Conversations were conducted in person in public spaces in South-East England, including London, Brighton, Reading and Cambridge, with eight conducted via Skype for women living beyond feasible travel boundaries. Conducting conversations with women in public space for a project focused on men's intrusion in public space gave rise to interesting opportunities for the phenomenon under investigation to play out in the research context. On route, during and returning from meeting participants I experienced men's intrusion, as did my participants. Where this had happened before meeting it helped bring an immediacy into the conversation. Where it happened afterwards for participants, many expressed pleasure in the follow-ups that they had the notebooks in which to record what had happened. For myself, it helped if occurring following the conversation to enable a 'testing out' of my own responses to and experience of intrusion, assisting in the iterative process of analysis. During the research process I also experienced men's stranger intrusion into online public spaces. The website used for recruitment remained online during the course of the project in order to enable ease of dissemination of findings to women who did not participate but had shown interest in the project. This decision revealed an unanticipated consequence of using online spaces for feminist projects as it was targeted by men's rights activists, following the publication of several media articles discussing the research and 'street harassment' more broadly (see Taylor, 2012; Topping, 2012). Over the course of a few hours the site received 36 comments ranging from threatening and abusive, to sarcastic and dismissive. After using internet search engines to trace the commentators and the research website, a YouTube video disparaging the research and encouraging others to troll the research website was discovered,[6] which contained an additional 52 derogatory comments about the project and myself. A growing body of evidence collected by activists and researchers is highlighting the experience of gendered abuse in online environments (Hardaker, 2010; Herring, Johnson & DiBenedetto, 1995; Henry & Powell, 2015; Herring, 1999, 2000; Herring, Job-Sluder, Scheckler & Barab, 2002; Jane, 2012; Reid, 1999). Given the similarities in practice, as well as in reasons given to invalidate concerns, further research on intrusion on women by men in public would benefit from including online contexts in order to explore the overlaps and differences – a modern day extension of Kelly's (1988) continuum of sexual violence.

Researching the ordinary: conversation and notebooks

The limitations of naming and defining practices create specific difficulties in using survey methodologies to capture ambiguous experiences, however attempts to come from women's experiential language also meet the limits of traditional, even semi-structured, interviewing. The principles of conversation provide opportunities that assist in overcoming these, as well as helping to counteract the processes of habituation. Conversation as method furthers the concept developed by Ann Oakley (2005) of conducting an interview *as if* it were a conversation, suggesting that for a feminist phenomenological project there is a benefit in moving beyond Oakley's concept to a joint exploration of research questions and towards conducting research *as* a conversation. This is not to deny the usefulness of all more traditional quantitative and qualitative methods, both needed for researching the powerful. Nor is it to make the unethical suggestion that comments made within a conversation not initiated as a form of research should later be used as research data. Rather it highlights that for particular questions, settings and research relationships, conversation as method may gain the most robust data and generate the most useful knowledge. Unlike an interview, all participants in conversation are involved in the active construction of meaning. The dynamic of power shifts as participants and researcher exchange, develop and bounce ideas between one another, rather than in the one-way exchange of conventional interviewing or even more participatory designs where, though participants interact, the structure and content remains defined by an outside source. Such a method builds on the work of Marjorie DeVault (1990), who moved beyond the traditional interview format to adopt an 'interactive approach' (Anderson & Jack, 1991). DeVault worked in collaboration with her respondents to 'co-construct' new words that accurately reflected their experiences, thoughts, and feelings. It is not that conversation removes the power dynamics inherent in the project of research; here, for example, the process of analysis and writing means that I ultimately recreate this co-creation, a process described by Coy (2006: 422) as 'my story of their stories'. There is, however, a more fluid exchange and co-creation of knowledge. In this way conversation as a research method echoes Beauvoir's theory of the situated self in two distinct yet associated senses: meaning is created and consolidated through active exchange with another (and the world); and, like the self, this meaning is best understood not separated out in quotes or stories, but in the context of the whole.

Each initial conversation opened with asking what interested the participant in the project, and from this developed, using the voices of other women and my own experiences instead of a topic guide, to encourage and expand the range of experiences that could be speakable. This resulted in a difficulty in analysing frequencies, as not all participants spoke about the same intrusions, however it did work to assist in combating habitual responses such as minimising or forgetting, an effect that was bolstered through the use of participant notebooks. The method of a notebook to record experiences of 'street harassment' had been previously used in June Larkin's (1997) study, however she found that '[d]espite the variations in their experiences, being harassed on the street was so routine that many hadn't bothered to include these incidents in their journals' (Larkin, 1997: 120). Building from Larkin's findings, in order to help in making these routine intrusions 'noteworthy', the notebooks were structured to guide participants to record the more common and/or ambiguous of men's intrusive practices.

This meant that the notebooks did in fact prefigure (some) of the stories that could be told, however this still appeared the best possible route into mundane experiences and habituated responses. Using an adaptation of the everyday incident analysis tool,[7] developed by Kelly and Westmarland (2015), individual participant notebooks were created to cover three categories that were understudied in the literature: 'space invaders' (unknown men intruding on space both physical and mental); 'the gaze' (both actual and anticipation of the gaze); and, in a phrase borrowed from Laniya (2005), 'verbal ejaculations' (including comments and noises). Each category asked specific questions designed to capture phenomenological detail through locating the experience temporally, in terms of before, during and after the incident, as well as encouraging detailed self-reflection regarding what participants were thinking, feeling and importantly doing. Women were also asked to record and reflect on how safe they felt and how free they felt throughout the encounter. In this way, the notebooks were more conventionally structured than the conversations, and they limited participants to capturing particular categories of intrusion. They were used mostly as a memory tool, enabling women in the follow-ups to reflect on intrusion with a level of immediacy which many were unable to summon during the initial conversations. Women brought their notebooks to the follow-up conversations and spoke with and through them, expanding on their own notes and often reflecting with surprise on the impacts they had recorded of particular intrusions – impacts that had frequently been forgotten even days after the encounter. They also submitted their notebooks at the end of participation which enabled, during analysis, a reflection both on what had been said during the follow-ups and on what, if anything, had been recorded at the time but silenced on reflection.

Representing the ordinary: poetic transcription

Analysis and data collection were thus enmeshed, enabling the latter conversations to also act as testing grounds for particular ways I was approaching the data. Analysis was best described as an ongoing process, not a discrete event – an iterative, inductive approach. Conversations were audio recorded and transcribed, with the transcripts returned to participants to check for accuracy and also to add or comment on their words so that what was represented for analysis was not only what was said but what they wanted to say.[8] The transcripts were then reviewed alongside the notebooks, for frequencies of particular intrusions. As the research design aimed particularly in the initial conversation to increase the spaces for women to define experience in their own terms, the categories used for analysis came from the participants, and not all forms of men's intrusive practices were covered in each conversation. Coming from the language of participants, 20 initial categories of men's intrusion were identified, and further analysis enabled the grouping into the six forms of men's stranger intrusion explored in Chapters 4 and 5: ordinary interruptions; verbal intrusions; the gaze, including 'creepshots'; physical intrusions; flashing and public masturbation; and the experience of being followed.[9] These categories, worked with when discussing the findings, are to be understood as analytical concepts developed with an awareness that the behaviours characterising men's intrusive practices were lived by participants as cumulative not isolated. The frequencies from the notebooks, alongside the qualitative responses given, were transformed into a spreadsheet and checked for themes, commonalities and differences. It was these differences, found both during the notebook stage and in the initial conversations, that led to the need for an analytic tool that would facilitate analysis of the connections and commonality between accounts, without collapsing the differences in individuals' social, political and personal locations in relation to the research topic: a tool able to 'elucidate patterns and uniformities in the women's responses, while striving to protect more unique experiences from disappearing in the analysis' (Jordan, 2005: 539). Given the sheer bizarreness of some men's intrusions, I also wanted to find a method of data representation whereby the breadth of the continuum of men's intrusion would be evident, a way of capturing the singularity. The answer to both aspirations was met through the creation of the poetic transcript, threaded through these chapters.[10]

The principles of poetic transcription and creative representation (Glesne, 1997; Faulkner, 2010; Prendergast, 2007; Richardson, 1992; Reilly, 2011) provide particular opportunities for researchers keen to retain the phenomenological, the experiential and evocative nature of qualitative data. Creative representation also suggests innovative opportunities to enable the apprehension of differing subjective experiences of shared social realities (West, 1987). Holding this in mind, I constructed a hybrid poem to explore such possibilities, with the poem then used as a dataset in itself to analyse alongside the full transcriptions of both initial and follow-up conversations and the data recorded in participant notebooks. Working through each transcript, comments from every particular intrusive encounter that women recalled were extracted, and every time women gave a general comment about the way they responded. The notebooks were not included as participants were able to recall with clarity particular responses to particular intrusions. The choice to use women's general responses over particular responses to individual instances was in part determined by participants themselves, many of whom were unable to remember specific reactions during the conversations. This choice revealed patterns that may have been lost in other forms of analysis, in particular participants' habitual embodied responses to the possibility of intrusion. In order to capture men's stranger intrusion as a shared social reality for women, the list of both particular encounters and general responses was randomised, with only the final two sentences ordered by design. Analysis was conducted both with and through the poetic transcript, identifying themes across the 50 initial conversations as well as representing in itself a form of data presentation that preserved the phenomenological detail of women's experiences of intrusion. Such a method is reminiscent of Beauvoir's use of fiction. For Beauvoir, there is a specific value in creative methods for relaying existential-phenomenological ideas, claiming that through fiction '[t]he reader interrogates, doubts, he takes sides and this hesitant elaboration of his thought is for him an enrichment that no doctrinal teaching could replace' (Beauvoir, 1946:

107). The poetic transcript seeks to do what structured writing cannot, to offer a useful means of producing a 'shared experience between research, audience, and participant' (Faulkner, 2009: 3), and to mirror in the reader's emotional response, aspects of the lived experience itself; its uninvited interruption, the repetition and relentlessness.

Sample characteristics

Ann J. Cahill has critiqued phenomenological analyses of embodiment such as that conducted by Iris Marion Young (2005) and Sandra Lee Bartky (1990) as being 'notoriously unraced' arguing that 'there are many different standards of femininity, that are particular to economic classes or ethnic groups' (Cahill, 2001: 153). Cahill acknowledges that modalities of embodiment for raced women's bodies may differ from that described in analyses that focus on the experiences of predominantly white women. Carrying Cahill's (2001) critique forward, embodied differences across ethnicities, ages and sexualities, influence both experiences of men's intrusions and their meanings, and that it is therefore analytically important to give the embodied characteristics of the women participating.

The research process enabled women to opt in or out at each point of participation. Of those participating in the initial conversations ($n=50$), 34 (65 per cent) went on to complete the notebook, with three of these notebooks being lost and one having nothing recorded in it,[11] leaving 30 notebooks (58 per cent of participants) for analysis. Just under two thirds (64 per cent, $n=32$) of participants completed a follow-up interview. Due to the unanticipated popularity of the project, as well as the iterative nature of analysis, saturation point was reached for the follow-up conversations after these 32 participants, with the remaining participants invited to give feedback through a form designed to be returned with their notebooks. An additional six participants chose to do this. A quarter of participants (27 per cent, $n=14$) did not participate beyond the initial conversation.

Given recent conversations about the dominance of white feminists in online spaces,[12] and the fact that the majority of research participants were recruited through online feminist networks,[13] almost three quarters (72 per cent) of the sample were women who identified as being from various white ethnic backgrounds[14] (see Figure 2.1). Whilst this is an under-representation of the national picture for England and Wales, where 86 per cent of census respondents are listed as coming from a white background, it is an over-representation for London, where the vast majority (78 per cent) of participants lived.[15] Census data for London has almost 60 per cent of the population identifying as white, just over 20 per cent as Asian, and close to 16 per cent as of Black and mixed-Black descent (ONS, 2011).

This over representation cannot be accounted for by online demographics in general, which are estimated to be roughly representative of the general population (Hamilton & Bowers, 2006). It may relate both to the predominance of white feminists in online spaces mentioned earlier (and thus to the demographics

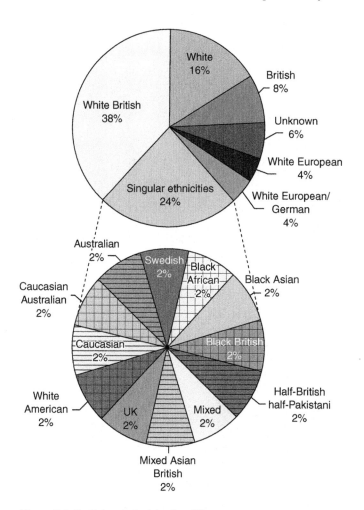

Figure 2.1 Participant ethnicity (*n*=50).

of women belonging to the networks through which the call for participants was disseminated), and/or reflect who felt they counted for the research and the research counted for them.

The age range (Figure 2.2) for participants showed a much greater breadth than anticipated; from 18–63 years, with just over a third (*n*=18) of participants aged 30 years and over.

The sexualities of participants also showed a greater range than anticipated (Figure 2.3), with almost a quarter identified as belonging to an LBQ group. Similar to ethnicity, participants were asked to self-define their sexuality, leading to some categories that sit outside of those comparable to other studies or to the national picture given by the census (ONS, 2011).

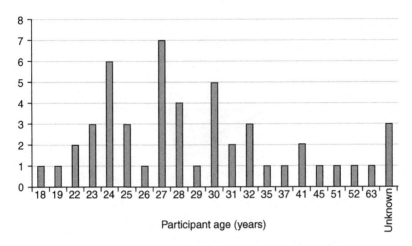

Figure 2.2 Participant age (*n*=50).

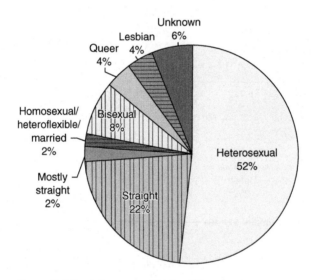

Figure 2.3 Participant sexuality (*n*=50).

The research sample recruited thus, though not representative, can still be considered a diverse group of women with a range of embodied differences. It did, however, generate limitations to what the study could explore. Given that there wasn't a large range of different ethnicities in the sample, the intersections of racist and sexist forms of men's stranger intrusions in public was not fully investigated. Where it did arise in the research, women of colour who participated spoke mostly of experiencing particular forms of intrusion from men who identified them as from their own communities, rather than of racist intrusions from white men. Josina, for example, was particularly aware of homophobia from Black and Latin American men who shared the communities of her and her girlfriend, whilst Shelley spoke of getting 'negative attention from Asian men' because of how she dressed in comparison to what was expected for a woman with her heritage. Whether such encounters stood out because the men practicing intrusion shared their communities, thus rendering the experiences memorable or remarkable in comparison to the seeming ubiquity of intrusion from white men, was unable to be explored in any depth, however provides interesting possibilities for future work.[16] Similarly, the absence of transgender women in the sample, particularly when seen alongside the findings around the impact of experiences in girlhood in Chapter 6, suggests an opening to explore the similarities and differences across individuals occupying different positions in the series of woman. Where our living experience of embodied selfhood is both corporeal and epistemological, both in our bodies and in our way of knowing the world, we need conceptual frames that are able to acknowledge how differences in material bodies may generate differences in the living experience of 'womanhood', without closing down the spaces of overlap and similarity.

It is to understand more fully the framework that is drawn on here to conceptualise women's embodiment, that the following chapter turns to a discussion of this study's theoretical foundations; Simone de Beauvoir's work on the situation and Maurice Merleau-Ponty on the body as lived.

Notes

1 Survey methodologies struggle to craft questions able to capture the ambiguity and complexity of particularly routine experiences of men's stranger intrusions. The requisite separations suggest either something has been experienced or it has not – which does not accurately reflect the way that many intrusions are experienced, as possibility or anticipation.

2 There is a resonance in the potential of phenomenology here, with that taken up by Frantz Fanon (2008) in outlining how the colonizing project of White Europe established the Black experience as an 'other' to define itself against.

3 Such a position is seen in Beauvoir's Introduction to the Second Volume of *The Second Sex*, making clear her desire to describe 'the common ground from which all singular feminine existence stems' (Beauvoir, 2011: 289).

4 Here I draw on the conceptualisation of the body made by Maurice Merleau-Ponty in his early phenomenology of the body-subject, *Phenomenology of Perception* (Merleau-Ponty, 2002), with the recognition that his later ontology of the flesh developed in *The Visible and Invisible* (Merleau-Ponty, 1968) sought to further dissolve the dualisms that plagued existential-phenomenology. For more on this see Beata Stawarska's (2002) critical examination of intersubjectivity in Merleau-Ponty's ontology.

5 Beauvoir's frequent claims that she was a writer, not a philosopher (see Simons, 1999), can be construed as a subversive act recognising knowledge as situated and refusing the hierarchies of power inherent in claims of a totalising system.

6 The term 'troll' refers to the fishing practice where a lure is dragged through the water with the intention of provoking a feeding frenzy amongst fish (Donath, 1998; Binns, 2012). There is no single agreed upon definition academically (see Hardaker, 2010 for

a discussion of terminology), and here the use of the 'troll' follows the broad definition given by Herring *et al.* (2002) as being a user of computer-mediated communication who is 'hostile to the purpose of forums, actively seeking to disrupt and undermine them' (357). This definition captures both the strategies of pseudo-sincerity and blatant abuse or flaming used to disrupt and instigate argument for the purposes of amusement, experienced during the research.

7   This tool is itself an adaptation of critical incident analysis, see Flanagan, 1954.

8   Only two participants took up the opportunity to comment on their transcripts, both using it as a space to expand on points they had been considering further since the initial conversation.

9   The 20 original categories measured were (in order of frequency reported): Ordinary interruptions (at this stage with a more limited range of practices included than in the final category); staring; sexualised comments; touched/groped; cheer up/smile; followed (definite); whistled/noises; flashed; followed (felt); abusive; blocked space; masturbated at; beeped; rape (known perpetrator); rape (stranger); car followed/solicited; intimate partner violence; photographed; childhood sexual abuse; and stalked. These were then further grouped separating out known from unknown men, and the intrusions from unknown men categorized into the six categories given above.

10 The poetic transcript has been previously published in full under the name of Fiona Elsgray (see Elsgray, 2014).

11 It is important to note that the empty notebook did not mean that the participant experienced no intrusions, simply that, like Larkin's (1997) participants, no experiences appeared 'noteworthy'.

12 In August, 2013, Mikki Kendall brought attention to the imbalances in online feminist media through the creation of a Twitter hashtag #solidarityisforwhitewomen (see Kendall, 2013).

13 The careful design of recruitment materials in order to avoid locating the research within an explicitly feminist paradigm did not help with the unexpected pick up of the call for participants through feminist social networks. Despite the care taken in terminology, the speed with which the call for participants circulated, and the networks through which it moved, resulted in the recruitment of a predominantly feminist sample. 36 per cent of participants (*n*= 18) explicitly cited being feminist as one of the motivations for participating in the study, with many more expressing a commitment to feminist principles during the conversations. That such a standpoint would be evident in participants is understandable given the topic under study, which may particularly interest women who have an acknowledged interest in gender inequality. It does mean, however, that the sample cannot be taken as representative of the experiences or opinions of women more generally and also that an additional dominant narrative needed consideration during analysis, that of feminist identified women always experiencing men's intrusion as 'harassment'.

14 Monitoring information was sent out to participants following initial conversations. Participants were asked to define their own ethnicity and sexuality rather than select from pre-defined options, hence the different terminologies used.

15 It may also reflect that not all of the women who participated were based in the United Kingdom; four women were living in cities in Egypt, Morocco, Germany and France, though all had previous experience of living in England.

16 Such possibilities are also suggested in the ways in which the ethnicities of intrusive men were only mentioned by participants when these: differed from their own (thus again becoming 'remarkable'); were directly connected to the intrusion itself (as in black and minority ethnic women being targeted by men from their own communities), or where the intrusion occurred whilst the woman was on holiday – again marking the experience as memorable. White men as a named group were absent in the narratives given.

References

Anderson, K., & Jack, D. C. (1991) 'Learning to Listen: Interview Techniques and Analysis', in Gluck, S. B., & Patai, D. (eds), *Women's Words: The Feminist Practice of Oral History*, Routledge, pp. 11–26.

Bartky, S. L. (1990) *Femininity and Domination*, Routledge.

Beauvoir, S. d. (1946) 'Littérature et métaphysique', *Les temps modernes*, 1 (7), pp. 1153–1163, translated in Fullbrook, E. & Fullbrook, K. (1998) 'Merleau-Ponty on Beauvoir's Literary-Philosophical Method', Twentieth World Congress of Philosophy, Boston, Massachusetts: August 10–15. Available at: www.bu.edu/wcp/Papers/Lite/LiteFull.htm, [accessed 8 May 2011].

Beauvoir, S. d. (2011) *The Second Sex*, Borde, C. & Malovany-Chevallier, S. (transl.), Vintage.

Binns, A. (2012) 'DON'T FEED THE TROLLS! Managing Troublemakers in Magazines' Online Communities', *Journalism Practice*, 6 (4), pp. 547–562.

Braidotti, R. (1993) 'Embodiment, Sexual Difference, and the Nomadic Subject', *Hypatia*, 8 (1), pp. 1–13.

Brison, S. J. (2002) *Aftermath: Violence and the Remaking of a Self*, Princeton University Press.

Brown, L. S. (1995) 'Not Outside the Range: One Feminist Perspective on Psychic Trauma', *Trauma: Explorations in Memory*, 100, pp. 100–101.

Brownmiller, S. (1975) *Against Our Will: Women and Rape*, Simon Schuster.

Burstow, B. (1992) *Radical Feminist Therapy: Working in the Context of Violence*, Sage.

Cahill, A. J. (2001) *Rethinking Rape*, Cornell University Press.

Collins, P. H. (2000) *Black Feminist Thought: Knowledge, Consciousness and the Politics of Empowerment* (2nd ed.), Routledge.

Cowburn, M., & Pringle, K. (2000) 'Pornography and Men's Practices', *Journal of Sexual Aggression*, 6 (1), pp. 52–66.

Coy, M. (2006) 'This Morning I'm a Researcher, This Afternoon I'm an Outreach Worker: Ethical Dilemmas in Practitioner Research', *International Journal of Social Research Methodology*, 9 (5), pp. 419–431.

Crenshaw, K. (1989) 'Demarginalizing the Intersection of Race and Sex: A Black Feminist Critique of Antidiscrimination Doctrine, Feminist Theory and Antiracist Politics', *The University of Chicago Legal Forum*, 1989, pp. 139–167, http://chicagounbound.uchicago.edu/uclf/vol1989/iss1/8.

Davhana-Maselesele, M. (2011) 'Trapped in the Cycle of Violence: A Phenomenological Study Describing the Stages of Coping with Domestic Violence', *Journal of Social Sciences*, 29 (1), pp. 1–8.

Denzin, N. K. (1984) 'Toward a Phenomenology of Domestic, Family Violence', *American Journal of Sociology*, 90 (3), pp. 483–513.

DeVault, M. L. (1990) 'Talking and Listening from Women's Standpoint: Feminist Strategies for Interviewing and Analysis', *Social Problems*, 37, pp. 96–116.

Donath, J. (1998) 'Identity and Deception in the Virtual Community', in Smith, M., & Kollock, P. (eds), *Communities in Cyberspace*, Routledge, pp. 29–59.

Du Toit, L. (2009). *A Philosophical Investigation of Rape: The Making and Unmaking of the Feminine Self*, Routledge.

Elsgray, F. (2014) 'You Need to Find a Version of the World You Can Be In: Experiencing the Continuum of Men's Intrusive Practices', *Qualitative Review*, 20 (4), pp. 507–519.

Fanon, F. (2008) *Black Skins, White Masks*, Philcox, R. (transl.), Grove Press.

Faulkner, S. L. (2009) 'Research/Poetry: Exploring Poet's Conceptualizations of Craft, Practice, and Good and Effective Poetry', *Educational Insights*, 13 (3), pp. 1–23.

Faulkner, S. L. (2010) *Poetry as Method: Conceptualizations of Craft, Research Poetry, and Practice*, Left Coast Press.

Flanagan, J. C. (1954) 'The Critical Incident Technique', *Psychological Bulletin*, 51 (4), 327.

Frank, A. (1995) *The Wounded Storyteller: Body, Illness and Ethics*, University of Chicago Press.

French, S. G., Teays, W., & Purdy, L. M. (eds) (1998) *Violence Against Women: Philosophical Perspectives*, Cornell University Press.

Garko, M. G. (1999) 'Existential Phenomenology and Feminist Research', *Psychology of Women Quarterly*, 23 (1), pp. 167–175.

Glesne, C. (1997) 'That Rare Feeling: Re-Presenting Research through Poetic Transcription', *Qualitative Inquiry*, 3 (2), pp. 202–221.

Greer, G. (1971) *The Female Eunuch*, Grand Publishing.

Grosz, E. (1993) 'Bodies and Knowledges: Feminism and the Crisis of Reason', in Alcoff, L., & Potter, E. (eds), *Feminist Epistemologies*, Routledge, pp. 187–216.

Hamilton, R. J., & Bowers, B. J. (2006) 'Internet Recruitment and E-Mail Interviews in Qualitative Studies', *Qualitative Health Research*, 16 (6), pp. 821–835.

Hanmer, J., & Saunders, S. (1984) *Well-Founded Fear: A Community Study of Violence to Women*, Hutchinson & Co.

Haraway, D. (1988) 'Situated Knowledges: The Science Question in Feminism and the Privilege of Partial Perspective', *Feminist Studies*, 14 (3), pp. 575–599.

Hardaker, C. (2010) 'Trolling in Asynchronous Computer-Mediated Communication: From User Discussions to Academic Definitions', *Journal of Politeness Research. Language, Behaviour, Culture*, 6 (2), pp. 215–242.

Harding, S. G. (1991) *Whose Science? Whose Knowledge?: Thinking from Women's Lives*, Cornell University Press.

Harris, A. P. (1990) 'Race and Essentialism in Feminist Legal Theory', *Stanford Law Review*, 42 (3), pp. 581–616.

Hartsock, N. C. (1983) 'The Feminist Standpoint: Developing the Ground for a Specifically Feminist Historical Materialism', in Harding, S., & Hintikka, M. B. (eds), *Discovering Reality*, D. Reidel Publishing Company, pp. 283–310.

Hartsock, N. C. (2006) 'Experience, Embodiment and Epistemologies', *Hypatia*, 21 (2), pp. 178–183.

Heben, T. (1994–95) 'Radical Reshaping of the Law: Interpreting and Remedying Street Harassment', *Southern California Review of Law and Women's Studies*, 183, pp. 183–220.

Heidegger, M. (1996) *Being and Time*, Stambaugh, J. (transl.), State University of New York Press.

Heinämaa, S. (2003) 'The Body as Instrument and as Expression', in Card, C. (ed.), *The Cambridge Companion to Simone de Beauvoir*, Cambridge University Press, pp. 66–86.

Heinämaa, S. (2006) 'Feminism' (Chapter 34), in Dreyfus, H. L. & Wrathall, M. A. (eds), *A Companion to Phenomenology and Existentialism*, Blackwell Publishing Ltd.

Henry, N., & Powell, A. (2015) 'Embodied Harms: Gender, Shame, and Technology-Facilitated Sexual Violence', *Violence Against Women*, 21 (6), pp. 758–779.

Herman, J. L. (1992) *Trauma and Recovery*, Basic Books.

Herring, S. (1999) 'The Rhetorical Dynamics of Gender Harassment On-Line', *The Information Society*, 15, pp. 151–167.

Herring, S. (2000) 'Gender Differences in CMC: Findings and Implications', *Computer Professionals for Social Responsibility Newsletter*, Winter, www.cpsr.org/publications/newsletters/issues/2000/Winter2000/index.html, [accessed 9 May 2011].

Herring, S., Job-Sluder, K., Scheckler, R., & Barab, S. (2002) 'Searching for Safety Online: Managing "Trolling" in a Feminist Forum', *The Information Society*, 18 (5), pp. 371–384.

Herring, S., Johnson, D. A., & DiBenedetto, T. (1995) ' "This Discussion is Going Too Far!": Male Resistance to Female Participation on the Internet', in Hall, K., & Bucholtz, M. (eds), *Gender Articulated: Language and the Socially Constructed Self*, Routledge, pp. 67–96.

Husserl, E. (1960) *Cartesian Meditations*, Cairns, D. (transl.), M. Nijhoff.

Husserl, E. (2001) *Logical Investigations* (Vol. 1). Findlay, N. J. (transl.), Psychology Press.

Jane, E. A. (2014) ' "Your a Ugly, Whorish, Slut" Understanding E-bile', *Feminist Media Studies*, 14 (4), pp. 531–546.

Jordan, J. (2005) 'What Would MacGyver Do? The Meaning(s) of Resistance and Survival', *Violence Against Women*, 11 (4), pp. 531–559.

Kelly, L. (1988) *Surviving Sexual Violence*, Polity Press.

Kelly, L. (1996) 'Weasel Words: Paedophiles and the Cycle of Abuse', *Trouble and Strife*, 33, www.troubleandstrife.org/articles/issue-33/weasel-words-paedophiles-and-the-cycle-ofabuse/ [accessed 1 February 2014].

Kelly, L. (2012) 'Preface', in Brown, J., & Walklate, S. (eds), *Handbook on Sexual Violence*, Routledge, pp. xvii–1.

Kelly, L., Burton, S., & Regan, L. (1994). 'Researching Women's Lives or Studying Women's Oppression? Reflections on what Constitutes Feminist Research', in Maynard, M., & Purvis, J. (eds) *Researching Women's Lives from a Feminist Perspective*, Taylor & Francis, pp. 27–48.

Kelly, L. & Westmarland, N. (2015) *Domestic Violence Perpetrator Programmes: Steps Towards Change*. Project Mirabal Final Report, London Metropolitan University and Durham University.

Kendall, M. (2013) '#SolidarityIsForWhiteWomen: Women of Color's Issue with Digital Feminism', *Guardian: Comment is Free*, 4 August 2013, www.theguardian.com/commentisfree/2013/aug/14/solidarityisforwhitewomenhashtag-feminism [accessed 6 August 2013].

Laniya, O. O. (2005) 'Street Smut: Gender, Media, and the Legal Power Dynamics of Street Harassment, or Hey Sexy and Other Verbal Ejaculations', *Columbia Journal of Gender & Law*, 14, pp. 91–142.

Larkin, J. (1997) 'Sexual Terrorism on the Street: The Moulding of Young Women into Subordination', in Thomas, A. M., & Kitzinger, C. (eds), *Sexual Harassment: Contemporary Feminist Perspectives*, Open University Press, pp. 115–130.

Mason, G. (2002) *The Spectacle of Violence*, Routledge.

McKenzie-Mohr, S., & Lafrance, M. N. (2011) 'Telling Stories Without the Words: "Tightrope Talk" in Women's Accounts of Coming to Live Well after Rape or Depression', *Feminism & Psychology*, 21 (1), pp. 49–73.

McNay, L. (2004) 'Agency and Experience: Gender as a Lived Relation', *The Sociological Review*, 52 (2), pp. 173–190.

Merleau-Ponty, M. (1968) *Visible and the Invisible*, Lingis, A. (transl.), Northwestern University Press.

Merleau-Ponty, M. (2002) *Phenomenology of Perception*, Smith, C. (transl.), Routledge.

Merry, S. E. (2006) *Human Rights and Gender Violence: Translating International Law into Local Justice*, University of Chicago Press.

Mui, C. (2005) 'A Feminist-Sartrean Approach to Understanding Rape Trauma', *Sartre Studies International*, 11(1–2), pp. 153–165.

Oakley, A. (ed.) (2005) *The Ann Oakley Reader: Gender, Women and Social Science*, The Policy Press.

Office for National Statistics (ONS) (2011) Census: Aggregate data (England and Wales), UK Data Service Census Support, http://infuse.mimas.ac.uk. This information is licensed under the terms of the Open Government Licence [www.nationalarchives.gov.uk/doc/open-government-licence/version/2] [accessed, 9 December 2013].

Pineau, L. (1989) 'Date Rape: A Feminist Analysis', *Law and Philosophy*, 8 (2), pp. 217–243.

Prendergast, M. (2007) 'Thinking Narrative (on the Vancouver Island ferry): A Hybrid Poem', *Qualitative Inquiry*, 13, pp. 743–744.

Price, L. S. (2005) *Feminist Frameworks: Building Theory on Violence Against Women*, Fernwood.

Reid, E. (1999) 'Hierarchy and Power: Social Control in Cyberspace', in Smith, M. A., & Kollock, P. (eds), *Communities in Cyberspace*, Routledge, pp. 107–133.

Reilly, R. C. (2011) ' "We Knew Her …" Murder in a Small Town: A Hybrid Work in Three Voices', *Qualitative Inquiry*, 17, pp. 599–601.

Richardson, L. (1992) 'The Consequences of Poetic Representation', in Ellis, C. & Flaherty, M. G. (eds), *Investigating Subjectivity: Research on Lived Experience*, Sage, pp. 125–137.

Simons, M. A. (1999) *Beauvoir and The Second Sex: Feminism, Race and the Origins of Existentialism*, Rowman & Littlefield.

Smith, D. E. (1987) *The Everyday World as Problematic: A Feminist Sociology*, University of Toronto Press.

Smith, D. E. (1990) *The Conceptual Practices of Power: A Feminist Sociology of Knowledge*, University of Toronto Press.

Stanko, E. (1985) *Intimate Intrusions: Women's Experience of Male Violence*, Unwin Hyman.

Stanley, L., & Wise, S. (1983) *Breaking Out: Feminist Consciousness and Feminist Research*, Routledge.

Stanley, L., & Wise, S. (1990) 'Method, Methodology and Epistemology in Feminist Research Processes', in Reinharz, S. (ed.), *Feminist Praxis: Research, Theory and Epistemology in Feminist Sociology*, Routledge, pp. 20–60.

Stanley, L., & Wise, S. (1993) *Breaking Out Again: Feminist Ontology and Epistemology*, Routledge.

Stawarska, B. (2002) 'Reversibility and Intersubjectivity in Merleau-Ponty's Ontology', *The Journal of the British Society for Phenomenology*, 33 (2), pp. 155–166.

Taylor, J. (2012) 'Catcalls, Whistles, Groping: The Everyday Picture of Sexual Harassment in London', *Independent*, www.independent.co.uk/news/uk/home-news/catcalls-whistles-groping-the-everyday-picture-of-sexual-harassment-in-london-7786185.html [accessed 4 March 2013].

Topping, A. (2012) 'Four in 10 Young Women Sexually Harassed in Public Spaces, Survey Finds', *Guardian*, www.guardian.co.uk/lifeandstyle/2012/may/25/four-10-women-sexually-harassed [accessed 4 March 2013].

Weeks, K. (1998) *Constituting Feminist Subjects*, Cornell University Press.

West, R. L. (1987) 'The Difference in Women's Hedonic Lives: A Phenomenological Critique of Feminist Legal Theory', *Wisconsin Women's Law Journal*, 3 (81), pp. 81–145.

Wise, S., & Stanley, L. (1987) *Georgie Porgie: Sexual Harassment in Everyday Life*, Pandora Press.

Young, I. M. (2005) *On Female Body Experience: 'Throwing Like a Girl' and Other Essays*, Oxford University Press.

I had one guy who mimicked a blowjob from the car window one time.
If you don't put make up on you can become quite invisible.
Someone did just literally stop and say oi love you should be on Weightwatchers.
I don't really like being in crowded places just in case.
He got out his penis and he was trying to make me touch it.
It wears you down in the end.

>He yelled after me you whore, you whore, that was a compliment
>why didn't you say thank you,
>his friend said he wants to dog you,
>and another one said you've got a face like shit.

He was going oh c'mon, just let me take a few pictures.
I'll try to avoid situations where I am going to be on my own.
He just reached up and grabbed my boob.
Look straight ahead and keep walking.
He pulled his trousers down and was having a wank.
I just refuse to let that stop me. I can't accept it.

And a guy came up from behind and attacked me
and stuck his hands underneath my
skirt and tried to assault me or did assault me.
The guy that date raped me kept asking me out for weeks afterwards.
My husband tried to strangle me.
He just said something really innocent at first.

This guy came up to me and said oh so you look nice,
I've never been with a fire-crotch before.
I won't like hit someone but I'll inch my elbows back.
One of them jumped out and went BOO like that.
I've developed what my friends call bitch face.
His arm was going back like going alright, up and down my leg.
I've just learnt to ignore them.

>Sexy lady, nice tits, hello baby, hello baby.
>He was chasing us and screaming at us.

>He decided he was going to lock me in the house.

This young guy stood opposite me just sort of jigging up and down.
Trying to walk less sexily, trying to not draw attention to myself.
He only just said hello beautiful.
I don't look at anybody ever.
All of a sudden this guy turns up and he's got it out and he's going for it,
like actually got it out properly.

This is not happening, I'm in a glass box.

I had a man wank off over me on the tube.
He was like no you don't understand my cock is huge.
There was this guy in a bush behind us jerking off.
He just repeated it again and again following me down the street.

He just came up to me and punched me in the gut.
I try to make myself feel not scared and fine.
Some guy just took a swig of water out of his water bottle and spat it in my face.
I just mock, in a banter kind of way.
He slowed down and watched me walk on a bit and then started following me.
I know where my keys are.

I heard footsteps behind me, fast approaching, running footsteps
and I turned around
and this guy just stopped in his tracks.

I went and hid under the porch bit and he didn't see me,
and he didn't see me under my house,
and he drove back really slowly
looking.

He was like oh come on get in the car I'll give you a lift.
I prepare myself by distracting myself.
A couple of guys actually moved seats to sit in front of me.
I usually try to sit next to women.
And as he went past he just flashed.
I can just power straight past them, with my head up and barely register.

They'd called me over to the car,
wound the window down and said I need some directions.
I asked him where to and
he pointed to his crotch.

3   The situated self

In order to maintain the complex and multiple ways in which the continuum of sexual violence impacts on the self as we live it, a conceptualisation of this self is required that can hold both the way we act on and the way we are acted on by the world. Such a view is needed to illuminate the shared aspects of women's experiences of men's stranger intrusions in order to make sense of and challenge it, as well as to explore how the social meanings of particular bodies open different avenues for and experiences of intrusion. This need is evident throughout feminist work on men's violence against women; a desire to resist removing women's agency in responding to men's violence and/or intrusion, without claiming that actions made within unequal conditions are expressions of absolute freedom. Simone de Beauvoir's development of the self as a situated body-subject provides a framework for balancing this tension. As such, returning to her conceptualisation of the situated self, offers a useful framework for addressing some of the questions about power and agency that trouble recent feminist thinking.

Situating Beauvoir

For Beauvoir, 'every concrete human being is always uniquely situated' (2011: 4), and it is her application and extension of this concept, together with the role of ambiguity, which shows such promise for theorists working on men's violence. Her account of the situated self enables recognition of our concrete freedom alongside the acknowledgement of how that core expression of this freedom, our agency, is rooted in real, often restrictive, contexts. Our choices, actions, even desires are not free-floating – they spring from our material bodies, located in ways that open and close particular possibilities to us. Our agency is situated.

In line with the numerous misrepresentations Beauvoir made of her own philosophical contributions, she credited Jean-Paul Sartre with originating the idea of situation – a misleading claim since both she and Sartre drew upon, and disagreed about, Heidegger's concept of being-in-situation.[1] Heidegger (1996) posited *Dasein* as 'delivered over' to the world and that through this human existence has the inescapable characteristic of *geworfenheit* or 'thrownness'. We are thrown without knowledge or choice into a world that was there before us and will remain after us, and in this thrownness we find ourselves in the world always already in a particular situation, and in relation to the Other who forms part of the conditions grounding our freedom; part of the conditions for our being a self at all. I was born as a white, able-bodied female in the early 1980s, in a small logging town on the North Island of New Zealand. None of these material conditions, their socio-historical meaning or indeed my entry into the world itself, are expressions of my freedom, however my freedom depends on their existence. My situation is what makes my freedom possible as well as being the starting point from which I choose my projects, projects which must have a meaning beyond me (both temporally and spatially) if they are to have meaning *for* me.[2] The influence of our situation on our choice of projects is seen in the way that situation acts to expand our possibilities in the world. A change to my birthplace would have changed my possibilities; a change to my body would have altered the starting point for my perspective on the world. Our situation does not constitute us, yet it does give us a location within the world through which it becomes meaningful – through which it becomes 'ours'.

Questions about how our situation can act not just as an expansion but also as the horizon for our projects are where Beauvoir significantly departs from Sartre and where she usefully employs the notion of ambiguity as the basis of human existence – a basis particularly expressed by the situation of 'woman'. In her exploration of ambiguity in the work of both Beauvoir and Merleau-Ponty, Monika Langer points to the need to let go of our insistence on achieving precision in our formation of the concept, quoting Merleau-Ponty's comments during a conference in 1951 that 'if one could conceive ambiguity with total clarity, it would no longer be ambiguous' (Langer, 2003: 90). Ambiguity is used throughout Beauvoir's writing to capture the uneasy relationship springing from of our freedom as situated and our existence as embodied. We are both freedom – that is a subject able to choose, act and make meaning of our life through the taking up of projects – and *facticity*, the term used to convey the material 'facts' of our existence, some of which become limiting factors for our freedom. To understand the possibilities in Beauvoir for theorising men's violence against women as part of women's situation, we need to carefully unpack where, historically, the singularity of her insights have been overlooked, beginning with this concept of ambiguity.

Situation and ambiguity

The particular usefulness of Beauvoir for thinking through female embodiment can be unearthed by a brief exploration of two other French theorists whose conceptual frameworks are often adopted and adapted by feminists wanting to explore the historically located inscription of social processes on the female body – Michel Foucault and Pierre Bourdieu.[3]

Foucault offers possibilities to feminist theorists keen to reconceptualise power as not being something possessed by one group over another but rather as what Bordo (1993) sees as a relational network consisting of practices, institutions and technologies (see Foucault 1979, 1980). Similarly, his genealogy of the political economy of body could provide a useful tool through which to examine the operations of the continuum of sexual violence as a disciplinary practice, though the uncritical deployment of his theory in this way may encounter obstacles.[4] However there are unresolved, maybe irresolvable, tensions in mobilising Foucault in feminist work on men's violence – most notably the risk of losing the multiple ways women find different levels of access to agency in and through the current gender order.[5] Carelessness could give weight to the accusation of 'victim feminism', levelled against feminists focusing on men's violence. The charge here is that concentrating on violence against women and girls as a context structuring, limiting, situating women's freedom undermines women's sexual agency. Such a perspective locks us into an unhelpful binary of oppression or action, moving further from articulating our experiences as lived. The complex, multiple and uneasy ways in which women individually and collectively live our agency in the current gender order is lost.

Increasingly critical of Foucault himself,[6] Pierre Bourdieu developed the concept of habitus through building on the phenomenological insights of Husserl. Habitus represents how social structures are embedded in our embodied selves, giving a conceptual tool for describing how social conditions and contexts set what we define as 'reasonable' actions, perceptions and thought processes within them (see Bourdieu, 1998). We can see here a resonance of situation in its Beauvoirian sense. The connections between the conceptual thinking of Beauvoir and Bourdieu have been commented on by Toril Moi (1991), and more broadly, the links between Merleau-Ponty, Martin Heidegger and Bourdieu have also been made (Crossley, 2001; Dreyfus & Rabinow, 1993; Young, 2005).[7] The concept has also been productively employed by feminist researchers working on men's violence. Maddy Coy's (2009) use of habitus enables an exploration of how women's experiences of the local authority care system are inscribed on the body in a way conducive to selling sexual access to the body. Michele Ruyters (2012) employs habitus to conceptualise how some women's experience of embodiment as vulnerability can be transformed through the pedagogic practice of self-defence training. Again, however, we're left with questions as to the possibilities Bourdieu sees for freedom and individual difference in the face of the totalising force of habitus – questions raised by Judith Butler (1997) and Iris Marion Young (2005).[8]

What remains to be seen across feminist employment of Foucault and Bourdieu is how we can hold their illuminations of the complexities of power without inadvertently rewriting what we experience as freedom into solely an effect of social processes. What is needed is a theory of the embodied self and embodied practices that is able to account for the different meanings given to, and created by, the individual through our living experience: a theory that can hold the ambiguity of the self as both a collection of social prescriptions and processes, and at the same time an agent with differing levels of access to freedom. The Beauvoirian concept of situation provides such a theoretical tool, enabling exploration of the ambiguous position of 'victim-survivor'[9] as an expression of both how women are both acted on by, and choose to act within and beyond, men's violence. Beauvoir heralds such ambiguity as embedded in human existence and, importantly, as fundamental to women's situation as the inessential Other.

> [W]hat singularly defines the situation of woman is that being, like all humans, an autonomous freedom, she discovers and chooses herself in a world where men force her to assume herself as Other.... Woman's drama lies in this conflict between the fundamental claim of every subject, which always posits itself as essential, and the demands of a situation that constitutes her as inessential.
>
> (Beauvoir, 2011: 17)

For Beauvoir, the situation of women under patriarchy expresses the ontological ambiguity of human beings more concretely than that of men. Beauvoir does not try to resolve the ambiguity, making us either a freely choosing subject or solely constructed through external forces. Instead, she believes existence is characterised by this conflict of being both, a continual struggle between our capacity for freedom and the alienating processes of socialisation.

Situation and freedom

Beauvoir's use of 'situation', then, refers to the meanings derived from the total context of our living experience, not just the meanings determined by the material 'facts' of our existence (our facticity) and its values within a particular historically located context. Recognising the material details of our embodiment as the basis from which our freedom both exists and is limited, means that situation, for Beauvoir, is also the ways in which these details emerge in light of our particular projects. The term 'project' has a particular meaning within the existentialist tradition, a meaning Beauvoir drew on. Our embodied being-in-the-world was seen by both Beauvoir and Jean-Paul Sartre as an act of self-creation, the permanent realisation of our possibilities. We are nothing outside of the undertakings made in light of our broader chosen projects; our existence 'nothing else but a series of enterprises' (Sartre, 1973: 57). This position is also found in one of Beauvoir's most famous, and most misinterpreted, statements from *The Second Sex*, that '[o]ne is not born, but rather becomes, woman' (Beauvoir, 2011: 293).[10] Our projects, including the project of gender, are acts of becoming, with these projects situated rather than free-floating and both our living body and the existence of the Other forming part of our situation. There is thus a crucial difference in how Beauvoir understands the freedom underlying our projects compared to the position of Sartre. Beauvoir recognises the embodied self as both free and constrained, claiming that 'the idea of freedom is not incompatible with the existence of certain constraints' (Beauvoir, 2011: 57). Human 'being' is such that we have the ability to act on the world and make it our own through the taking up of meaningful projects, where for a project to be meaningful it must be one which could be taken up by the Other (and thus one which supports their freedom). At the same time our situation is constituted by forces that are not of our making, forces that may act to limit the projects we choose. Our embodiment is one of these. Our embodiment forms part of our facticity, outside of our freedom to change. We can, for example, choose to alter our bodies but we cannot choose to not be embodied. Our corporeal body then, that which we did not choose, already forms a situation in itself, creating and limiting our possibilities in the world. Her use of 'becoming' is thus substantially different from that of Sartre who upheld an absolute ontological freedom whereby even under material constraints, we are always free to choose the meaning we give our situation (Sartre, 2007).

Beauvoir had already begun to conceptualise freedom as situated and crucially interdependent in her early ethical essays *Pyrrhus and Cineas* (2004) and *The Ethics of Ambiguity* (1976). In her early autobiography, *The Prime of Life* (1962), she reveals that her break with Sartre's ontological freedom was grounded in the living experience of gender inequality.

> I maintained that, from the point of view of freedom, as Sartre defined it ... not every situation is equal: what transcendence is possible for a woman locked up in a harem? Even such a cloistered existence could be lived in several different ways, Sartre said. I clung to my opinion for a long time and then made only a token submission. Basically I was right. But to have been able to defend my position, I would have had to abandon the terrain of individualist, thus idealist, morality, where we stood.
>
> (Beauvoir, 1962: 346)

That Beauvoir remained relatively quiet on the ways in which her theory of freedom significantly broke with that of Sartre has had particular consequences for Beauvoir's legacy. Judith Butler has both notably developed and critiqued Beauvoir's concept of the self in putting forward her performative theory of gender (Butler, 1985, 1986). For Butler, Beauvoir's statement on becoming a woman is an assertion of 'the non-coincidence of natural and gendered identity' (Butler, 1987: 128). Following this, Butler was able to claim that 'Simone de Beauvoir's formulation distinguishes sex from gender and suggests that gender is an aspect of identity gradually acquired' (Butler, 1986: 35).

> For Simone de Beauvoir, it seems, the verb 'become' contains a consequential ambiguity. Gender is not only a cultural construction imposed upon identity, but in some sense gender is a process of constructing ourselves. To become a woman is a purposive and appropriate set of acts, the acquisition of a skill, a 'project' to use Sartrian terms, to assume a certain corporal style and significance. When 'become' is taken to mean 'purposefully assume or embody', it seems that Simone de Beauvoir is appealing to a voluntaristic account of gender.
>
> (Butler, 1986: 36)

There is a subtle misstep here in collapsing together the Beauvoirian and Sartrean concepts of freedom which underwrite our ability to choose a project, a result of the limited protests Beauvoir herself made of the divergence and of the fact that Butler was writing here before the 'scholarly renaissance' (Simons, 2010: 910) that has taken place since Beauvoir's death in 1986.[11] There is also no acknowledgment of the ways in which the Beauvoirian project has a relational rather than individual nature. Beauvoir's theory of situated freedom in fact marked a critical departure from Sartre in its assertion that not everyone has the same capacity to freely choose their project from a range of possibilities. Freedom, for Beauvoir, exists in situation, an ambiguous foundation of both expression and constraint. Basing theory in living experiences means a necessary acknowledgment of the impact of our situation in both limiting and expanding our possibilities and our freedom to choose amongst them. Butler's claim that 'Simone de Beauvoir's view of gender as an incessant project, a daily act of reconstitution and interpretation, draws upon Sartre's doctrine of pre-reflective choice' (Butler, 1985: 508), hides the ways in which Beauvoir's writing signalled a departure from, not an exercise in, a Sartrean vision of existential choice. Beauvoir does not assert freedom as an ontological category of being where all expressions of agency are equal. Women have a situated freedom, constituted within socio-historical locations, which are structured both by and beyond us. Sonia Kruks (1992) highlights the ways in which Butler's reading of Beauvoir loses this difference, 'the point where Beauvoir breaks with Sartre in arguing that, for the oppressed, a "project" can cease to be possible' (Kruks, 1992: 101, note 23).

Situated agency

Beauvoir is thus useful for current feminist theorising seeking to conceptualise the ambiguous balance of women's agency, particularly though not solely sexual agency, as it is lived in an unequal gender order (see Coy & Garner, 2012; Gill, 2007, 2008). For Kathy Miriam (2005: 14), discussions of agency must hold forefront how the term is 'defined as a capacity to negotiate with a situation that is itself taken for granted as inevitable'. Building on Beauvoir's situated freedom, we can posit that our agency is situated, with 'situated' here a direct development of 'situation' in its Beauvoirian sense – that is where the body is understood as a situation itself.

The terminology of 'situated agency' exists within welfare economics (see Peter, 2003), and is also employed by Barbara Herman (1991) in her discussion of Kantian ethics in the context of understanding the difference between agency and autonomy.

> Autonomy is the condition of the will that makes agency possible.... But *agency* is not completely described by identifying a will as rational. As human agents we are not distinct from our contingent ends, our culture, our history, or our actual (and possible) relations to others. Agency is situated.
> (Herman, 1991: 795)

Seen in this way, autonomy is expressed through our situated agency, with acknowledgement of the limits of particular situations not therefore resulting in a denial of autonomy. The concept of situated agency gives us a tool for exploring women's agency under an unequal gender order, drawing on the ambiguity of human existence to avoid binaries of freedom or constraint, subject or object, actor or victim. Recognising agency as situated helps to heed the warning of Bina Agarwal (1997) that emphasising the restrictions on women's agency risks undermining the multitude of ways women act within these restrictions, alongside refusing to promote the individualist notion of all actions as equal regardless of structural inequalities experienced between actors. It responds to Iris Marion Young's (2005) call for the need to include a theory of embodiment in any analysis of agency and also rises to the challenge posed by McNay (2004) of rethinking an idea of agency around a non-reductive notion of experience, where 'experience', conceptualised through Beauvoir's situation, is an ambiguous blend of the structural and the material.

Similar to situated agency, Evan Stark sees the constraints imposed on women by controlling partners as limiting their opportunities to 'enact their life projects, not on their capacity to do so' (Stark, 2009: 1514). Stark claims that in reconceptualising domestic violence from an assault-based model to one of experienced reality, 'no challenge was more formidable than conveying the extent of women's resiliency, resistance, capacity and courage in the face of coercive control without minimising the comprehensiveness of the strategy' (Stark, 2009: 1514). His conceptualisation of coercive control as continuous, cumulative, persistent and invisible in plain sight, rather than focusing on episodic, incident-based injury, has parallels to the operations of men's stranger intrusion. Such a claim connects to Beauvoir's 'situation', where situation refers to the total context in which and through which we give our life meaning through our choice of projects. For Stark, as for Beauvoir, freedom and agency are situated. A space is thus opened for feminists wanting to talk about men's violence as a constraining context for women, without forfeiting women's autonomy and our acts of resistance and resilience.

Situation, sex and gender

There is a second concern with Butler's early reading of Beauvoir, one that leads into a discussion of the living body. Sara Heinämaa has argued that Butler's interpretation of Beauvoir holds a problematic starting position of *The Second Sex* as being 'a thesis about the sex/gender relationship' (Heinämaa, 1997: 20). Again, Beauvoir's declination to explicitly signal her breaks with her male colleagues, in particular but not only Sartre, has meant that many of the ways she has been taken up subsequently have lost the uniqueness of her insights. The Beauvoirian self is a situated and thus necessarily embodied self, a 'body-subject' or 'bodily-self' not a pure, disembodied consciousness. The sex/gender distinction that Judith Butler claims was one of the pivotal contributions of Beauvoir's *Second Sex*, though useful in challenging essentialist arguments for specific regimes of gender inequality, reiterates culture/nature and mind/body dichotomies, leaving the body outside history. This Cartesian replication also supports the notion of a separate, disembodied 'self', an unhelpful theorisation for feminist theory on violence and one not supported by Beauvoir's theory of situation.

Beauvoir maintained that the body is a situation and that the human being is an historical idea. As early as in the *Ethics of Ambiguity*, Beauvoir states her belief that 'the body itself is not a brute fact. It expresses our relationship to the world' (Beauvoir, 1976: 41). This demonstrates how the lived or living body for Beauvoir is always experienced as both the biological and the social, and always in relation. This is, however, at odds with the common usage of Beauvoir's work to usher in the sex/gender distinction. Toril Moi (1999) makes a compelling argument for how the heuristic distinction between sex and gender, as popularly understood, conflicts with Beauvoir's view of the body-subject, a conflict that Butler acknowledges yet seems to over-ride in her presentation of Beauvoir's contributions (Butler, 1986). For Moi, separating sex from gender has the consequence of turning 'sex into an ahistorical and curiously disembodied entity divorced from concrete historical and social meanings' (1999: 30), a separation crucially in tension with Beauvoir's understanding of the ambiguity of human existence.[12] Lois McNay (2004) also uses the situatedness of being, the idea that 'abstract forces only reveal themselves in the lived reality of social relations' (175), to suggest gender is a lived social relation rather than structural location. McNay uses Bourdieu's social phenomenology rather than Beauvoir's situation to develop her argument, though she does signal to the ways in which Bourdieu's arguments resemble Beauvoir's. Additionally, feminist standpoint theorist Nancy Hartsock argues for a move beyond the theoretical divide between sex and gender, claiming that the work of Judith Butler has contributed to the language allowing such a move by 'recognizing that bodies are both natural and cultural and neither, and that they are created in discursive and physical ways and intertwined to the point where they cannot be separated' (Hartsock, 2006: 182). This recognition, however, formed one of the fundamental components of Beauvoir's concept of the situated self, though it was lost in an interpretation, supported by Butler (1985), of 'born' and 'becoming' as representing a binary of biological sex against or apart from the social meanings of bodies.

In her more recent work, Sara Heinämaa argues that the similarities between the Beauvoirian body-subject intertwined in the social and natural worlds and Butler's assertion that the materiality of sexed bodies itself is socially constituted, are lost due to Butler's conflation of Beauvoirian and Sartrean concepts of the self. Heinämaa (2001) suggests that close study of the Beauvoirian self reveals it is actually closer to Merleau-Ponty's concept of a body-subject intertwined with the world. Butler's early work recognises the significance of Beauvoir's Merleau-Pontian understanding of the body, however she does not unearth the uniqueness in Beauvoir's gendered application of his insights.

In Merleau-Ponty's reflections in *The Phenomenology of Perception* on 'the body in its sexual being', he ... claims that the body is 'an historical idea' rather than a 'natural species'. Significantly, it is this claim that Simone de Beauvoir cites in *The Second Sex* when she sets the stage for her claim that 'woman', and by extension, any gender, is an historical situation rather than a natural fact.

(Butler, 1988: 520)

What is lost in the claim of 'historical situation rather than natural fact' is the ambiguity Beauvoir believed to be so fundamental to human existence and so particularly expressed by women's situation. Combined with her theory of the self as situated, Beauvoir's welcoming of the ambiguity of existence can be used to dissolve the binary of sex and gender in line with Butler's own project, rather than establish it. For Beauvoir, there is no body-subject outside of our historical situation. She conceptualises the body as living, the self as a living bodily-self. In effect, there are no 'natural facts of the body' as this presupposes the possibility of the body existing outside it being lived, and the self existing beyond its being embodied, both claims Beauvoir would refute. Our situation derives from the *total context* of our living experience, thus including the materiality of the body rather than being posited against it. This is where Butler's reading of Beauvoir subtly misrepresents the concept of situation.

> If gender is a way of 'existing' one's body, and one's body is a 'situation', a field of cultural possibilities both received and reinterpreted, then gender seems to be a thoroughly cultural affair. That one becomes one's gender seems now to imply more than the distinction between sex and gender. Not only is gender no longer dictated by anatomy, but anatomy does not seem to pose any necessary limits to the possibilities of gender.
>
> (Butler, 1986: 45)

It is by reconceptualising Beauvoir's model of situation as being *solely* a field of cultural possibilities, rather than as the total context of these combined with our facticity and our projects, that enables the separation of sex and gender into unambiguous, independent categories. This separation then allows Butler to be able to assert that gender is 'thoroughly cultural'. It is not that Beauvoir claims our anatomy has meaning outside of our particular historical situation. For Beauvoir, '[p]resence in the world vigorously implies the positing of a body that is both a thing of the world and a point of view on this world: but this body need not possess this or that particular structure' (Beauvoir, 2011: 24). At the same time, however, she holds that we cannot experience our bodies in any way outside of this situation. In her discussion of what Beauvoir can offer to current feminist debates on the politics of privilege, Sonia Kruks (2005) highlights how we cannot shed our skins or our personal histories. Kruks suggests that Beauvoir sees social processes as being taken in through the body, becoming 'elements of a lived experience that is deeply embedded in one's selfhood' (Kruks, 2005: 187). The bodily-self thus becomes immeasurably important as it is what enables us to grasp the world and for the world to grasp us.

Our living body

The second volume of *The Second Sex* is devoted to women's lived experience, '*l'expérience vécue*', mistranslated until 2011 in the English edition as '*The Woman's Life Today*' (Beauvoir, 1989). As outlined above, the heuristic distinction between sex and gender, where the former refers to biological sex and the latter to the social meanings of sexual difference, is often misattributed to *The Second Sex*. Beauvoir's understanding of the body as a living, situated and relational bodily-self, however, actually provides an alternative to the individualistic and dualistic thinking of the sex/gender distinction (Moi, 1999; Kruks, 2000; Young, 2005).

> To consider the body as a situation ... is to consider both the fact of being a specific kind of body and the meaning that concrete body has for the situated individual. This is not the equivalent of either sex or gender. The same is true for 'lived experience' which encompasses our experience of all kinds of situations (race, class, nationality etc.) and is a far more wide-ranging concept than the highly psychologizing concept of gender identity.
>
> (Moi, 1999: 81)

Building on Moi (1999), Iris Marion Young (2005) explains in detail the particular possibilities the concept of the 'lived body' raises for feminist theorising today.

> The idea of the lived body thus does the work the category 'gender' has done, but better and more. It does this work better because the category of the lived body allows a description of the habitus and interactions of men with women, women with women, and men with men in ways that can attend to the plural possibilities of comportment, without necessary reduction to the normative heterosexual binary of 'masculine' and 'feminine.' It does more because it helps avoid a problem generated by use of ascriptive general categories such as 'gender', 'race', 'nationality', 'sexual orientation', to describe the constructed identities of individuals, namely the additive character that identities appear to have under this.
>
> (Young, 2005: 18)

The lived body thus assists in the project of intersectionality, able to capture the whole experience of a person. Though Young has been criticised for not recognising Beauvoir's prior gendered adaptation of Merleau-Ponty (Chisholm, 2008), there is benefit in drawing on both Beauvoir and Merleau-Ponty to provide a full account of women's concrete experience of the continuum of sexual violence.

The 'lived body' has a particular meaning in existential-phenomenology, a meaning drawn on here through the slightly altered terminology of 'our living body' and 'our bodily-self'. The terminology of 'our' is not used here to suggest a shared body, rather to represent the characteristic of *mineness*. As seen throughout this chapter, Beauvoir's concept of the self as situated highlights the role of our body as that through which the world takes hold of us and we take hold of it. In the position adopted by Beauvoir, 'that of Heidegger, Sartre and Merleau-Ponty ... the body is not a *thing*, it is a situation: it is our grasp on the world and the outline for our projects' (Beauvoir, 2011: 46). Despite Beauvoir's naming of Martin Heidegger here, Heidegger's main philosophical treatise *Being and Time* (1996) did not give a thematic account of the body.[13] This absence is particularly notable given that Edmund Husserl, whose phenomenological insights were expanded on by Heidegger, developed the concept of *Leib* (Husserl, 2001), translated alternatively as the 'lived' or 'living' body. Writing in the *Cartesian Meditations*, Husserl signalled the difference between the body as instrument and the body as material as being one whereby the living body (*Leib*) is my body, uniquely singled out among other bodies (*Körper*) for me as 'the only one in which I immediately have free rein (*schalte und walte*)' (Husserl, 1960: 97). This characteristic of 'mineness' that applies to our living experience of our body is highlighted by Gail Weiss (1999) in the introduction to her book exploring the Merleau-Pontian concept of the body image.

> [T]he use of the definite article suggests that the body and the body image are themselves neutral phenomena, unaffected by the gender, race, age, and changing abilities of the body. Put simply there is no such thing as 'the' body or even 'the' body image. Instead, whenever we are referring to an individual's body, that body is always responded to in a particularized fashion ... these images of the body are not discrete but form a series of overlapping identities whereby one or more aspects of that body appear to be especially salient at any given point in time.
>
> (Weiss, 1999: 1)

In order to capture this characteristic of the body, and to avoid the misrepresentation of the Beauvoirian self seen in the parting of the 'sexed' body from the 'gendered' self, I use the plural possessive pronoun 'our' in referring to our living body, mirroring the similar terminology in use around 'our'self. My purpose here is similar to that expressed by Rosi Braidotti in relation to the subject 'woman'. 'Our living body' is used not to represent 'a monolithic essence defined once and for all, but rather the site of multiple, complex, and potentially contradictory sets of experience defined by overlapping variables' (Braidotti, 1993: 7). It is 'a' body, but a body that is uniquely singled out for us among all others as our very means of being-in-the-world at all.

This resonates with Beauvoir's careful deconstruction of the concept of 'woman' in the first book of *The Second Sex*, which she discards as a patriarchal myth, holding instead that we grow to become a woman (see Moi, 2010). It is in this sense that 'our' is used here, with the intention to capture through this the singularity of each body that is 'ours'. The terms 'living body' and 'living experience' are also used instead of the conventional 'lived', to further emphasise our active processes. Our living body, like our dying body, represents a process, not an event. Our living body is necessarily spatially and temporally located, experienced differently across age and in different spaces. Such use sits closer to replicating in English, Beauvoir's conception of our self as in a continual mode of becoming. This shift is argued by Sara Heinämaa (1999) to also represent more fully Husserl's original differentiation between the body as expression or instrument (*Leib*) and the body as physical presence or object (*Körper*), built on by both Simone de Beauvoir and Maurice Merleau-Ponty. Heinämaa signals the ways in which translations between German, French and English have moved Husserl's original concept of *Leib* or living body, to that of lived body.

> Merleau-Ponty's discussion of *corps vivant* or *corps vécu (Leib)* is often translated with the term 'lived body'. I do not follow this convention because my intention is to illuminate the methodological and conceptual connections among Husserl, Merleau-Ponty and Beauvoir. So I follow Carr's procedure and use the term 'living body' for both the German *Leib* and the French *corps vécu*.
>
> (Heinämaa, 1999: 128)

The reasons behind my choice in terminology here vary slightly in intention from Heinämaa, though both are attempts to get closer to the meaning of the term within the phenomenological tradition. To speak of the lived body has the implication of past tense. The role of our situated agency in creating, adapting and developing meaning is lost. 'Living body' helps to represent a bodily-self always in situation, in flux. It is the body as we live it, a living that changes not only based on age, health, but also on social environmental factors, including the meeting of other embodied subjects. The ways in which men's stranger intrusion can thus affect our living body are opened up, without reducing our embodied selfhood to an effect. 'Living' linguistically moves from the past participle to a verb, a move for theory from essential *being* to experiential *doing*, and thus assists in maintaining the transformative vision of Beauvoir's thought.

> The scope of the verb *to be* must be understood; bad faith means giving it a substantive value, when in fact it has the essence of the Hegelian dynamic: *to be* is to have become, to have been made as one manifests oneself. Yes, women in general *are* today inferior to men; that is, their situation provides them with fewer possibilities: the question is whether this state of affairs must be perpetuated.
>
> (Beauvoir, 2011: 13)

For Beauvoir as for Sartre, there is no set human essence, 'woman is not a fixed reality but a becoming' (Beauvoir, 2011: 46). We define ourselves through our existence and thus are in principle unpredictable (for an exception to this see the discussion on habit in this chapter) as long as we are living; bringing forward our situated agency. Toril Moi highlights how for this perspective: '(d)eath is the only thing that deprives us of the possibility of change' (Moi, 1999: 76). 'Living' experience/body also provides greater opportunity to recognise difference between, rather than the suggestion of one grand 'lived' experience shared by all.

Our bodily-self

In holding that the foundational situation of every self is that we are embodied, Beauvoir again departed from Sartre, aligning instead with Merleau-Ponty's conceptualisation of the embodied subject. This move towards the inseparable body-subject circumvents what Butler (1985) has called Sartre's 'Cartesian ghosts', the remaining traces of dualism evident in Sartre's account of the body. For Beauvoir: 'it is not the body-object described by scientists that exists concretely but the body as lived by the subject' (Beauvoir, 2011: 50). Our living body is always at the same time a bodily-self, our body indivisible from our self 'living' it. This brings together self and body, entangled with and in each other conceptually in the same way in which they are lived. The intertwined nature of body and subject is a key tenant in the conceptualisation of the lived body developed by Merleau-Ponty, and extended by Beauvoir. Merleau-Ponty attempted to challenge the residual dualism in Husserl, where the Cartesian mind-body problem was replaced with another categorical distinction between 'immanence' and 'transcendence',[14] through his development of the concept of the body-subject.[15] For Merleau-Ponty, the body is not only singled out in terms of being that which I have control over, the locus of my perceptions or 'mineness'. It is also the primordial horizon of our having perception at all, the original locus of our intentionality, and 'our general medium for having a world' (Merleau-Ponty, 2002: 169).

This position is also found in psychoanalysis,[16] with Freud's claim that '[t]he ego is first and foremost a bodily ego' (1962: 26), capturing what Kathleen Lennon (2010) refers to as the ways in which we live the material contours of the body as formative of the self. More recently, psychoanalyst Susie Orbach who has written extensively on the body (1978, 1993, 2003, 2009b), described how bringing together the bodily-self is foundational for work on women's embodiment.

> Where does the self get located if the body is okay? Hopefully we would be getting close to a notion that we couldn't divide these categories up ... I'm only discussing a body qua body because we need to discuss something that hasn't been looked at in this way. I don't really want to discuss it because I think it's mad. My speech production is both a physical, emotional, mental activity so there is no division between those two. So that's where I'm hoping we would get to, that we would have, we could be, corporeal beings. We would *be* embodied.
>
> (Orbach, 2009a, emphasis added)

Rosi Braidotti (1993) also reasserts the revolutionary possibilities of bringing back the 'bodily roots' of subjectivity and rejecting traditional views of the subject as universal or neutral, stating that this 'situated way of seeing the subject states that the most important location or situation is the rooting of the subject into the spatial frame of the body. The first and foremost of locations in reality is one's own embodiment' (Braidotti, 1993: 7). Though Braidotti argues that the phenomenological approach is, at the end, weighted in essentialism (see Heinämaa, 2006), the similarities between her position here and that of Beauvoir are evident. Beauvoir took the claim that the situated self is always a bodily-self further, claiming that our material body forms a situation *itself*, opening up and closing down possibilities for our embodied self. Remembering the positive ambiguity infusing Beauvoir's writing, this claim is that the body is a limitation on our possibilities, without infusing such limitation with any necessary or universal meaning outside of our situation.

Increasingly it is argued that Beauvoir's discussion of the female body needs to be understood in the context of this theory of the body as situation (see Heinämaa, 2003a, 2003b; Moi, 1999; Ward, 1995). Beauvoir's seemingly condemning analysis of the female body in *The Second Sex* has historically been subject to feminist criticism for its negative descriptions of women's bodies (Hartsock, 1983) or has been avoided in studies of the phenomenology of women's embodiment in favour of Merleau-Ponty (see for example Grosz, 1994; Young, 2005; Weiss, 1999). The criticism here is based on a claim that Beauvoir's analysis is essentialist and masculinist, falling into the trap of Cartesian dualism through employing the concepts of immanence and transcendence, and, as suggested by Judith Butler (1986), an exercise in Sartre's voluntarist conception of subjectivity. Indeed, the modern day English language reader of *The Second Sex* may find passages such as the following (taken from the original and most widespread English language translation) sit uneasily, if read as Beauvoir talking about immutable 'facts' of the female body.

> The young girl may succeed in accepting the fact of her desires, but usually they retain a cast of shame. Her whole body is a source of embarrassment. The mistrust that as a small child she felt in regard to her 'insides' helps to give to the menstrual crisis the dubious character that renders it odious to her. It is because of the psychic state induced by her menstrual slavery that it constitutes a heavy handicap.... Because her body seems suspect to her, and because she views it with alarm, it seems to her to be sick: it is sick.
>
> (Beauvoir, 1989: 332)

That the revised English translation by Constance Borde and Sheila Malovany-Chevallier goes some of the way towards correcting the English language mistranslation can be seen in its version of the same section.

> The girl can succeed in accepting her desires: but most often they retain a shameful nature. Her whole body is experienced as embarrassment. The

defiance she felt as a child regarding her 'insides' contributes to giving the menstrual crisis the dubious nature that renders it loathsome. The psychic attitude evoked by menstrual servitude constitutes a heavy handicap.... Because her body is suspect to her, she scrutinises it with anxiety and sees it as sick: it is sick.

(Beauvoir, 2011: 356)

It is evident in comparing the two passages above how subtle differences in translation, for example, 'her whole body *is a source of* embarrassment' (1989, emphasis added) in comparison to 'her whole body *is experienced as* embarrassment' (2011, emphasis added), have influenced the ways Beauvoir has been taken up and critiqued by English language theorists. In the Parshley translation (Beauvoir, 1989) the body is the source, with the implication of an essence preceding or outside of our experience. Such a conceptualisation is at odds with Beauvoir's detailed theory of the body as situation. The recent English translation of *The Second Sex* also reinstates the introduction to the second volume in its correct place; in the original English translation it was moved to the beginning of the first volume.

When I use the words 'woman' or 'feminine' I obviously refer to no archetype, to no immutable essence; 'in the present state of education and customs' must be understood to follow most of my affirmations. There is no question of expressing eternal truths here, but of describing the common ground from which all singular feminine existence stems.

(Beauvoir, 2011: 289)

This introduction to her discussion of lived experience makes clear Beauvoir's non-essentialist position. Its displacement in the Parshley translation may have led to years of misinterpretations of her work. If the self is thus entangled with the body, the way we live our body gives us clues about how we understand and live our self. When focusing particularly on women's experiences of the continuum of men's intrusive practices, what becomes important is an illumination of how we perceive our bodies, the body image, how we live our bodies, the body schema and habit body, and what this then means for our bodily-self in relationship to the embodied selves of others and our world.

Body image and body schema

Beauvoir's gendered exploration of the female body-subject aligns closely with Merleau-Ponty's conceptualisation of embodiment. For both there is recognition that the body is our means of grasping the world and that which makes it possible for us to have a world at all. In Merleau-Ponty, as in Beauvoir, the body is always situated, in constant engagement with the world. In *The Phenomenology of Perception* (Merleau-Ponty, 2002), Merleau-Ponty offered a radical revisioning of our bodies, with two particular areas that will be drawn on here; the corporeal schema, including the body schema/image distinction, and the habit body.

Our body image is the way we internally perceive our bodies, frequently delimited into positive and negative evaluations and usually understood as self-attitudes or perceptions based on our body's appearance and not its capacities. In the context of this study, body image refers to women's internal perceptions of their body as seen from the outside in public space, women's 'external perspective' (see Chapter 7). There is a move away from understanding body image as existing at an individual level towards viewing it as a dynamic between individuals and between individuals and their social and cultural context, is a shift that has been influenced by a gender and cultural studies perspective (Riley, 2013). A phenomenological perspective on men's violence against women suggests moving the discussion further towards understanding not only how men's intrusive practices impact on women's body image, but also to look to how the embodied practices developed as a response to men's intrusion influence women's experience of the capacities their bodily-selves – the body schema.

Merleau-Ponty used the terms 'body image', 'body schema' and 'corporeal schema' interchangeably (see Weiss, 1999), where modern day philosopher of mind Shaun Gallagher (1986) marks a distinction between the two, with the body image being the appearance of the body in the perceptual field and the body schema as the ways in which the body shapes the perceptual field. For Griffin (2012), this distinction is particularly useful in helping to broaden out discussion of our 'body confidence' from one focused on external appearance to a conceptualisation including the experience of our body's abilities.

> Because body image is such a familiar term, discussion of the experience of a body often returns to social standards of beauty, whether one accepts herself, and the like. This account, though, draws attention away from the very real experience of inhabiting the world in various bodily forms, and the way one interacts with her environment on a physical or physiological (and likely subconscious) level ... the body image/schema distinction helps to explain my experience in the world as both informed by physical states and bodily characteristics as well as what I think, feel, or perceive of those characteristics.
>
> (Griffin, 2012: 378)

Using Beauvoir to balance the ambiguity of our body as a situation that is both experienced as a body image and as a body schema helps to avoid the separation into a dichotomy where at any one time we experience our bodily selves only as one or the other. Instead, the difference between the two can be maintained whilst acknowledging that they are lived as interdependent, with our body image impacted on by our body schema and our body schema influenced by our body image. In addition, Gail Weiss (1999) suggests that the use of the definite article and a singular instance, 'the body image' or 'the body schema' is to falsely presume that we live our bodies as cohesive, coherent and uniform. Weiss argues that in experiential terms we have 'a multiplicity of body images, body images that are co-present in any given individual, and which are themselves constructed through a series of corporeal exchanges that take place both within and outside of specific bodies' (Weiss, 1999: 2). In this way, the modalities of our embodiment are conceptualised as contextual and temporal: a living relation. For both Merleau-Ponty and Beauvoir, our body schemas are not solely the way the mind maps the body, but also the ways in which we experience our living body as this contextual body, entangled with the world. Merleau-Ponty outlines the ways in which his use of body schema applies not solely to our mapping of the body, but the ways in which this mapping includes our environment; the ways in which our being is always a being-in-the-world. Again, this *in* is of a particular kind. Our body, for Merleau-Ponty, 'appears to me as an attitude directed towards a certain existing or possible task. And indeed its spatiality is not, like that of external objects or like that of "spatial sensations", a *spatiality of position* but a *spatiality of situation*' (Merleau-Ponty, 2002: 114–115, emphasis in original). Susie Orbach, draws on this concept of our living body to claim that the body

> is not a thing in and of itself, not even the integral or material basis of an individual's life, but the body, much like the psyche, has relational and object relational elements to it. The body is only made in relationship.
>
> (Orbach, 2003: 11)

For Merleau-Ponty (2002), this relationship between the world, others and the embodied self is expressed through the concept of a 'bodily intentionality' whereby the bodily senses form a pre-reflective 'intentional arc' projecting towards an anticipated world.[17] The body schema incorporates not just our immediate physical body, but also the ways in which this bodily intentionality enmeshes our body in the world, extended beyond the material confines of our skin. In the context under consideration here, the extended embodiment of the body schema is seen in the ways in which public space is moved through or used by women's bodily-self, women's 'external awareness'. For Griffin (2012) this external awareness and our external perspective together form our embodiment through 'feedback loops' (376). Conceptualising embodiment in this way helps to limit the remaining influence of Cartesian dualism, moving towards a theory of embodied cognition of the bodily-self. It also signals the importance of exploring how particular situations give rise to particular modalities of embodiment through habitual embodied practices; a perspective seen in Coy's (2009) work in relation to the development of a habit body from childhood sexual abuse to selling sex.

The habit body

Our habits play a key role in any examination of living experience. In her review of the concept of 'everyday life', Rita Felski (2000) discusses the role of habit in crystallising our experience of dailiness.

> Habit describes not simply an action but an attitude: habits are often carried out in a semi-automatic, distracted or involuntary manner. Certain forms of

behaviour are inscribed upon the body, part of a deeply ingrained somatic memory. We drive to work, buy groceries, or type a routine letter in a semi-conscious, often dream-like state. Our bodies go through the motions while our minds are elsewhere. Particular habits may be intentionally cultivated or may build up imperceptibly over time. In either case, they often acquire a life of their own, shaping us as much as we shape them.

(Felski, 2000: 26)

Where habit connotes routine, repeated action, often performed without conscious awareness, Merleau-Ponty's 'habit body' concerns the capturing of a movement by the body and giving it meaning through its interaction with the world (Hamington, 2008). For Merleau-Ponty: 'habit is neither a form of knowledge nor an involuntary action' (Merleau-Ponty, 2002: 166). It is an understanding in the body, and one that cannot be detached from the bodily effort that reveals it. Nick Crossley describes Merleau-Ponty's point here as being that '[t]o acquire a habit is to grasp and incorporate, within one's body schema, a tacit and practical "principle"' (Crossley, 2001: 106). Habit is thus not simply a mechanical response to external or internal stimulus but rather is a form of embodied and practical understanding, a bodily know-how which shapes the way we make sense of our environment. For Merleau-Ponty, our habituated embodied practices have their 'abode neither in thought nor in the objective body, but in the body as mediator of a world' (Merleau-Ponty, 2002: 167). Through habit the true nature of the body as expression and instrument, a living 'bodily-self' entangled in the world, is revealed.

Bourdieu's (1977) concept of habitus offers a route into talking about the ways in which cultural and social structures are embodied, what Lois McNay (1999: 99) terms 'the incorporation of the social into the corporeal', however the foundational, encompassing role Bourdieu attributes to the habitus in an individual's life hides the 'specificity of each individual's bodily experiences' (Weiss, 1999: 233). A conceptualisation that recognises an agency situated by the particular social structures it is expressed within can be constructed by mobilising Merleau-Ponty's concept of the habit body through the insights of Beauvoir on the gendered body-subject.[18] Drawing on Merleau-Ponty's conceptualisation of the habit body, Bourdieu claimed that '[w]hat is "learned by the body" is not something one has, like knowledge that can be brandished, but something that one is' (Bourdieu, 1990: 73). Wendy Parkins (2000) builds on this suggestion, applying Merleau-Ponty's discussion of habit to a gendered analysis of the body. Parkins highlights how 'arising from our own history of personal acts in particular situations, habits develop which give us "stable dispositional tendencies" ... resources for acting meaningfully in the world' (Parkins, 2000: 60). Absent from many discussions of women's embodiment, however, is concentrated empirical work focused on the relationship between men's violence against women and women's habitual embodied practices. A key exception is the work of Maddy Coy (2008, 2009) focusing on Merleau-Ponty's concept of a 'habit body', together with prostitution, (dis)embodiment and young women's experiences in local authority care. Coy explores in depth the ways in which previous experiences of men's sexually violent practices can be conceptualised as creating a template for how 'women act with their bodies and demarcate boundaries of ownership and use, which are absorbed into the embodied sense of self' (Coy, 2009: 66). Like Coy, Beauvoir also connected the development of gendered bodily habits in *The Second Sex* in relation to men's practices.

> If girl students run through the streets in happy groups as boys do, they attract attention; striding along, singing, talking and laughing loudly or eating an apple are provocations, and they will be insulted or followed or approached. Light-heartedness immediately becomes a lack of decorum. This self-control imposed on the woman becomes second nature for the 'well-bred girl' and kills spontaneity; lively exuberance is crushed.
>
> (Beauvoir, 2011: 358)

In this formulation, men's intrusive practices create particular habitual bodily dispositions for women, habits both generated by and themselves generating ways of living the body – similar to Ann Cahill's (2001) work on the impact of 'rape culture' on feminine bodily comportment. These pre-reflective habits then shape our conscious perceptions, including perceptions of our bodily-selves. This is not to replicate the determinism of Bourdieu, but rather, following Beauvoir, to remember our self, including our habituated embodied self, as always in the mode of 'becoming'.

Beauvoir's situated self thus provides a theory of embodied selfhood that also accounts for the different meanings given to the individual and generated by the individual through their socio-historical location; including the ways our habitual embodied practices shape our conscious perceptions; perceptions of our environment, our bodily appearance and our bodily capacity. When thinking about building a feminist phenomenological understanding of violence against women, such a conceptualisation of the self suggests the importance of examining the ordinary experiences of the continuum of men's intrusive practices, how these experiences are captured and given meaning through women's habitual modes of embodiment, and what this then reveals of women's situated self. It is with these questions in mind that we enter the empirical findings of this study.

Notes

1 See Simons (2010) for an outline of the ways in which Beauvoir derailed suggestions of her philosophical import, such as crediting Sartre with the concept of 'situation' in *Force of Circumstance* (Beauvoir, 1992). Simons highlights how Beauvoir's posthumously published war diaries and letters show Sartre and Beauvoir disagreeing on the concept of situation, which Beauvoir supported and Sartre rejected.

2 This point on the relational nature of both our projects and situation is particularly indebted to the participants at the Beauvoir workshop of Jonathan Webber's Rethinking Existentialism project at Cardiff University.

3 See for example the collected work in Diamond and Quinby, 1988; Adkins and Skeggs, 2004.

4 Most notably in the recognition of Foucault's blindness when it comes to 'those disciplines that produce a modality of embodiment that is peculiarly feminine' (Bartky, 1990: 65).

5 Nancy Hartsock claims for example that 'Foucault's is a world in which things move, rather than people, a world in which subjects become obliterated or, rather, recreated as passive objects, a world in which passivity or refusal represent the only possible choices' (1989: 167).

6 For more on Bourdieu's growing critique of Foucault see Callewaert, 2006.

7 Sociologist Michael Burawoy (2010) goes further, arguing that despite his vocal contempt for her work, Bourdieu appropriated much of Beauvoir's conceptual thinking

8 For a response to the critique of determinism in Bourdieu's habitus using the phenomenological insights of Edmund Husserl and Maurice Merleau-Ponty, see Crossley (2001).

9 See Kelly, Burton and Regan (1996) for a discussion of the debates on use of victim or survivor. Here I use victim-survivor to represent a connected rather than dichotomous relationship.

10 Toril Moi (2010) argues against this English translation, from the original '(o)n ne naît pas femme: on le devient' (Beauvoir, 1949), claiming that Borde & Malovany-Chevallier use 'woman' and 'the woman' interchangeably as if there were no difference. For Moi, '[t]his error makes Beauvoir sound as if she were committed to a theory of women's difference' (Moi, 2010: 5). If we take 'woman' as referring to a category defined by its inessential otherness, we see that what Beauvoir is saying here is that there is nothing in the thrownness of female embodiment in itself that forces the inessential otherness that this term 'woman' represents.

11 Margaret A. Simons (2010) provides a detailed overview of the ways in which the posthumous publication of Sylvie Le Bon de Beauvoir's edition of Beauvoir's war diary (Beauvoir, 1990) and letters to both Sartre (Beauvoir, 1991) and Nelson Algren (Beauvoir, 1998), together with biographies from Kate Fullbrook and Edward Fullbrook (1993), and Toril Moi (2008), have started a move in Beauvoirian scholarship towards reclaiming the uniqueness of her philosophical contributions.

12 In an extended essay on Beauvoir appearing in her book 'What is a Woman?' (1999), Moi suggests that the very distinction of sex from gender arises from the limitations of the English language, demonstrating that the need for such a distinction is absent in many other languages, including the French of Beauvoir's original text.

13 Responding to Sartre's critique of the lack of attention paid to *Dasein* as embodied, Heidegger gave a series of lectures held between 1959–69 at the home of one of his close friends and colleagues, Medard Boss (see Heidegger, 2001). Kevin A. Aho (2005) suggests that the theory of embodiment Heidegger presented at these lectures bears striking similarities to that developed by Maurice Merleau-Ponty (and I would add Simone de Beauvoir who extended Heidegger's concept of 'being-in-situation'), though Heidegger himself directed his response primarily at Sartre.

14 The complexity of the categories of immanence and transcendence as used by both Beauvoir and Sartre is made clearer through Gail Weiss's claim that immanence is associated with '*living* one's body as a being-in-itself or a being-for-others' while transcendence refers to our '*existing* as a conscious being-for-itself' (Weiss, 1999: 45, emphasis in original). It is important however, to counter the binary (a reworking of the concept of mind/body) that could be suggested results from this distinction. Beauvoir, using her theory of ambiguity, held the two together, claiming 'In truth, all human existence is transcendence and immanence *at the same time*; to go beyond itself, it must maintain itself; and while relating to others, it must confirm itself in itself' (Beauvoir, 2011: 455. Emphasis added).

15 For a discussion of the ways in which Merleau-Ponty's phenomenology represents a radical departure from the Husserlian project that inspired it, as well as Husserl's residual metaphysical dualism, see Carman (1999).

16 An unsurprising resonance given Beauvoir's interest in psychotherapy and Merleau-Ponty's training in psychology.
17 The notion that our embodiment is extended into the world through our bodily intentionality was developed in Merleau-Ponty's later work into his theory of 'Flesh', where all bodies, whether celestial, human or animal, were viewed as belonging to the whole of 'Being' (what Merleau-Ponty termed 'Flesh'), governed by the principle of reflexivity (Merleau-Ponty, 1968; see also Stawarska, 2002 and Slatman, 2005 for discussions of Merleau-Ponty's later philosophy).
18 Beauvoir did not detail the role or impact of habit on women's bodily-self in *The Second Sex*, though she did attend to it in the third volume of her autobiography, *The Coming of Age* (1996), where she claimed that embodied habits, rooted in the past yet open to change, transform the binaries of freedom and determinism into lived ambiguities (for more see Cuffari, 2011).

References

Adkins, L., & Skeggs, B. (eds) (2004) *Feminism after Bourdieu*, Blackwell.

Agarwal, B. (1997) 'Bargaining and Gender Relations: Within and Beyond the Household', *Feminist Economics*, 3 (1), pp. 1–51.

Aho, K. A. (2005) 'The Missing Dialogue between Heidegger and Merleau-Ponty: On the Importance of the Zollikon Seminars', *Body & Society*, 11 (2), pp. 1–23.

Bartky, S. L. (1990) *Femininity and Domination*, Routledge.

Beauvoir, S. d. (1949) *Le Deuxième Sexe: Tome 2, L'expérience vécue*, Gallimard.

Beauvoir, S. d. (1962) *The Prime of Life*, Green, P. (transl.), World Publishing Co.

Beauvoir, S. d. (1976) *The Ethics of Ambiguity*, Frechtman, B. (transl.), Citadel Press.

Beauvoir, S. d. (1989) *The Second Sex*, Parshley, H.M. (transl.), Vintage.

Beauvoir, S. d. (1990) *Journal de guerre: Septembre 1939–Janvier, 1941*, Le bon de Beauvoir, S. (ed.), Gallimard.

Beauvoir, S. d. (1991) *Letters to Sartre*, Hoare, Q. (transl.), Arcade.

Beauvoir, S. d. (1992) *Force of Circumstance: Vol. 2, Hard Times, 1952–1962*, Howard, R. (transl.), Paragon House.

Beauvoir, S. d. (1996) *The Coming of Age*, W. W. Norton.

Beauvoir, S. d. (1998) *A Transatlantic Love Affair: Letters to Nelson Algren*, Le Bon de Beauvoir, S. (transl.), The New Press.

Beauvoir, S. d. (2004) 'Pyrrhus and Cineas', in Simons, M. A. (ed.), *Simone de Beauvoir: Philosophical Writings*, University of Chicago Press.

Beauvoir, S. d. (2011) *The Second Sex*, Borde, C. & Malovany-Chevallier, S. (transl.), Vintage.

Bordo, S. (1993) *Unbearable Weight: Feminism, Western Culture, and the Body*, University of California Press.

Bourdieu, P. (1977) *Outline of a Theory of Practice*, Nice, R. (transl.), Cambridge Studies in Social and Cultural Anthropology, 16, Cambridge University Press.

Bourdieu, P. (1990) *The Logic of Practice*, Nice, R. (transl.), Polity Press.

Bourdieu, P. (1998) *Practical Reason: On the Theory of Action*, Stanford University Press.

Braidotti, R. (1993) 'Embodiment, Sexual Difference, and the Nomadic Subject', *Hypatia*, 8 (1), pp. 1–13.

Burawoy (2010) 'The Antinomies of Feminism: Beauvoir meets Bourdieu', in *Conversations with Pierre Bourdieu: The Johannesburg Moment*, Lecture series number 6, http://burawoy.berkeley.edu/Bourdieu/7.Beauvoir.pdf [accessed 10 January 2011].

Butler, J. (1987) 'Variations of Sex and Gender: Beauvoir, Wittig and Foucault', in Benhabib, S., & Cornell, D. (eds), *Feminism as Critique: Essays on the Politics of Gender in Late Capitalist Societies*, Polity Press, pp. 128–142.

Butler, J. (1986) 'Sex and Gender in Simone de Beauvoir's Second Sex', *Yale French Studies*, 72, pp. 35–49.

Butler, J. (1988) 'Performative Acts and Gender Constitution: An Essay in Phenomenology and Feminist Theory', *Theatre Journal*, 40 (4), pp. 519–531.

Butler, J. (1990) *Gender Trouble: Feminism and the Subversion of Identity*, Routledge.

Butler, J. (1997) *Excitable Speech: A Politics of the Performative*, Routledge.

Cahill, A. J. (2001) *Rethinking Rape*, Cornell University Press.

Callewaert, S. (2006) 'Bourdieu, Critic of Foucault: The Case of Empirical Social Science against Double-Game-Philosophy', *Theory, Culture & Society*, 23 (6), pp. 73–98.

Carman, T. (1999) 'The Body in Husserl and Merleau-Ponty', *Philosophical Topics*, 27 (2), pp. 205–226.

Chisholm, D. (2008) 'Climbing Like a Girl: An Exemplary Adventure in Feminist Phenomenology' *Hypatia*, 23 (1), pp. 9–40.

Coy, M. (2008) 'Young Women, Local Authority Care and Selling Sex: Findings from Research', *British Journal of Social Work*, 38 (7), 1408–1424.

Coy, M. (2009) 'This Body Which is Not Mine: The Notion of the Habit Body, Prostitution and (Dis)Embodiment', *Feminist Theory*, 10 (1), pp. 61–75.

Coy, M., & Garner, M. (2012) 'Definitions, Discourses and Dilemmas: Policy and Academic Engagement with the Sexualisation of Popular Culture', *Gender and Education*, 24 (3), pp. 285–301.

Crossley, N. (2001). 'The Phenomenological Habitus and its Construction', *Theory and Society*, 30, pp. 81–120.

Cuffari, E. (2011) 'Habits of Transformation', *Hypatia*, 26 (3), pp. 535–553.

Diamond, I., & Quinby, L. (1988) *Feminism & Foucault: Reflections on Resistance*, Northeastern University Press.

Dreyfus, H., & Rabinow, P. (1993) 'Can There be a Science of Existential Structure and Social Meaning?', in Calhoun, C., LiPuma, E., & Postone, M. (eds), *Bourdieu: Critical Perspectives*, Polity Press, pp. 35–45.

Felski, R. (2000) *Doing Time: Feminist Theory and Postmodern Culture*, NYU Press.

Foucault, M. (1979) *Discipline and Punish: The Birth of the Prison*, Sheridan, A. (transl.), Vintage.

Foucault, M. (1980) *Power/Knowledge: Selected Interviews and Writings*, Pantheon Books.

Freud, S. (1962) *The Ego and the Id*, Riviere, J. (transl.), W. W. Norton.

Fullbrook, E., & Fullbrook, K. (1993) *Simone de Beauvoir and Jean-Paul Sartre: The Remaking of a Twentieth-Century Legend*, Harvester.

Gallagher, S. (1986) 'Body Image and Body Schema: A Conceptual Clarification', *Journal of Mind and Behavior*, 7, pp. 541–554.

Gill, R. C. (2007) 'Critical Respect: The Difficulties and Dilemmas of Agency and "Choice" for Feminism', *European Journal of Women's Studies*, 14 (1), pp. 69–80.

Gill, R. C. (2008) 'Empowerment/Sexism: Figuring Female Sexual Agency in Contemporary Advertising', *Feminism & Psychology*, 18 (1), pp. 35–60.

Griffin, M. (2012) 'Ruptured Feedback Loops: Body Image/Schema and Food Journaling Technologies', *Feminism & Psychology*, 22 (3), pp. 376–387.

Grosz, E. (1994) *Volatile Bodies: Toward a Corporeal Feminism*, Indiana University Press.

Hamington, M. (2008) 'Resources for Feminist Care Ethics in Merleau-Ponty's Phenomenology of the Body', in Weiss, G. (ed.), *Intertwinings: Interdisciplinary Encounters with Merleau-Ponty*, State University of New York Press, pp. 203–220.

Hartsock, N. C. (1983) 'The Feminist Standpoint: Developing the Ground for a Specifically Feminist Historical Materialism', in Harding, S., & Hintikka, M. B. (eds), *Discovering Reality*, D. Reidel Publishing Company, pp. 283–310.

Hartsock, N. C. (1989) 'Postmodernism and Political Change: Issues for Feminist Theory', *Cultural Critique*, 14, pp. 15–33.

Hartsock, N. C. (2006) 'Experience, Embodiment and Epistemologies', *Hypatia*, 21 (2), pp. 178–183.

Heidegger, M. (1996) *Being and Time*, Stambaugh, J. (transl.), State University of New York Press.

Heidegger, M. (2001) *Zollikon Seminars: Protocols, Conversations, Letters*, Northwestern University Press.

Heinämaa, S. (1997) 'What is a Woman? Butler and Beauvoir on the Foundations of the Sexual Difference', *Hypatia*, 12 (1), pp. 20–39.

Heinämaa, S. (1999) 'Simone de Beauvoir's Phenomenology of Sexual Difference', *Hypatia*, 14 (4), pp. 114–132.

Heinämaa, S. (2003a) 'The Body as Instrument and as Expression', in Card, C. (ed.), *The Cambridge Companion to Simone de Beauvoir*, Cambridge University Press, pp. 66–86.

Heinämaa, S. (2003b) *Toward a Phenomenology of Sexual Difference: Husserl, Merleau-Ponty, Beauvoir*, Rowman & Littlefield.

Heinämaa, S. (2006) 'Feminism' (Chapter 34), in Dreyfus, H. L., & Wrathall, M. A. (eds), *A Companion to Phenomenology and Existentialism*, Blackwell.

Herman, B. (1991) 'Agency, Attachment, and Difference', *Ethics*, 101 (4), pp. 775–797.

Husserl, E. (1960) *Cartesian Meditations*, Cairns, D. (transl.), M. Nijhoff.

Husserl, E. (2001) *Logical Investigations* (Vol. 1), Findlay, N. J. (transl.), Psychology Press.

Kelly, L., Burton, S., & Regan, L. (1996) 'Beyond Victim or Survivor: Sexual Violence, Identity and Feminist Theory and Practice', in Adkins, L., & Merchant, V. (eds), *Sexualizing the Social: Power and the Organization of Sexuality*, Macmillan, pp. 77–101.

Kruks, S. (1992) 'Gender and Subjectivity: Simone de Beauvoir and Contemporary Feminism', *Signs*, pp. 89–110.

Kruks, S. (2000) 'Existentialism and Phenomenology', in Code, L., Jaggar, A., & Young, I. (eds), *A Companion to Feminist Philosophy*, Blackwell, pp. 66–74.

Kruks, S. (2005) 'Simone de Beauvoir and the Politics of Privilege', *Hypatia*, 20 (1), pp. 178–205.

Langer, M. (2003) 'Beauvoir and Merleau-Ponty on Ambiguity', in Card, C. (ed.), *The Cambridge Companion to Simone de Beauvoir*, Cambridge University Press, pp. 87–106.

Lennon, K. (2010) 'Feminist Perspectives on the Body', in Zalta, E. N. (ed.), *The Stanford Encyclopedia of Philosophy*, Fall 2010, http://plato.stanford.edu/archives/fall2010/entries/feminist-body/ [accessed 19 November 2012].

McNay, L. (1999) 'Gender, Habitus and the Field Pierre Bourdieu and the Limits of Reflexivity', *Theory, Culture & Society*, 16 (1), pp. 95–117.

McNay, L. (2004) 'Agency and Experience: Gender as a Lived Relation', *The Sociological Review*, 52 (2), pp. 173–190.

Merleau-Ponty, M. (1968) *The Visible and the Invisible: Followed by Working Notes*, Lefort, C. (ed.), Lingis, A. (transl.), Northwestern University Press.

Merleau-Ponty, M. (2002) *Phenomenology of Perception*, Smith, C. (transl.), Routledge.

Miriam, K. (2005) 'Stopping the Traffic in Women: Power, Agency and Abolition in Feminist Debates over Sex-Trafficking', *Journal of Social Philosophy*, 36 (1), pp. 1–17.

Moi, T. (1991) 'Appropriating Bourdieu: Feminist Theory and Pierre Bourdieu's Sociology of Culture', *New Literary History*, 22 (4), pp. 1017–1049.

Moi, T. (1999) *What is a Woman? And Other Essays*, Oxford University Press.

Moi, T. (2008) *Simone de Beauvoir: The Making of an Intellectual Woman*, Oxford University Press.

Moi, T. (2010) 'The Adulteress Wife: Review of a New Edition of The Second Sex', in *The London Review of Books*, 32, pp. 3–6.

Orbach, S. (1978) *Fat is a Feminist Issue: A Self-Help Guide for Compulsive Eaters*, Berkley-Paddington.

Orbach, S. (1993) *Hunger Strike: The Anorectic's Struggle as a Metaphor for our Age*, Karnac Books.

Orbach, S. (2003) 'Part I: There is No Such Thing as a Body', *British Journal of Psychotherapy*, 20 (1), pp. 3–16.

Orbach, S. (2009a) *Bodies*, Lecture presented at the London School of Economics and Political Science, 16 November 2009, www.youtube.com/watch?feature=player_embedded&v=bOfo_U2tIHw#t=4454 [accessed 20 April 2012].

Orbach, S. (2009b) *Bodies*, Profile.

Parkins, W. (2000) 'Protesting like a Girl: Embodiment, Dissent and Feminist Agency', *Feminist Theory*, 1 (1), pp. 59–78.

Peter, F. (2003) 'Gender and the Foundations of Social Choice: The Role of Situated Agency', *Feminist Economics*, 9 (2–3), pp. 13–32.

Riley, S. (2014) 'A Gender & Cultural Studies Perspective on Body Image: Evidence, Understanding & Policy', *Report to Jo Swinson Minister for Women and Equalities: Current Stage of Research on Body Image*, www.gov.uk/government/publications/body-confidence-a-rapid-evidence-assessment-of-the-literature [accessed 10 February 2014].

Ruyters, M. (2012) *Vulnerable Bodies and Gendered Habitus: The Prospects for Transforming Exercise*, Doctoral Thesis, RMIT University.

Sartre, J. P. (1973) *Existentialism and Humanism*, Mairet, P. (transl.), Eye Methuen.

Sartre, J. P. (2007) *Being and Nothingness*, Routledge.

Simons, M. A. (ed.) (2010) *Feminist Interpretations of Simone de Beauvoir*, Penn State Press.

Slatman, J. (2005) 'The Sense of Life: Husserl and Merleau-Ponty on Touching and Being Touched', *Chiasmi International*, 7, pp. 305–325.

Stark, E. (2009) 'Rethinking Coercive Control', *Violence Against Women*, 15 (12), pp. 1509–1525.

Stawarska, B. (2002) 'Reversibility and Intersubjectivity in Merleau-Ponty's Ontology', *The Journal of the British Society for Phenomenology*, 33 (2), pp. 155–166.

Ward, J. K. (1995) 'Beauvoir's Two Senses of "Body" in The Second Sex', in Simons, M.A. (ed.), *Feminist Interpretations of Simone de Beauvoir*, The Pennsylvania State University Press, pp. 223–242.

Weiss, G. (1999) *Body Images: Embodiment as Intercorporeality*, Routledge.

Young, I. M. (2005) *On Female Body Experience: 'Throwing Like a Girl' and Other Essays*, Oxford University Press.

This other guy just came out of the shadows of a doorway and just grabbed me,
was just holding onto me.
He'd said something about me having epic tits.

I had somebody rubbing themselves on me.
I'll like sit somewhere else, change seats.
This guy just literally pulled down his trousers and started wanking.
I normally go at the end of the carriage.
He did a comment like oh you know, you can flirt as much as you want
but no one really wants you anyway.

I look down, I don't look at them.

Young boys like 14, 15 year olds,
coming up to us saying
are you lesbians? Kiss then.

I had one guy burp in my face.
I'll try to cross the street.
He kept saying my cunt stinks, about me.
You've got to have a book with you.
A car came up, slowed down a little bit, wound the window down, and screamed.
I just try to ignore. I don't engage.

This man just came up to our table and starting banging on it
and was like I want some chicken nuggets,
give me some fucking chicken nuggets.
You fucking bitch I'll kill you. If I see you again I'll kill you.
He was just staring at me as I walked past.

This man one time grabbed my leg.
You've got to stay polite, stay quiet and be agreeable.
He just said something about me having nice tits.
I don't walk down there at night.
And he came up behind me and grabbed both of my arms.

Never smile, never,
just never make any kind of contact at all with any men.

And he got out his dick and wanked off in front of me.
This guy stands outside the window and takes a picture of me.
He started jerking off while he was sitting next to me
They might catch me unawares but they will never catch me without an answer.

This man came up to me and put his arm around me.
I'll pretend to text.
He took his hand underneath my hand and held it there.
I've got this thing that I call the stare.
A guy came up and literally went ugh, and walked away.

                                        I get this feeling of guilt sometimes.

They weren't subtle they said it like in audible range
and they were like what do you reckon mate, an 8 out of 10?
He raped me.
He kind of like run his hand down my back.
I basically have been hiding myself for the last 6, 7 years.
He was so obviously looking just at my boobs.
I always listen to music.
Some guy just wound down his window and started shouting at me.
I'd probably forget about it.

These two guys probably 40 walked past and said
oo you'll have a nice body on you
when you're 16.

He was like, I don't mind if you've got a baby.
I do make the choice if there is one to sit with women.
He started putting his hand on my leg.
Sometimes I'll just close my eyes.

4   Living men's intrusion
Part one

A feminist phenomenology of violence against women and girls calls for the need to shift both our theoretical and empirical focus from a world that exists objectively out there, to the specifics of a woman's concrete, living experience. When such a shift is applied to the continuum of men's intrusive practices, what moves to the forefront are the daily, mundane intrusions, 'the noises, the tsst' (Josina), which were recounted as simply part of occupying public space for participants. Interrogations about the existence of a male partner, a train journey spent pretending to read to block out the man staring two seats over – experiences lived as routine and thus unremarkable, minimised and forgotten, 'nothing really happened' (Kelly & Radford, 1990). The routine intrusions explored below are those that many women struggled to remember in the particular, and yet were lived by all of the participants as the unremarkable backdrop to being a woman in public. Such trivialisation is challenged by a phenomenological approach where the key role routine intrusions play in how women experience their freedom and safety in public spaces is revealed. Here we find the access point into the findings of this study. Ordinary interruptions, verbal intrusions and the gaze, were the intrusive practices most commonly experienced by participants in public space, and those most often discounted. They form the first three of the six categories of intrusion to be considered in detail. Given the breadth of experiences within even a similarly defined category, women's accounts provide the necessary definitional and experiential meaning to make sense of the connections, divisions and frequencies in and between categories. In light of this, across the following chapters, the findings are read through participant voices to give the living detail of each category.

Ordinary interruptions

The category of 'ordinary interruptions' captures the practices that are most often dismissed as trivial, discarded as a 'daily hassle' (Esacove, 1998). Carol Brooks Gardner (1995) uses Erving Goffman's concept of 'open persons' to describe such a phenomenon, where particular characteristics are perceived as inviting a break from the 'civil inattention' (Goffman, 1990) typical of interactions between strangers in public space. Gardner develops Goffman's examples of attributes such as having a dog or a baby in public space, or carrying something particularly unusual such as a large plant or a wardrobe, to argue that women as a group are perceived as open persons in public space. The experiences of participants support Gardner's claim; all reported experiencing ordinary interruptions from unknown men in public (Table 4.1).

The category itself is one of the broadest of the analytical concepts worked with here, including a range of practices such as wolf-whistles, catcalls and car beeping, alongside comments such as uninvited greetings, usually attached to a diminutive such as 'love' or 'beautiful', or prolonged one-sided conversation. A practice was categorised as an ordinary interruption if women described experiencing it as a mundane extension of how the current gender order affirms men's power to act on and through women's bodies (Coy & Garner, 2012). Ordinary interruptions were thus expressed by participants as being demonstrative of this, rather than figured as a form of violence against women, and understood as motivated by men's need to make them aware that they have been seen and that their bodies can be acted on.

> [Y]ou are more interrupted being a woman because people generally feel they can. There's this weird general sense whereby what women do isn't as important and can be interrupted, what women look like is much more important and everybody has a right to comment on it or have an opinion.
>
> (Viola)

That such intrusion is experienced as 'ordinary' led to a difficulty in recording frequencies; just over two thirds of participants were unable to recall particular instances but stated they experienced ordinary intrusions either regularly or occasionally. This suggests that the phenomenological detail of such practices, their frequency and impact, can be missed when research methodologies ask women only to *recall* rather than *record* particular intrusive experiences. June Larkin's (1997) research is unique in the literature in its use of notebooks, though participants were not first asked to recount their histories of men's intrusion. The findings of this study, where women were asked to do both, revealed a disjuncture between both projected frequency (with the notebooks finding less than anticipated episodes of intrusion), and claims of impact (with the notebooks

Table 4.1 Ordinary interruptions: frequency (*n*=50)

Frequency	Number	%
Regularly (no number given)	25	50
Occasionally (no number given)	9	18
Three or more	6	12
Twice	6	12
Once	4	8
Total	50	100

recording a greater impact for women of these mundane encounters than they remembered when relaying past experiences in the initial conversations). This disjuncture will be discussed in more detail when we move to the exploration of the impact of men's intrusion on women's habitual modes of embodiment in Chapter 7.

Where specific instances of ordinary interruptions were remembered in the initial conversations it was most often where the intrusion contained comments and extended over time, with a recurring context for this being when participants were alone on public transport. Across participants' accounts, men engaged in interrogations of women in such a context. For Laura, this extended over the course of a transatlantic flight.

> [P]ublic transport is a great example where guys sit uncomfortably close to you on a bus and they'll just be really invading your personal space but you don't say anything because it might be busy and you're just trying to read your paper. The worst one actually was on a plane, this guy on a plane. Transatlantic flight so I was there for quite a while, completely stuck. And I was on the window and he was on the middle seat and there was this armrest there and he was leaning all over it and trying to talk to me and I was trying to be polite and friendly but then after a while I felt a bit like he was, because it went on for so long he was really just starting to get on my nerves and I just wanted to be left alone to watch my film or whatever, and he was constantly leaning over and being like 'where are you going?' and 'what are you doing?' and 'is this a holiday?' and 'have you got a boyfriend?'
>
> (Laura)

Lisa was faced with similar intrusive questioning during a bus journey home.

> When there's other seats or when it's an empty bus, but they will come and sit next to me and we will have a very long extended conversation whether I want to or not ... I was finishing an essay at school and was getting the bus back and this very drunk man got on and he was getting off at my stop so I had to wait and get off at the next stop because I didn't want him to, well where my house was you could go the long way round or you could go down an alleyway which was behind some shops and I didn't want him to know that I was going to go down that dark and dingy alleyway. So I just got off at the next stop and went around ... I think he was talking about how he's had a really good night and then he was like 'oh do you have a boyfriend?' so I was like 'yep I have a boyfriend.' And then he kept pestering me about him, 'where's your boyfriend? Where's your boyfriend tonight?'
>
> (Lisa)

The routine way in which Lisa speaks of changing her intended route home based on both the intrusion itself and what it signals in the possibility for escalation, is also seen in Luella's description of an experience that almost replicates Lisa's.

I was going [across city] and the bus was basically empty there were about four people, so there were plenty of seats to sit at, and I was sitting right next to the window. And this man gets on and just heads for the seat right next to me.... To be honest when I saw that he looked at me and headed to my seat I thought, 'here we go'. It's not even, I didn't feel scared because I was on the bus. I was so tired, it was late, I'd had a drink. I was just enjoying my night bus ride with some music in my ears and he started talking to me and I had my headphones in so I ignored him the first time. And then he said something else and I didn't want to act like a bitch because I don't want to provoke them in any way, so I took my headphone out and I can't even remember what he was saying, it was like, 'where are you coming from?' or something like that, and I said to him I was out with some friends, and he asked what I did and I told him I was at university, and he asked 'what year?' and I said 'first year'. So clearly the man understands that he's twice my age. And he kept trying to engage me in conversation.... And I was thinking 'where the hell is he going to get off? What bus stop is he getting off at?' Because I didn't want to squeeze past him either because I was scared he'd grab me or something like that.

(Luella)

Luella's account here shows the ways in which, similar to Lisa, ordinary interruptions were often experienced as connected to the potential for criminalised forms of men's intrusion. Lisa gets off a stop later than usual to combat the possibility of being followed, while Luella also checks that she will be getting off the bus after the intrusive man to avoid being 'grabbed'. For some participants this connection had been experienced within the encounter, with men practicing several forms of intrusion. Delilah's account of an experience of escalation after a man moved next to her on public transport, describes this.

I was just sat on a train. Minding my own business again, and a guy came up to me and sat down and said 'so what line of work are you in?' And I was like 'excuse me?' And he said, 'what do you do?' And I was like 'I'd rather not talk to you if that's ok' and he said 'oh whatever line of work you're in it's a waste of your time.' And I'm like 'what the hell? Who are you?' And he said something about me being destined to work in topless modelling.... He was sitting a few chairs down and he slowly moved towards me and then he was sitting right next to me and that's when I was like ok this is very threatening, very late at night. It wasn't an empty train but there weren't very many people and I was going to get off at the last stop so I could be possibly the last one off the train. So I think my initial thing was I'm in trouble and secondly I thought 'why me? Is it something I'm giving off?' So yeah it does go in that cycle ... I think it was his stop eventually. Because he tried to get me to get off at his stop. He was going 'oh c'mon, just let me take a few pictures'.

(Delilah)

Such escalation, from interrupting with intrusive questioning, to physically encroaching, as seen with both Delilah and Laura, was understood as an ever-present potential. As such, many participants responded to ordinary interruptions using an 'escalation calculation', building on a bodily knowledge of men's intrusion to evaluate their safest response – often drawn from the limited options of ignore, engage, challenge or leave. There is thus an expression of agency here, seen in the differences between women's general responses to men's intrusion, however the agency is located within the total context of our situation. The escalation calculation conducted in response to men's stranger intrusions reveals some of the factors underlying this total situation; our living body and the possibilities and limitations thus opened, as well as a recognition of how the Other forms part of the conditions grounding our ability to act.

The ordinariness of such intrusions, how they fade into the background becoming an aspect of unexamined, unremarkable everyday life, has specific importance when attempting to understand the impact of men's intrusive practices on women's experience of their embodiment. On the simplest level such encounters worked to remind participants that they were seeable and seen, and through this disrupted their ability to *be* embodied in public space. Hannah describes the result of this as a feeling of loss.

> [A] lot of the time your commute is the only time you get to yourself. Whether you're wanting to read of listen to music or something, it's an infringement on that. You always feel a bit robbed.
>
> (Hannah)

Anna, Jan, Claire and Sophie also spoke about how they experienced ordinary interruptions as breaking into their internal world, a recurring disruption not only of their time to their self but their time *in* their self.

> When it first happens I feel really quite taken aback and it really throws you as well because you're, as everyone is when you're walking around, you're in your own world and got your own interior monologue going on and when somebody just says something … it really throws me.
>
> (Anna)

> You're in your little dream, thinking your own thoughts, quite happy, not hurting anybody, minding your own business, and they step into your world, unasked and unwanted. And that's, you could say that's not sexual, that's not harmful in any way, but there's a boundary there I think and they were treading over it.
>
> (Jan)

> For me it's just that thing about someone intruding, I'm a million miles away, I'm in my own thought, and someone snapping me straight back out … it's an absolute invasion of your getting on with your daily task. It's

someone breaking into that and demanding your attention and it's just infuriating.

(Claire)

[I]t can be really distracting if you're thinking about something and it's just something there, suddenly, it's in your consciousness, there's a person a few metres away from you who, they want something from you. They either want to look at you or want to talk to you, they want to interrupt you in some way. And they almost want acknowledgment some of them, by you looking up or by you being like, 'what?'

(Sophie)

Following Beauvoir, participants are describing here the experience of the embodied self as a for-itself (Beauvoir's *en-soi*), and the impact of men's intrusion in forcing a return to the materiality of the body; a movement in Heideggerian terms from the body as lived to the body as corpse.[1] Women's internal world is disrupted and their awareness moved to their being embodied, at the same time as external contextual factors such as the fleetingness of the encounter, or the ambiguity of whom the noises were intended for, often undermined their ability to respond. In addition, calculating the possibility of escalation forced women to alternate between the self and the other, adjusting actions and responses in relation to those projected by and for the other. The inner world of one doing this was engaged in a tripartite process of experiencing the corporeality of the embodied self, alongside a diminishment of one's ability as a subject to make sense of the world, while at the same time attempting to anticipate the actions of the other. Such interiority was thus experienced as routinely interrupted *regardless* of an external interruption by men, suggesting part of the reason behind the disjuncture between anticipated and recorded intrusions for participants.

Verbal intrusions

The range within the category of verbal intrusions demonstrates some of the difficulty encountered in measuring different practices. There is a danger in collapsing the particularities of encounters under broader categories, particularly as participants spoke of different impacts across different types of comments. Recalling the previous chapter's discussion on our living body, whilst grouping experiences together sheds light on women's shared situations, this is not to be mistaken for a totalised or universal situation of 'woman'. Rather, as argued by Stevi Jackson (2001), key to understanding the differences between women is an understanding of both structural and social inequalities as manifested in everyday social practices. To balance the competing impulses of bringing experiences together whilst maintaining their particularities, verbal intrusions were coded into three broad categories: sexualised comments; comments commanding happiness in women's demeanour; and insulting or explicitly threatening comments.

Table 4.2 Verbal intrusions: frequency (n=50)

Type of commentary	Sexual		'Cheer up'		Insults/threats	
Frequency	Number	%	Number	%	Number	%
Once	15	30	7	14	10	20
Twice	7	14	5	10	5	10
Three or more	3	6	1	2	1	2
Regularly (no number given)	13	26	13	26	4	8
Happens (no frequency given)	1	2	4	8	3	6
Rarely	–	–	1	2	–	–
Explicitly stated never happened	–	–	7	14	3	6
Total recording practice (n=50)	39	78	31	62	23	46

Ninety-six per cent of participants ($n=48$) reported experiencing at least one of these forms, with almost half ($n=23$) experiencing comments from two categories, and a quarter having experienced all three ($n=12$). Table 4.2 shows the frequencies of the particular forms of verbal intrusions.

'You've got a really nice ass, I'd like to wrap my cock in it':[2] *sexual commentary*

The most common form of verbal intrusions from unknown men in public was sexual commentary, experienced by 78 per cent ($n=39$) of participants (see Table 4.2). The regularity of sexualised comments meant that many women could not recall specific instances, making frequency often an approximation. Unlike ordinary interruptions, an almost equivalent number of women were able to remember and explicitly recount one particular incident.

There was a wide range within this category, including sexualised evaluations on body parts such as the breasts, bottom or genitals, or graphic comments intimating sexual relations between the unknown man and the woman or, for women identified as lesbian, between themselves and their partner. All were understood by participants as having an explicitly sexual motivation, an impetus described as experientially different from that of ordinary interruptions.

> [P]eople saying things like 'alright Blondie, alright sweetheart' doesn't bother me as much as someone coming up to me and saying 'nice stockings babe', because there's a totally different tone about it. However I don't know if the men who are saying 'alright gorgeous' are rapists or might assault me or are being sexually predatory, but contextually I don't see those things as being as threatening as someone talking about my appearance in a different way.
>
> (Alice)

This commentary thus operated in a similar way to that which will be seen in the discussion of the gaze, encouraging women to experience a constant, conscious awareness of the vulnerability of having a woman's body. The sexualised element, however, introduced a more palpable fear based on what is experienced as the imminent potentiality of men's sexual violence.

The content of sexualised speech generally focused on the man's penis, the woman's breasts or invitations for sex. An unknown man followed Abbey and her female friends home one night.

> He was clearly drunk and kept talking about his huge fucking cock and how we were really missing out that we weren't going home with him and one of my friends was like 'just fuck off' and he was like 'no you don't understand my cock is huge'.
>
> (Abbey)

Hannah was also walking home with female friends when she was asked by a man standing outside of a pub with his male friends for directions to an underground station.

> I said 'oh yeah it's down there and through there'. And he turned around to me and said 'can you do me a favour?' which I thought was odd. I mean initially he hadn't really been speaking to me, he'd been speaking to my friend. Now in context this makes sense because the other two of my friends are quite big chested, and they were wearing, not revealing, but they tend to wear nice dresses and stuff like that. I had a big hoodie on, my chest completely covered, and he said 'can you do me a favour?' and I said 'what?' as we were walking away, and he said 'can I cum on your tits?'
>
> (Hannah)

Both Bec and Kirsten were propositioned by unknown men in public, Bec in a public bar and Kirsten in an underground station.

> I remember one night it was crowded, there were lots of staff, and some of them were guys, some were girls, I know them, they know me, and I felt so humiliated when this guy said, really loud so everybody heard, something like 'can I fuck you?' or 'I want to fuck you' something like that. Because I had leaned over to hear what he wanted because it was really loud and he said it really loudly and everybody heard it, and I think I felt so humiliated because he'd said that to me in front of my staff. It made me feel like a really small person that wasn't worth anything.
>
> (Bec)

> I was in [city] after my year abroad I'd just been travelling and I was queuing to buy a tube ticket and this man was standing right behind me and he started whispering into my ear 'you're so sexy. I want to have sex with you'.
>
> (Kirsten)

For Josina, being in public space with her girlfriend led to sexualised comments that did not intimate sexual activity between intrusive men/boys and herself, but between herself and her partner.

> [Y]oung boys like 14, 15 year olds, coming up to us saying, 'are you lesbians? Kiss then'.... And then the one that really pissed me off, and me and my girlfriend had a different reaction to, was this guy who; we were waiting at a bus stop and he walked past us and went 'oh my god, lesbians, wow' and got really close to us and was like 'oh are you two lesbians?... You should be happy. Your girlfriend looks happy, why aren't you happy? You should kiss your girlfriend.' And it took a long time of saying look I don't

want to talk to you, you're being really disrespectful, go away … he just thought lesbians was something for him to interact with.

(Josina)

The basis of men's intrusion in the heteronormativity of the current gender order is revealed through the ways in which invoking an absent male partner, as seen in Lisa's account earlier in this chapter, was understood by many participants as more useful in discouraging men's intrusion than the presence in Josina's experience of a real female partner. Across the accounts of Abbey, Kirsten, Bec, Hannah and Josina there is a commonality in that not only are these men feeling entitled to sexualise an unknown woman, 'but also to *announce it to her*' (Kotzin, 1993: 167, emphasis in original). The lived experience here is more nuanced than the framework of 'objectification' suggests. For Bartky it is that 'I must be *made* to know that I am a "nice piece of ass"; I must be made to see myself as they see me' (Bartky, 1990: 27). This forced awareness of our corporeality, what Bartky terms 'being-made-to-be-aware of one's own flesh' (ibid.), is evident in Sophie's account of her friend's experience of sexualised commentary.

I wanted to tell you about my friend and she had enormous breasts, like H, F? Something huge, and she had a breast reduction on the NHS because of all the unwanted male attention that she used to get, and back pain, and I was talking to her about the fact that I was going to come and see you and I said 'what was it like before?' and she said 'people used to look at my boobs and be like "look at the tits on that".' And she said 'that's exactly how it used to make me feel, like a that, not a person. I'm a thing, I'm two walking boobs on legs'.

(Sophie)

Taryn spoke of similar experiences, where 'people would just refer to me like I was my breasts'. This reduction of women to their sexualised body parts was also something that was notably, though not solely, racialised. Participants who were identifiably from black and minority ethnic communities spoke with regularity of having their breasts and bottom commented on. For both Nisha and Delilah this crossed over from unknown to known men and from public to private spaces.

I think when you're larger breasted guys just narrow in on that. And we were out and [a friend of a friend] just kept staring at my chest. So I made a point of saying, he makes me feel really uncomfortable so I'm going to get lost for a bit. And [my friend] was like 'oh no, it's nothing, it's harmless, you've got to get used to that kind of thing because people are just going to stare.' And I thought, you don't really understand that when I'm alone somewhere and the same thing is happening then it is a threatening situation. And the fact I can pick that up more than he can made me worry because I thought oh hang on this is actually affecting the way I feel in public because he thinks I should feel ok but I don't.

(Delilah)

I'm like a F/G now and I've always had this thing where people just can't keep, they just look at them, even, like I was at a party the other day and this guy made a shit comment to me like oh someone was playing the bongos and I said 'there's too many fucking bongos at this party man,' and this guy was like 'I think you brought the bongos.' And I didn't even get it at first, I was just like 'huh? Nah I'm pretty sure you brought them mate,' and just carried on the joke and he said: 'No [looking at her chest] you brought them.'

(Nisha)

Sexualised commentary operated to force an awareness of women's corporeality in a way that was experienced as discounting their embodied selfhood. That such commentary was most regularly experienced by women of colour points to the wider connections, mostly unexplored here, between men's stranger intrusions on women in public and histories of racism that seek to reduce the colonised subject to the body.

'You'd look so much better if you smiled':[3] comments on women's demeanour

Over 60 per cent ($n=31$) of those receiving comments from unknown men in public had been told to cheer up or smile, with close to half ($n=13$) stating that they experienced this regularly (see Table 4.2). Unlike other forms of intrusion, commands to be demonstrably happy in public spaces comment on women's interiority. In this way, they have a particularly revealing role in exploring the relationship between men's intrusion and how women enact modalities of embodiment. Where women are experiencing the body as their grasp on the world, commands for women to be happy are commands that this grasp be adjusted, that the body be lived as a thing distinct from, rather than a reflection of, their internal world. Many participants encountering this perceived that an evaluative external perspective revealed something of their embodied self, even where it was inconsistent with their internal awareness; the (men's) view from outside is privileged.

[T]hey must think that's a good line with me. I must always look miserable.

(Katielou)

I learnt that I have a miserable face apparently, from men saying to smile.

(Gail)

Initially I was a bit naïve and thought that maybe I did just look a bit miserable. Then I realised I probably was smiling.

(Carolyn)

I think my default face when I'm not thinking about anything, it's just not very approachable I guess, I look annoyed or something. And so I've tried to walk around not looking quite so unhappy all the time which is not something that I am all the time, it just happens to be the way my muscles relax ... so I walk a little different now and I do different things with my face when I realise I'm starting to look annoyed, keeping the eyes wide and that sort of thing.

(Abbey)

Abbey's account in particular demonstrates how this privileging leads to a conscious adaptation: a bodily self-consciousness. The regular experience of commentary on her demeanour resulted in Abbey actively attempting to alter her embodiment to project the appearance of a set inner world, rather than living her corporeality as a fluid reflection of her inner world. The body is no longer 'expressing the conscious subject, but a vase, a receptacle made of inert matter and the plaything of mechanical caprices' (Beauvoir, 2011: 409). This works alongside the disruption and devaluing of women's internal world to undermine the experience of being an embodied subject, exemplified in Emma's account below, of being told to cheer up on the day she discovered she had miscarried.

There's no acknowledgement that you're a person that has other things happening rather than just existing for them to look at ... I was just really angry, because I wasn't being treated like a person.

(Emma)

Without recourse to an appropriate response, participants spoke of the difficulty in reasserting their embodied selfhood. Experiencing their interiority as penetrated and the privileging of men's evaluation of their internal world over their own experience, resulted in several participants claiming calls to 'cheer up' are among the most crippling of men's intrusive practices.

Cheer up is just worse than almost everything else. Because if I'm, if I'm say standing at the junction and waiting for the green light or something and somebody decides that it's their right to come to me and tell me to smile, give me orders about how I should keep my expression ... it's not the degrading feeling that you get from whistles and comments like 'hey sexy' and everything like that. It's more that, 'how dare they? What? Who do you think you are that you can tell me that?'

(Ginger)

'[O]h smile love,' that's the worst actually. I hate that, I hate that. Because you don't even know what to say, it's not even, like when someone says 'oh beautiful' you can say shut up. But when someone says 'oh smile love' there isn't a response for that, there's nothing. You could say 'shut up' but it doesn't really fit. So yeah that's probably the worst one.

(Jeannine)

I was on my way to work one day and passed some builders who said the 'alright gorgeous, it's not that bad, smile'. And I hate that, I almost hate that more because they think that they're being kind and paying you a compliment when actually it's just as bad really. Something negative, it's still having attention drawn to you, you haven't asked for it, you haven't even made eye contact, but still they're picking you out.

(Claire)

Exploring women's accounts through a feminist phenomenological framework enables an understanding of how such a seemingly innocuous comment is experienced as 'the worst one'. Commands to 'cheer up' are comments on the rare moments where participants felt embodied in public space and a judgment penetrating this inner world and encouraging a split between body and mind – a valuing of women not as a for-itself but in their being-for-others.

'You've got a face like shit':[4] insults and threats

One of the unexpected findings from the initial conversations was the extent of insulting and/or threatening comments: experienced by almost half of participants (n=23). Of these, over half (n=13) had experienced this type of intrusion more than once, with over a quarter (n=6) explicitly recounting multiple incidents. The range and contexts of insulting or threatening comments is largely absent from the literature on 'street harassment', demonstrating how terminology combines with mainstream framings of the phenomenon as complimentary or as sexual harassment to hide the extent of men's intrusion. Participants understood insults and threats to be practiced by men both on a retaliatory basis after women's refusal to participate in an intrusive encounter was expressed verbally or through the body, and also arbitrarily. Insults were directed at women's bodies as deficient in some way, most often in regards to their weight.

I've been called fat so many times, by [male] strangers. Slut, I've had that too.

(Taryn)

I was walking down past this pub and there were these middle aged men outside and they shouted out 'stick insect' to me ... I just remember it was a really nice sunny day and I was just walking along and it was a really weird thing to say but I remember the look on his face was horrible, like I was really unattractive.

(Anna)

I've had other incidents where people have been really insulting, like called me fat and stuff out of a car window ... I think that sort of thing definitely – my self confidence, from people saying things like that, definitely has damaged it a bit. Just because when it's a stranger as well it feels like my body offends you that much that you need to tell me that I'm unattractive to you, why do you need to tell me that?

(Lucy)

Women also spoke of appearance-related abusive comments that did not focus on weight but still pronounced an uninvited negative evaluation. Jane was insulted after a man approached her in public.

I was going to a bar with a friend and I had a guy ask me if I wanted to go with him and I said 'no,' and he said 'well fuck you, you're ugly anyway'.

(Jane)

Anne, who along with Ginger spoke of experiencing regular comments from unknown men about her red hair, spoke about experiencing a range of abusive comments from unknown men.

Someone called me crab face. They pointed and went 'crab face' and it didn't make sense. That was the biggest thing about it. I think I spent a long time thinking about that one, trying to work out what it was. But the ones that do affect me I think the most emotionally are when people shout out comments about your appearance. Things like 'oi ugly' ... 'Oi bitch', I've been called that.

(Anne)

The range of insults used also illustrates the grounding of such practices in misogyny. Where comments were not based on women's bodies, they revolved around archetypal gendered insults such as bitch and slut, as well as, particularly in Charlie's account, explicit negative reference to female genitalia.

He kept saying '[your] cunt stinks', about me. He was saying 'women, you're disgusting', really hateful, really nasty stuff ... I just sat there and thought 'ok, well you can't answer, you just do what you always do and look away', but [the tube] was so packed and nobody said anything.

(Charlie)

I had a guy call me a slut in Camden markets. He just walked straight past me and I was wearing, well I wasn't showing a great deal of flesh, and this guy walked past me, this was recent about six months ago, and this guy walked past me and just said 'slut'. Just like that.

(Alice)

I was sitting on the tube, there were like loads of people on the tube, men as well, and this sort of like 50-, 60-year-old Rasta guy gets on and he's sort of like murmuring to himself, obviously off his face, and he basically sits opposite me and he starts just like shouting at me going 'bitch, bitch', calling me a bitch. I was kind of ignoring it and I can't remember the exact sequence of events but basically I moved down to another carriage and he continued to shout abuse at me ... he just kept calling me a bitch.

(Anna)

For Anna, as for Rosalyn's similar experience below, physically removing the bodily-self was unsuccessful in combating abusive comments.

[H]e followed me down the tube, sat down opposite me again and carried on and at that point I was like 'look leave me alone, I don't want to talk to you, stop talking to me' and he did this whole like 'oh, oh, oh' thing, like I was being a bitch. And then we stopped, we got to where we were going and he got off and he called me 'a tranny and a minger' and walked off.

(Rosalyn)

Where physically removing the self does not work, many participants spoke about the strategic use of bodily alienation to experientially distance the body being abused. Referred to in Charlie's account above as 'just do what you always do and look away', this is where a habitualised mode of alienated embodiment as a response to men's stranger intrusions begins to enter women's accounts.

'We can see you':[5] the gaze

Almost all (94 per cent) of participants mentioned experiencing being stared at as a form of men's stranger intrusion in public space. Similar to ordinary interruptions, it was difficult for participants to recall individual episodes, with just nine able in the initial conversations to recount one or more particular instances (see Table 4.3).

Participants described the experience of men's intrusive staring as one of a distinct bodily-self consciousness.

I feel like I'm on a catwalk as I walk by because they're all lined up and I'm walking by ... I notice them from far away and I start to become really

Table 4.3 The gaze: frequency ($n=50$)

Frequency	Number	%
Regularly (no number given)	23	46
Occasionally (no number given)	13	26
Once	4	8
Three or more	3	6
Twice	2	4
Rarely (no number given)	2	4
Not mentioned	2	4
Not recorded	1	2
Total	50	100

conscious of how I'm walking and what I'm wearing and how I'm looking as I'm approaching them and as I'm walking by. And try really hard not to look at any of them.

(Abbey)

I remember being very aware of my body, and how I was, well I guess I felt like I was performing, which was weird because I didn't want to perform, and that was really unpleasant.

(Alice)

[H]e was looking at me in a way that was just like, you are just a piece of meat and I'm loving the show.

(Bec)

They're looking at me. They're looking at parts of my body I don't want them to be looking at. And also I'm a person, I'm not a body. The thing I'm most proud of myself for isn't having legs or a body, that's a given, it's not all of me.

(Lucy)

What participants express here is a bodily-self consciousness, an awareness of their embodiment marked by the experience of *having* not *being* one's body (Carman, 1999). As described by Lucy, her body is not experienced wholly as an embodied subjectivity, but rather as a necessary part of herself – a part she 'has'.

Recalling Heidegger's analogy where *Dasein* is not *in* the world as water is *in* a glass, participant accounts of the experience of being stared at by unknown men suggest the dislocation of feeling as though one *is* in the world as water is in a glass, seen through a transparent barrier, observable from the outside. The analogy can also be applied to the relationship expressed between the self and the body, where the body comes to be lived as this glass, a container that 'we' have for the self rather than the very means of our being at all. The danger here is that we are pulled towards a Cartesian view of the mind and the body as separate entities; encouraged to experience our body as a thing. This living experience is of the body 'as shape and flesh that presents itself as the potential object of another subject's intentions and manipulations, rather than as a living manifestation of action and intention' (Young, 2005: 184), an attitude towards the female body that is compounded in popular and consumer culture. These combine to encourage a relationship to the body as a physical presence or object (*Körper*), marked by control rather than care. For Sandra Lee Bartky, this continued forced awareness of the materiality of one's body is humiliating, 'like being made to apologise' (1990: 27). This feeling of shame is particularly explored in existential-phenomenological accounts of the gaze.

For Simone de Beauvoir 'nothing is more ambiguous than a look; it exists at a distance, and that distance makes it seem respectable: but insidiously it takes hold of the perceived image' (Beauvoir, 2011: 375). This ambiguity, and its insidiousness, is captured in the way that Ginger described the particular impact of the gaze.

> [I]t makes me feel really, really helpless. Because if somebody does something actively you can do something about it. You know if somebody touches you, you can go 'hey don't touch me,' you can hit them, you can talk to them, and they can't pretend they didn't do it. But if somebody's looking at you, well imagine a guy's staring at you from across the seat, you could tell them 'what are you looking at?' and his answer is 'nothing.' Unless he really wants to say something, a lot of times if he feels ashamed or if he doesn't feel comfortable he's going to say that I'm imagining it. And that's another one of those things, so I've become one of those people who imagine everybody's looking at them and it's my problem, because I'm the one who's imagining that everybody's paying attention to me and obviously there has to be something wrong with myself not with the people who are looking.
>
> (Ginger)

Jean-Paul Sartre devoted an entire section to the phenomenology of 'the Look' in *Being and Nothingness* (2007). His insights are valuable here, particularly that the Sartrean 'Look' does not necessarily refer to the actual experience of being looked at; rather it refers to a consciousness of the *possibility* of the gaze. This possibility was manifest for participants in contexts where unknown men, particularly in groups, were anticipated, such as Meg's description of passing a building site.

> There's a big massive building work going on there at the moment and my brother's gym is there so I go and see him and every time I walk past you can just feel the eyes on you. It's a really long walk as well and you just think about it the whole way.
>
> (Meg)

Events such as these remind us of the possibility that we can be looked at and in doing so provokes a phenomenological response *as if we were* being looked at. As with ordinary interruptions, where participant's internal world in public space was regularly experienced as interrupted because of the potentiality of men's intrusion, public spaces also represented for many participants the imminent potentiality of the gaze of unknown men. Following Sartre, this possibility has the same philosophical import as being constantly watched.

> I try to walk around if I want to, when I want to, and not have it in my head you should go home now, it's dark, watch your back, but you always do and it's something about always knowing who's around you and how you're behaving and being alert and a constant feeling of being observed.
>
> (Claire)

[T]his idea of the gaze generally does stop me from doing things ... it's a little bit like you're under observation, it's a bit big brotherly. You don't know why they're looking at you or what they're thinking. It's the unknown I guess.

(Viola)

The look then, whether actual or possible, disrupts what Sartre terms our non-thetic self-consciousness,[6] the pre-reflective cogito where our awareness is wholly of our acts and not a consciousness of the self *in* those acts. The gaze of the other forces us to become aware of our bodily-self, Sartre's claim that 'I see myself because somebody sees me' (2007: 260). Importantly, in the case of men's stranger intrusion, this awareness of our embodiment is experienced through the body image not through the body as a field of intentionality. As Sartre acknowledges, there is a particular vulnerability that comes with the acknowledgement of ourselves as a body that can be seen, and that can be hurt.

What I apprehend immediately when I hear the branches crackling behind me is not that *there is someone there*; it is that I am vulnerable, that I have a body which can be hurt, that I occupy a place and that I can not in any case escape from the space in which I am without defense – in short, that *I am seen.*

(Sartre, 2007: 282, emphasis in original)

This vulnerability is heightened when combined with the tripartite diminishment of our embodied subjectivity discussed earlier. The impact of the gaze of the other is further complicated when moved out of a degendered discussion and into the concrete particulars of the meanings attributed to female embodiment under patriarchy. For Rosalyn, her experiences of bodily-self consciousness under the gaze resulted in a desire to diminish her woman's body, to become 'less conspicuous' as a woman and through this to feel safer.

[T]here's another bit of me that also wishes, because having a skinny boyish figure means you can wear certain types of clothes and we're all supposed to want to be like that, but I think there's a bit of me that wishes that because, I guess because you feel like it's a kind of less conspicuous sexuality about that kind of body on a woman.

(Rosalyn)

For participants the apprehension 'that I have a body which can be hurt' (Sartre, 2007: 282) is gendered. It is the recognition that in the current gender order a woman's body is targeted for a particular form of hurt, referred to in the literature as a 'fear of rape' but conceptualised here as the imminent potentiality of rape; a potential embedded in women's living experience of their embodiment.

'*I just have to take a picture*':[7] *creepshots*

The role of new technologies in expanding the continuum of men's intrusive practices also has a place in a discussion of the gaze. As covered in the introduction, the opportunities for men's intrusion given through the advent of new technologies, and their connection to other forms of violence against women, are beginning to be made. The recent emergence of affordable smart phones has created new opportunities for men's stranger intrusions with five of the women participating in this project reporting experiencing an unknown man taking or attempting to take their photograph without their consent in public space. Popularly termed 'creepshots', such a practice is promoted through internet forums and social media accounts which encourage men to photograph unknown women in public space, without their consent, often focusing on sexualised body parts such as the breasts or the bottom.[8] For Taryn this was clearly connected to the routineness of the gaze and the ways she had habituated herself to it.

> Men just openly stare at your tits. Or you'll be on the tube sitting down and they'll be standing up just openly staring at your tits. I remember one of my exes nearly got up and punched a guy once … this guy was just standing there and we were talking and I hadn't noticed and she looked up just as he took a photo of my cleavage. She was furious. I was like 'don't worry it happens all the time' and she just couldn't believe that someone could be so openly rude. And it struck me at the time that I just thought that was quite normal whereas she was astounded.
>
> (Taryn)

Rosalyn and Meg remembered a specific instance when they had either been photographed, or a man had attempted to take their photograph in public space, as particularly wrapped in a sense of uncertainty about the purpose of the intrusion.

> When we were outside [of the bar] my friend was like oh my God that man is outside across the road taking pictures of us, it was just like what are you doing? And he came up closer and tried to do it again and we just kind of looked away, it was just really weird. You hope they're not going to do anything with the pictures … I mean people who do this stuff I just think 'why do you do it?' That's the big question isn't it.
>
> (Meg)

> When I was in the British museum and I was meeting a friend but I had an hour beforehand so I went to look at the stuff and I was in one of their medieval rooms and I was just looking at things and there's this guy next to me who was sort of, you know going around at the same pace as me, but it wasn't just that? That feeling when you know that he's looking at me as much as the stuff. And you're just waiting. And it went on and on and I

couldn't do what I was doing, like I couldn't, I was there to look at the stuff and I couldn't, I couldn't concentrate, because the whole time I was thinking when are you going to talk to me, what are you going to say, what's the deal here ... eventually he did speak to me. He leaned over and asked if he could take my photograph. I just looked at him and said 'no'. And then he was like 'I'm sorry I'm sorry' and ran out of the room ... it's only at that point I think that you really become like angry as well like, because for that first time you're so focused on what's going on here, feeling anxious I think, that when you reach that crisis point where they actually do speak to you and you're like 'no leave me alone I'm just doing my thing. You cannot take my photograph.' What the fuck? Why does he want a stranger's photograph?

(Rosalyn)

Marly and Luella had multiple experiences of being photographed in public space by men without their permission. When permission was requested, as for Rosalyn above, Marly was able to refuse the intrusion. Both her and Luella, however, remembered times where permission was not sought.

Actually, just the other day I was sitting in a takeaway on [street], minding my own business, and this guy stands outside the window and takes a picture of me. It was the same actually I was in [city] I was standing, staring, waiting for something. And this guy was like 'oh my God, look at your profile, it's so beautiful I just have to take a picture', and I'm like 'no you don't just have to take a picture', and he was like 'no I do I just have to take and picture' and I'm 'no you really don't, I don't want you to take a picture of me. Fuck off.'

(Marly)

I've had men trying to take pictures of me. One of those things happened really early when I was about 15, 16, I was just in a shop in my local high street, I was wearing a pair of shorts, ooo such a harlot, and I was just minding my own business, and this guy walked in, took a look, snapped like his phone, a picture on his phone and walked back out. And it happened in the space of like 5 seconds. And I was like 'what!' I was just standing with my face to the wall looking at whatever was on there, and then I just turned my head, I saw him, he snapped a picture and then walked back out, he didn't run, he just walked back out really casual as if he'd just strolled in. I was so taken aback I was just like 'did that actually happen?' I mean this is the middle of the day, there's a shopkeeper in the shop, I don't know. It just kind of stung because that was the first time that happened to me, and then the thought followed, 'what on earth is he going to do with that?' I just don't want to think about it.

(Luella)

Creepshots and photographs make literal Simone de Beauvoir's claim that the look 'takes hold' of the perceived image, and this is the concern expressed so clearly by Luella above. The fleeting moment of the gaze becomes in itself an object, a lasting record of one's reduction to a body that continues beyond and outside of the moment of intrusion. It thus has a specific permanence that is unseen across other forms of intrusion. There is also a sense in which women experience themselves as being part of public space, a thing or event to be recorded, rather than as actors within it. Though relatively small numbers of women reported the practice in this study, as the popularity and technical ability of smartphones grows, including the introduction of applications where a photo can be taken without the phone's screen showing that the camera is open,[9] this form of intrusion requires further research, a key part of the overlaps between men's stranger intrusions in physical and online public space.

Notes

1 For more on this differentiation see Thoibisana (2008).
2 Direct quote: Lucy.
3 Direct quote: Taryn.
4 Direct quote: Rosalyn.
5 Direct quote: Claire.
6 Sartre holds our non-thetic self-consciousness to be those moments when we lose ourselves in the world to the point where we are no longer conscious of the self in the world. It can be seen in the level of awareness we have, for example, in reading an engrossing novel. Rarely are we aware of ourselves reading the book, rather our self-awareness is wholly taken over and we are *in* the world.
7 Direct quote: Marly.
8 See, for example, American hosted site www.creepshots.com, the Reddit hub for 'Upskirt creepshots' www.reddit.com/r/upskirt and the Tumblr page http://creepshots.tumblr.com [all accessed 24 November 2015]. There are also a number of Twitter profiles devoted to the practice including the following which were all live at the time of writing: @CreepBJ; @CreepFan; @timetocreep; @creep_town; @womensbehinds; @im_just_lookin; @tokyocreeper; @XRayCreepin; @PeepersCreepers; and @CreepShot which is an offshoot of the creepshot.com site.
9 There are many applications like this openly available and at very low cost. The QuickShot HD ($3), is reviewed as being 'for you creep shot lovers out there. Pictures could be taken while leaving you the excuse that you don't have anything open should you get caught.' See http://androidappscene.blogspot.co.uk/2012/11/the-ultimate-camera-app.html [accessed 4 July 2013].

References

Bartky, S. L. (1990) *Femininity and Domination*, Routledge.
Beauvoir, S. d. (2011) *The Second Sex*, Borde, C., & Malovany-Chevallier, S. (transl.), Vintage.
Carman, T. (1999) 'The Body in Husserl and Merleau-Ponty', *Philosophical Topics*, 27 (2), pp. 205–226.
Coy, M., & Garner, M. (2012) 'Definitions, Discourses and Dilemmas: Policy and Academic Engagement with the Sexualisation of Popular Culture', *Gender and Education*, 24 (3), pp. 285–301.
Esacove, A. W. (1998) 'A Diminishing of the Self: Women's Experiences of Unwanted Sexual Attention', *Health Care for Women International*, 19 (3), pp. 181–192.

Gardner, C. B. (1995) *Passing by: Gender and Public Harassment*, University of California Press.

Goffman, E. (1990) *The Presentation of Self in Everyday Life*, Penguin.

Jackson, S. (2001) 'Why a Materialist Feminism is (Still) Possible—and Necessary', *Women's Studies International Forum*, 24 (3), pp. 283–293.

Kelly, L., & Radford, J. (1990). ' "Nothing Really Happened": The Invalidation of Women's Experiences of Sexual Violence', *Critical Social Policy*, 10 (30), pp. 39–53.

Kotzin, R. H. (1993) 'Bribery and Intimidation: A Discussion of Sandra Lee Bartky's Femininity and Domination: Studies in the Phenomenology of Oppression', *Hypatia*, 8 (1), pp. 164–172.

Larkin, J. (1997) 'Sexual Terrorism on the Street: The Moulding of Young Women into Subordination', in Thomas, A. M., & Kitzinger, C. (eds), *Sexual Harassment: Contemporary Feminist Perspectives*, Open University Press, pp. 115–130.

Sartre, J. P. (2007) *Being and Nothingness*, Routledge.

Thoibisana, A. (2008) 'Heidegger on the Notion of Dasein as Habited Body', *Indo-Pacific Journal of Phenomenology*, 8 (2), pp. 1–5.

Young, I. M. (2005) *On Female Body Experience: 'Throwing Like a Girl' And Other Essays*, Oxford University Press.

And then I felt someone's hands on my butt cheek.
I now stay away from the colour red
I had someone wind down their window and say oi love you dropped something,
and I looked down,
and they said it's your pants.

He was like oh do you have a boyfriend?
If I don't acknowledge him, it'll turn nasty.
He kind of stopped, said I just want you to know that you're a very beautiful woman.
I still have my earplugs in, even if the music isn't on.
This guy had come up to me and been like oh give us a smile
If I want someone to get past me I try to get my back to a wall.

This guy had actually snuck behind her
and put his hand down in a way that I'd think it was her
and then she saw too and I was just like oh my God
because he'd actually touched me

there.

He just sort of pulled his trousers down.
I walk quicker or I phone someone.
Guy walks past me and starts whispering shit in my ear.
I carry my keys between my hand so I can stab.
As we left he slapped my bum.
I wish I could just wear exactly what I wanted.

    They wouldn't let me get around the car, they kept reversing if I tried to go
          behind and pushing forward, so effectively trapping
               me as I tried to cross the road.

A dodgy guy stood next to me on the platform on the tube.
I always try to look like I know where I'm going.
He was just following me up the hill.
I take a key and I have the sharp part in between my fingers.
Some guys told me to leave my boyfriend and get in the car.
I don't really do anything.

       They circled around the block and met us on the other side
             and were there waiting for us
             when we got down to the end.

So there was one guy who was like 'come over here I want to buy you a drink'
I use my shadow on the floor, if I'm on the street I can tell how close they are.
He took a step back and he touched my hair.
Be polite but not too polite that they want to continue talking to me.
He was making this weird noise, like a clicking noise or something.
I dress with scarves and things to just cover, take the focus away.

Some guy, very seriously in a trench coat, was following myself and a friend of
mine from school halfway up that hill,
in the forest, into a green space
and then actually exposed himself.

He started talking to me more like saying oh where are you going?
I normally ignore it and then get angry at myself.
He followed us for like half a block telling us that his flat was around the corner.
I'll purposely just look straight ahead

He pointed and went crab face.
I tend to check my phone.

He even texted my daughter saying what he wanted to do to her,
what he wanted to do to both of us.
This guy walked past me and just said

                                                                                                    slut.

5 Living men's intrusion

Part two

The connective mechanisms across the continuum of men's intrusive practices, discussed in detail at the end of this chapter, highlights how the separation of categories is not as clear as their division into two parts may suggest. There are, however, particularities about the experience of the intrusions categorised here, that meant that for many participants these were remembered in a different way than the more routine intrusions of the previous chapter. This means many of the practices were easier to measure. Most of the intrusions given below have a physical element, either restricting women's physical movement in public space or being related to the physicality of the male stranger. They thus had a particular quality that touched the vulnerability of being embodied in a different way; not only a knowledge but an experience of the bodily boundary of the self as one that can be transgressed. Included in this chapter are intrusions named as rape,[1] sexual assault and/or physical assault, alongside behaviours where unknown men blocked women's way or touched them. In addition, practices where attention was drawn most palpably to the imminent potentiality of rape, such as flashing or following are also included. By framing experiences as located on the continuum of men's practices, the separation of practices such as rape or sexual assault into 'completed' and 'attempted', or practices such as following into 'actual' or 'perceived' is avoided, a separation that can operate to discount women's resistance and is often unhelpful given the similarity in impacts. The practice is analysed, not the outcome.

Physical intrusions

Attempts to measure the frequency of physical intrusions can lose women's successful resistance – a practice which may be experienced as following for example is lost if a woman's response successfully evades this escalating – a point we will return to. Despite this, it is useful to count what is known, with an eye kept on what is missed. Just over three quarters of participants (76 per cent) had experienced being groped or touched by unknown men in public space, almost a third had experienced men physically blocking their space for movement, and 10 per cent had experienced an unknown man rape or attempt to rape them (see Table 5.1).

Table 5.1 Physical intrusions: frequency (n=50)

Type of physical intrusion	Touched/groped		Blocked space		Rape (stranger only)	
Frequency	Number	%	Number	%	Number	%
Once	19	38	9	18	5	10
Twice	12	24	4	8	–	–
Three or more	3	6	1	2	–	–
Regularly (no number given)	2	4	1	2	–	–
Occasionally (no number given)	1	2	–	–	–	–
Happens but no frequency given	1	2	1	2	–	–
Never happened (explicit)	1	2	–	–	6	12
Not mentioned	11	22	33	66	39	78
Not recorded	–	–	1	2	–	–
Total	50	100	50	100	50	100
Total recording practice (n=50)	38	76	16	32	5	10

Similar to the discussion of the gaze, men's physical intrusions were an experience for women of living the paradox of the bodily-self as both subject and object. Anne describes an experience on holiday as a teenager.

> I went on holiday with my family when I was 18 again to [city]. And one day we got the bus and it was a really busy, crowded bus and there was this old man in front of me and everyone squeezed in, it was a bit like on the tube and then the bus turned the corner and this guy leaned into me, and you know you don't think anything when a bus is cornering, and after it had righted itself again he stayed leaning into me, was rubbing his crotch against me and he had an erection. I nervously smiled after it and then he smiled back and kept doing it more. This old Italian guy just rubbing himself on me on a bus.
>
> (Anne)

As seen in Anne's account, in physically intruding men express their bodily intentionality at the same time as women experience the materiality of their bodily-self. Here, as with the discussion of the gaze, the experience again is one of feeling as though one is in the world as water is in a glass. Anne continues her account to describe how she felt unable to act through her body at the time of intrusion.

> [A]t first I didn't really realise what was going on, and then I did. And then it was like, 'oh god what do I do? I don't know what to do?' And you get stuck because you're unsure how to deal with the situation. You don't know what's going to happen if you try to get out of it. Will this guy react badly or …? It just makes you feel really incapable of dealing with what's going on. It just makes you feel powerless, I don't know what to do, I don't know how to deal with this situation. Because it's not like it's something you can prepare for, and it shouldn't be. You shouldn't have to prepare for it. It shouldn't happen. But it happens in an ambiguous situation which is why they choose that.
>
> (Anne)

Unable to physically move away from the intrusive man for fear of escalation, Anne's experience of her embodiment as a 'body-for-others' is compounded through ways in which early experiences of men's intrusion had taught her to doubt her experiential reality, considered more fully in the following chapter. Such doubt combines with men using particular contexts to practice physical intrusions in ways participants found difficult to confirm, Anne's 'ambiguous situations'.

> I was in a massive crowd of people because it's like a huge station so you're all like getting off the tube and in the station, and this guy came up behind me and grabbed me between my legs, like properly grabbed me and I was

wearing a skirt and he was right behind me so I couldn't see him and I just felt this person grabbing and it was that thing again of shock, I can't believe someone just did that to me in this crowd of people. Like, how did that happen? And then I turned around and there was this guy behind me, quite short old guy who looked a bit weird. I wasn't even sure it was him because ... how do you know?

(Rosalyn)

I've had lots of men press themselves into me, loads of times, on the tube. It's really difficult to tell though. If they get too close I tell them 'don't do that' and they back off but you know some men are really clever, they do that as you're getting on and then they move away.

(New Mum)

There is a diminishment of Anne, Rosalyn and New Mum's ability to claim what is being done to them and by whom, something also seen in several accounts given by women of behaviours that are criminalised, though spoken about as ordinary or even forgotten. Here the particular use of conversation helped in unearthing experiences that may be lost in survey research or traditional interview guides. After initially saying she had not experienced any kind of physical intrusion, Delilah recalled being bitten on the lip and punched in the stomach by two separate unknown men in clubs, as well as the following encounter in a supermarket.

Someone undid one of my top buttons once on this shirt that I was wearing, in a supermarket of all places. He literally just came up to me and I thought at first something must be on my top, I don't know why this stranger feels the need to do it but at the time you're thinking 'ok that must be really embarrassing something's on my top'. But he literally just came up to me and undid my top button.

(Delilah)

Emma also recounted having an unknown man, at 17, pin her down on public transport and attempt to take off her skirt, immediately after claiming she had 'never had anything really bad before'.

I had a guy sit down next to me, it was a sufficiently busy train carriage that that didn't ring alarm bells, and asked me the time which I gave him, and while I was looking away he leaned across me and pinned me back and tried to take off my skirt and we got to, I don't know which train station it was because I'd just got to [the city] but he tried to drag me off the train but I got away.

(Emma)

The linked processes of minimisation and normalisation are similarly seen in a physical intrusion related by Viola, where a man circled the block three times when she was walking and each time tried to, in Viola's words, 'grab my ass'.

I was really shaken up and in hindsight, I still regret not having called the police. Not because I think they would have done anything or could have done anything but I think for myself I would have felt more in control, or like I was doing something about it, rather than running home and hiding ... I think they couldn't do anything anyway and nothing really happened either. He didn't even really touch me in the end and I think I would have felt very silly as well, talking to the police because it seemed like such a non-issue, though at the same time it did make me feel really panicky and quite unsafe.

(Viola)

This 'non-issue' in fact has significant impacts, giving living detail to Sandra Lee Bartky's claim that '[w]oman's space is not a field in which her bodily intentionality can be freely realized but an enclosure in which she feels positioned and by which she is confined' (Bartky, 1990: 66). Instead of the world experienced as a field within which to express one's own bodily intentionality, the movements of the body are constrained. An early experience with a physically intrusive man highlighted this for Jan.

I remember once in a cinema, I must have been 12 or 13 and I was sitting with a friend and a guy next to me started groping my knee. And I said to my friend, 'this guy's touching me'. And she said first of all 'don't make a fuss'. And I thought, 'I can't'. So we moved. But it was me making a fuss, not him being an asshole.

(Jan)

The operations of physical intrusions in restricting women's movements in public space are most literally seen in the practice of blocking women's space, a practice that also raises what can be missed in framing experiences within narrow definitions of 'harassment'.

Late at night I was with two friends and these two guys stopped their car because they wanted my number. We were on the street and we were trying to cross the road and they wouldn't let me get around the car, they kept reversing if I tried to go behind and pushing forward, so effectively trapping me as I tried to cross the road because they wanted my number. And I pretended I didn't have a phone but then took their number down just to get them to go away. And they must have been quite (a lot) older because they were driving and I was 14 or 15.

(Josina)

This was two guys in a car and we were walking on the pavement and they'd driven by, slowed down as they got close you know and yelled out the window. So we weren't interested at all so we thought ok we'll turn down a side street that wasn't allowed to have any cars on it. A one way street and they couldn't drive up it. So we're like 'we'll get away from them'. But they circled around the block and met us on the other side and were there waiting for us when we got down to the end and that was very uncomfortable because that for me, that took some extra effort on their part to call out some more, you know, it was that forward planning, and that was the bit that scared me.

(Sophia)

This physical blocking of space combines with feminist theory on how men's practices can constrain women's 'space for action' (Jeffner, 2000) to create a modality of female embodiment in public space characterised by what Young (2005) termed 'inhibited intentionality'. Young showed how the modalities of feminine embodiment illustrate a split between mind (aim) and body (enactment), finding that

[i]n those motions which when properly performed require the coordination and directedness of the whole body upon some definite end, women frequently move in a contradictory way. Their bodies project the aim to be enacted, but at the same time stiffen against the performance of the task.

(2005: 14)

Women's bodily intentionality is thus inhibited by a persistent disbelief in their capacity, and undermined by an anxious focus upon the processes of bodily movement. Exploring the impacts of intrusion for participants supports Young's finding, and suggests that this 'split' here (between self, body and world) operates as a distancing developed in response to, and in order to cope with, the continuum of men's intrusive practices.

Flashing and masturbation

The experience of flashing, whereby an unknown man exposes their penis intentionally to (predominantly) women and children in public space, forms a significant part of participants' early encounters with the continuum of men's intrusive practices. Almost half of participants ($n=21$) had experienced flashing at least once as given in Table 5.2.

Table 5.2 Flashing: frequency ($n=50$)

Frequency	Number	%
Once	14	28
Never happened (explicit)	5	10
Regularly (no number given)	3	6
Twice	2	4
Happens (no frequency given)	1	2
Three or more	1	2
Not mentioned	24	48
Total	50	100

The layered power dynamics of generation and gender played a key role for participant understandings, with many suggesting their age was the motivating factor for this type of intrusion. Nine participants reported an encounter before the age of 18, for some this was in childhood.

> [T]here was also another incident probably about a year after that when someone stopped the car and asked me for directions but they had no trousers on. They'd called me over to the car, wound the window down and said, 'I need some directions'. I asked him where to and he pointed [to his crotch]. So yeah [I] was about 8 or 9.
>
> (Claire)

> We were quite young about 8, or 9. But it was so impactful so it was quite the story to remember. It was the middle of the day and some guy, very seriously in a trench coat, was following myself and a friend of mine from school halfway up that hill, in the forest, into a green space and then actually exposed himself.
>
> (Cathrin)

Alice, who is in her early twenties, spoke of her numerous experiences of being flashed as related to her youthful appearance.

> [T]he one thing that I've experienced the most in London is being flashed because I look really young I think and I've been flashed at least six or seven times, on the tube mostly … it's probably about once every year it happens to me.
>
> (Alice)

For other women experiencing flashing before the age of 18, the particular impacts of the experience were often framed in terms of being the first time they had seen a penis – a point we will explore in the following chapter.

Men's public masturbation directed at women, and particularly at girls, is also a significant part of the practice of flashing. Over half (58 per cent) of participants who explicitly recalled experiences of flashing were masturbated at as part of the encounter. For some this was not preceded by an act where just the genitals themselves were exposed, however as the definition used to categorise the behaviours was the deliberate exposure of the penis, all encounters with men masturbating at/over women were also acts of flashing. Masturbation emerged as a practice that particularly targeted girls, even though it did occur to some women over the age of 18, as June's experience at university shows.

> [H]e was like 'excuse me do you know where this place is?' and I was like 'no, I don't'. And he said 'I've got a problem' and I thought that it might be maybe can I borrow your phone or something, and then he was like 'I like to expose myself to beautiful women' and I looked down and he essentially

had his cock out and basically ejaculated all over the lawn right in front of me.

(June)

When context was mentioned, the most common public spaces for men to practice both masturbation and exposure were open public spaces such as beaches or parks ($n=10$) or public transport ($n=8$), with four reports occurring on the street, two in a public swimming pool, and one in a supermarket on a Sunday morning.

I think the one that really upset me was when I was in Morrisons, on a Sunday morning, and I was just buying some ale or something and my normal weekly shop. And there was this guy and he was shuffling around, and I said to my partner, 'is he doing what I think he's doing?' ... [H]e was proper looking at me. And I had a bit of a low cut top on, like not loads, just a normal top, and he was doing it again, and I was like [to my partner] 'look mate, he's definitely having a wank, he's definitely doing it. In Morrisons'.

(Nisha)

Across accounts, participants expressed a range of emotional responses, from confusion to pity, humour when the practice was experienced with friends, and fear where the woman experienced the practice as suggestive of the possibility of further intrusion, as seen in Laura's account below.

[M]y friend turned around who was in front of me and said 'look over there!' and so I looked and between the houses that were facing the beach there was this little alleyway and there was this guy who had been sat next to us on the beach, stood with his trousers around his ankles just jerking off. And we were just like, we were laughing, he was probably far enough away for us to be like this is weird but the thing was it was quite funny so we starting laughing, but then it got horrible because he was obviously a local and he'd obviously gone around some back route and had come around and so we were on our way back to the flat on the hill and he'd come round and was stood under the bridge doing the same thing so we were like, that's creepy, that's really weird, this isn't funny anymore. So we carried on walking instead of going home and went and sat in a café and had another drink.

(Laura)

Sandra McNeil's (1987) study of the impact of flashing found that women experienced the threat in the exposed penis as the threat of rape. For some participants here the threat was not experienced only in the exposed penis, but through a combination of factors, both internal and external. In Laura's experience above, the threat is reduced when she is with friends and at a distance however it increases when they realise the man is purposefully seeking them out. The meaning of the intrusion abruptly changes at the point where it becomes clear that *he wants to be seen*. The decision made by Laura and her friends at the point of experiencing this shift was to remove the embodied self. Where this was not physically possible, women spoke of enacting a mode of embodiment whereby the body and world was held at a distance as seen in the accounts of Nisha, Jan and Theodora.

> I had a man wank off over me on the tube … I felt like I couldn't move, I felt like I didn't know what to do. Do I get up? Do I move? Do I just sit here, do I pretend nothing's happening? What do I do? There's hardly anyone else on the carriage … I sat there for a bit and then we came into the station and I jumped off. And I was really worried he was going to follow me. I was really frightened, like really shaken.
>
> (Nisha)

> [I]t was only me and him in the carriage, young guy, and he got out his dick and wanked off in front of me. I got off at the next station because I thought this could be anything. I felt quite scared. I didn't let him know that I'd seen him. I didn't acknowledge it in any way but I thought that could be nasty, if he can do that what else will he do?
>
> (Jan)

> I was on the tube again when I was quite young … he sat on the corner of the chair and again, legs akimbo, whipped it out, had a go … and I just thought, because there was no one else on the carriage, I can't make eye contact with him because if I do he'll think I'm coming onto him. I can't make any contact with him whatsoever, I've just got to pretend that I can't see him. Just put the wall up.
>
> (Theodora)

Theodora's 'wall' is her way of distancing the self from the body and the world. This refusal to acknowledge or to be *in* the world is a form of strategic alienation, enacted until one can physically remove themselves. These three encounters also suggest particular contexts are chosen by men. Similar to the accounts of ordinary interruptions, there is a repeated context for men's intrusion of women travelling alone on public transport. This suggests that rather than resulting from coincidental circumstances or uncontrollable desire, men who choose to intrude onto and into women are in control of both their self and the setting.

Following

As illustrated by Jan's experience of flashing, the possibility of escalation between different intrusive practices plays a key role in how women strategised responses, perhaps most palpable in the category of 'following'. Ambiguity was expressed by participants in relation to following, with a separation made between externally verified experience, where the feeling of being followed was somehow confirmed,

Table 5.3 Following (externally verified and unverified): frequency (*n*=50)

Frequency	Experiential externally verified		Experiential unverified	
	Number	%	Number	%
Once	15	30	7	14
Twice	9	18	1	2
Three or more	3	6	–	–
Regularly (no number given)	1	2	4	8
Happens (no frequency given)	1	2	9	18
Never happened (explicit)	9	18	3	6
Not mentioned	11	22	25	50
Not recorded	1	2	1	2
Total	50	100	50	100

and experiential unverified following where the feeling of being followed was not confirmed externally. What qualified as external verification will be discussed in more detail below. Table 5.3 shows that just over three quarters (*n*=39) of participants reported at least one experience of following.

Of these reports, most participants spoke of experiences that they had verified as a definite instance of following (*n*=29), and over half (*n*=24) reported experiences they were unable to verify.

> I have felt like it, I don't know if I've ever actually been followed. But you only know if you have been if they approach you. I've had like that thing about someone walking too close behind you. I've had that and it's horrible. Because you feel like if I turn around they could just be walking behind me and then you feel like you're being paranoid and that you're getting worked up over nothing. Or you don't want to turn around in case they are following you. And it becomes about avoiding a bad situation, again. So I walk quicker or I phone someone.
>
> (Anne)

As seen in Anne's account, the possibility of escalation was embedded in participant's sense making of following to the extent that for many if the practice did not escalate, despite their subjective experience, participants felt unable to verify that something had happened. Key here is how the possibility of escalation for many participants foregrounds the experiential connections between different practices on the continuum. For both Alice and Abbey, reminiscent of McNeil's (1987) findings on flashing, experiencing the possibility of being followed is simultaneously an experience of the possibility of rape.

> [A] guy followed me, now I say followed but he was just walking down the same alleyway as me … I remember looking over my shoulder, not at him

but being deliberately aware of where he was and checking the mirrors that came up on the windows how far away he was from me, and somebody joined us at the other end, it was another guy and, God this actually went through my mind, the other guy came at the other end and I actually thought 'fuck me this is a trap, fuck ok, no it's fine, be rational, it's probably nothing'. He walked past me and I thought 'phew', and then a woman came at the other end and I was like 'thank God, everything's fine, you're not going to be raped'.

(Alice)

I got followed, briefly only for like a few blocks probably, just shouting things like 'hey honey how you doing? Don't you want to talk to me? Are you having a good night? Don't you want to have some fun?' That kind of stuff and kind of, yeah, kind of terrifying actually ... even though I knew that probably nothing was going to happen, because one of them was in broad daylight and the other two I was in a busy area with a lot of people so probably nothing would have happened but I was ... I mean I guess, to put it incredibly bluntly scared of being assaulted. Although I've never come close to anything like that happening to me ... it's the first thing I think of when something like that happens.

(Abbey)

For Abbey as for Alice, both nothing and something happened (Kelly & Radford, 1990). Nothing happened in respect to anticipated escalation, but their internal world experienced not only the possibility that they were being followed but also the possibility of sexual assault. Such an account is reminiscent of Beauvoir's claims that ambiguity grounds the human condition (Beauvoir, 1976), and that women embody this ambiguity more explicitly than men (Beauvoir, 2011). Moving away from an either/or framing, Beauvoir's theory of ambiguity allows for an exploration of both/and, where both these possibilities are lived in the body. Participants attempted to reconcile this ambiguity through prioritising the external perspective on the bodily-self, a habituated bodily strategy. This is shown in Bea's detailed account below where her experience of being followed evoked an embodied response, regardless of the unknown man's intentions.

... [M]e and my sister were getting the night bus home one night and we think quite similarly, and I was convinced this guy was looking over at us and he was and then he happened to get off at the same bus stop as us and so we started walking, we hold hands and stand closer and that kind of stuff and I think I was more panicked than she was but she was like 'yep ok let's walk faster', and he walked faster. I was convinced he was following us, so I said 'let's just run, let's run home it'll take five minutes', so we started running and I was wearing these strange shoes and I slipped over in the middle of the road. And this happened like two years ago but I really hurt my hip, I slipped over, went into like the half splits, ripped this ligament, had to call my dad, and the guy just walked straight on past so he wasn't, maybe he was, maybe he wasn't, you'll never know.

(Bea)

The impact of regularly experiencing such uncertain situations, the claim of 'maybe he was, maybe he wasn't, you'll never know', contributes to the diminishment of Bea's subjectivity through her feeling unable to make meaning of the situation. The habitual dismissal of the capacity of women's embodied selfhood – to act through rather than be acted on – is further shown in the ways in which the possibility of Bea's agency in disrupting the following is minimised in her account. This was found across the ways participants spoke about experiences of intrusion, devaluing their own embodied practices whilst deferring to men's actions in their sense-making of an encounter. Throughout accounts of following, there was evidence of responses born of women's situated agency in preventing both intrusion and escalation.

This one time in [city] a couple of years ago, I was basically just walking home from a night out, it was about 5 o'clock in the morning, but people walk home there because it's like a little village and it's safe most of the time. And this strange guy was walking up the street in front of me and then he slowed down and watched me walk on a bit and then started following me, so I just picked up my phone and pretended I was ringing someone and I stopped, turned around and looked at him, on my phone, and he just walked down this side street.

(Shelley)

I might go a different way or I might drop back ... one night I remember it was quite late I was walking home behind a guy but he seemed to be slowing down or something? And he also seemed to have a piece of wood in his hands which was slightly concerning to me, but anyway so it'd probably be the same regardless of what he was carrying but he seemed to be slowing down as if he wanted me to pass him, and this could be in my head, he might just be dawdling, but you know I wouldn't, I'll hold back or again play with my phone and pretend ring somebody, that kind of thing.

(Katielou)

Despite their active responses and the experiential reality for Bea, Shelley and Katielou of *being* followed, the ambiguity remains. It may be that their responses disrupted an intrusive encounter. The power to define what counts as an experience, however, was deferred by participants to men's practices and in particular whether or not they escalated because of women's actions. This creates a problem in attempts to measure the practice. If following does not escalate it risks being discounted in its ambiguity as 'nothing really happened' (see Kelly & Radford, 1990). If following escalates it risks being absorbed into the further intrusion, for example Bec who was followed over different train lines by a man who eventually tried to rape her. In recounting the experience, Bec labels this an experience of attempted rape over, and sometimes to the exclusion of, it being an experience of following. For Lucy, Jeannine and Emma below, experiences of following led to further forms of intrusion, demonstrating the ways in which practices along the continuum bleed in and out of each other.

> [M]e and my friend thought this guy was following us and we were really drunk and on my road and we thought 'oh we'll sit down', because we were drunk, and we thought 'oh we'll just sit and talk'. And as he went past he just flashed. And we were like 'whoa'. This was like a year, or half a year ago.
>
> (Lucy)

> [H]e started following me down the street and I didn't hear him because I had my iPod in. He lived across the street from me and he came up behind me and grabbed both of my arms. And I screamed and threw my arms which I don't think he was expecting.
>
> (Jeannine)

> He decided to follow me through the train. He tried to pick me up and then was not really taking no for an answer, and it had kind of gotten physical by the time the guards had come across us. He was following me, clearly following me between train carriages ... I don't know if he'd cornered me yet or was just about to but it clearly looked dodgy to the security, the train guards.
>
> (Emma)

Categorisation is complicated here, due to the ways in which different intrusive practices are experienced within the same encounter. Across their accounts, women were most able to verify the practice of following and count it as a stand-alone practice where men's escalation was witnessed but not experienced because women physically removed themselves. Such witnessing came about as a direct effect of women's agency in responding.

> I was walking home from school, no it was the evening, maybe I was walking to my friend's house, and very noticeably a van slowed down behind me and he peered out and looked me up and down and I just thought something bad was going to happen. So I saw where he was going to turn around and went and hid ... I was only across the road from my house so I went and hid in the porch bit and he didn't see me under my house, and he drove back really slowly looking.
>
> (Carolyn)

> I was 14, on my way to ballet class at night and this man was following me, and he was really drunk and then I started to run and he came running after

me. By that time I'd reached the ballet hall and I started knocking on the door because it was locked and my ballet teacher opened it from the inside and she let me in and then I started crying ... I got really scared when that happened, I was panicking. I thought I was going to die.

(Kirsten)

I've been followed by a guy once but that's probably because I was with another girl at the time and we were kissing in the streets and this guy had seen us in the nightclub and he decided to follow us home. In the end we started running and he came banging on our front door, so we closed it. That was quite scary.

(Marly)

The role of fear in these accounts, together with how all three women respond to initially ambiguous practices through the potentiality of escalation, suggests a difficulty in a marking a definitive separation between the *experience* of intrusion and its *practice* – culminating in an understanding of the living experience of individual instances of men's intrusion as interconnected.

'When is it going to happen to me?':[2] rape, the fortunate lack

There are two primary connective mechanisms across the continuum of men's intrusive practices. The first, that different intrusive practices are experienced within the same encounter, is evident across many of the individual accounts given above – where men move from verbal intrusions to following to touching. To understand the second, that numerous forms of different practices from different men are experienced by the same woman, the analytical categories need to be pulled together. All 50 women in this study experienced at least four of the 20 initial categories measured, with the majority recounting experiences of between seven and 10 different forms of intrusion. As the sample was self-selecting, motivated by desire to talk about how men responded to them in public space, these findings cannot be generalised as applicable to a broader population of women. Mobilising the Beauvoirian concept of a situated, embodied self, however, enables discussion of commonalities between women's situations (and embodiments) without substituting a single universal situation for all women across all socio-historical contexts.

Within the dataset itself, an interesting pattern emerges when comparing women who have experienced the breadth of different forms of intrusive behaviour, from both unknown and known men. Those who reported experiences of the forms of men's intrusion that are the most documented and legislated against (e.g. rape and intimate partner violence), were also those who reported the greatest breadth of intrusive practices. Here it is important to pull together the intrusive practices of known and unknown men as, for participants in this study, intrusion from known men was a key context in their understandings of intrusion from unknown men. Of the 12 women who reported experiencing ten or more different types of intrusive practices from men (24 per cent of total sample), half ($n=6$) had also experienced rape and/or attempted rape and close to half ($n=5$) had experienced intimate partner violence.

Four women reported experiencing the largest range in intrusive practices, between 11 and 14 different forms. All of these women had also experienced rape and/or attempted rape, with two also having additional experience of intimate partner violence. That this sub-sample contains an over-representation of victim-survivors of rape and intimate partner violence becomes apparent in reviewing the experiences of those women reporting fewer than ten different types of intrusive practices. Here, victim-survivors of rape make up just over ten per cent ($n=4$) of the remaining 38 women, while victim-survivors of intimate partner violence make up just five per cent ($n=2$). The reasons for this over representation is connected to the ways in which participants drew on Kelly's (1988) concept of the continuum of sexual violence to situate their own experiences. Women who had not experienced rape or contact sexual abuse in childhood often expressed this through an appeal to notions of luck or fortune. Interesting here is that not being raped is seen as a *fortunate lack* rather than an unfortunate addition, alluding to women's understandings of rape as not just a possibility of their situation but more of an imminent potentiality.

> I think I've been quite lucky and I don't think from me you'll get like a shock story, I don't have a big, I'm grateful for that don't get me wrong, there's no big story.
>
> (Sophie)

> I was very, very fortunate, I never had any horrific experiences, I had the I know it's a really awful thing to say, I had the usual ones like being groped on the tube and I do know in my mind it's awful that women feel like that's a normal experience. Like every girl I know has had it at some point, at least once.
>
> (Theodora)

> [F]ortunately I've never had a proper assault or anything.
>
> (Meg)

> Luckily I've never had anything really bad before, well I was talking to a friend about this and we were both saying it's actually really hard to know when it's a big deal, and when it's just the way of life and you should put up with it.
>
> (Emma)

For Mariag, the perceived inevitability of sexual assault for women, and thus the luck at its absence, develops through the messages received as part of growing up a girl.

You can have at that [young] age a really precarious feeling of when is it going to happen to me? Not harassment but actual assault. When is it going to happen because I can't control it, I can't tell who is going to do it.

(Mariag)

A similar feeling was seen in Katie's account of how she experienced public space after being raped by an unknown man in a park in the middle of the day after he had said hello to her. Katie's direct words were lost for this study as the phone on which we were recording was stolen during the conversation,[3] however notes taken during our meeting revealed that Katie expressed a feeling close to relief at having had 'the worst thing' happen. Believing that no one would be unlucky enough to be raped twice by a stranger in public, surviving the rape gave Katie a feeling of freedom in public space, that, following Mariag, at least now it *had* happened, the 'wait' was over and she felt back in control. This idea of regularity, the mundanity of experiencing sexual violence as a woman, was also apparent in the narratives of other participants who identified as having been raped; again signalling a recognition that such an act is experienced as an ever-present potentiality both for themselves and for other women they knew. In speaking about being raped by an acquaintance, Taryn contextualised her experience through her knowledge of rape as routine.

Obviously when I was young date rape wasn't something that people talked about and yet every girl I know got date raped.

(Taryn)

This understanding of sexual violence as ordinary in women's lives is also found in women's responses to practices along the continuum of men's intrusion.

I've spoken to some girls about it and they're like, 'oh I don't really get it very much' and I'm like, 'ok'. And then they're like, 'oh but there was this time, and that time and something else'. And so there's something where you're just so used to it. It's just so part and parcel of being female. It's nothing special. It just happens all the time.

(Charlie)

I just kind of accepted it and it always makes you feel quite bad when guys shout at the street or tell you to cheer up but perhaps I'd just sort of, it's just part of life.

(Carolyn)

Bec describes her reaction on being confronted by the man mentioned in the section on following, who attempted to rape her having tracked her over three different underground lines after saying hello to her at a station.

I turned around and just ran as fast as I could, back down my street, back towards the main street and there was nobody there. I didn't know where I would go or anything but that was all I could think of to do, but he ran faster than me, and around in front of me and trapped me against the wall. So I screamed at him again to go away and he was just laughing and that's what freaked me out the most. Because he knew. He and I both knew that there was nothing I could do. And then he pulled down his pants. And my reaction then was so funny because I just went (sigh) 'really? Are you for real?'

(Bec)

Bec's response can be read as almost resignation due to the monotony of men's violence against women. This is similar to the strategy evoked by Sophia to comfort a friend after they were both flashed at by an unknown man in Belgium. Sophia describes how she reconceptualised the encounter to move it away from sexual threat through focusing on its mundanity; turning the penis from the threat of rape, back to flesh.

[S]he just got really upset and was like 'oh no, I just feel so uncomfortable'. And I just tried to explain to her, if you just see it for what it is, some guy thinking he is either severely bored or he doesn't have anything else to do today. You know, imagine if you were to decide one day, today I'm going to like flash my tits at someone. And she's like 'oh yeah actually that doesn't make much sense' and I'm like, 'it doesn't'. It's not funny, well it is funny but it's not scary. If you see it as what it is, a body part, then it removes that whole, it removes the sex from it, it removes the connotation, it removes the fear, it removes the intimidation.

(Sophia)

The division of men's intrusive practices into criminal and normal, with normal being nothing to worry about, is thus complicated in the ways in which criminal practices *are also* experienced by many women as normal. Such understanding raises interesting points for debates about the low number of women who report practices of criminal intrusion such as rape or flashing compared to those who experience them. This may not be solely to do with perceptions of the criminal justice system, or even the perniciousness of myths of victim precipitation (Walklate, 2013). It may be that part of what is happening is that reducing the criminal to the mundane is a way for women to cope with what feels like the inevitability of men's violence and intrusion.

'It works together doesn't it?':[4] connecting the continuum

The connections between forms are lived most palpably in how women structure their responses to intrusion, both that practiced and anticipated. Participants who had experiences of rape and/or intimate partner violence recognised the connection between the continuum of intrusive practices as grounded in what Coy

(2009) terms an 'experiential template of risk'. This troubles a popular discourse that suggests women experiencing criminal forms of intrusion/violence become involved in a 'cycle of abuse', whereby they seek out perpetrators and/or perpetrators are able to identify 'victims' through an embodied vulnerability. In a rare link in the literature between 'street harassment' and women's histories of sexual violence, Bowman suggested that: 'women who have been victims of rape are especially vulnerable to the harms that street harassment inflicts' (1993: 8). The connection found in this study is more complicated than a cyclical model, and does not wholly support Bowman's claim of a particular susceptibility to harm. Instead, the relationship between experience of criminalised forms of men's intrusion and those of mundane intrusions in public space may be embedded in perceptions of 'what counts'. Outlining Kelly's (1988) concept of the continuum in relation to the practices of 'street harassment', Bianca Fileborn (2013) describes the complicated process through which behaviours are experienced as harmful.

> [W]hether these behaviours are experienced as harmful (and *how* harmful they are) may vary depending on a range of contextual, personal and other factors, such as previous victimisation experiences. Further, the harm caused by an incident of sexual violence is not static, but is rather fluid and subject to change over time. That is, for example, the harm of an incident may decline over time. Alternatively, an experience that was previously understood as unproblematic may be reinterpreted as constituting sexual harassment or street harassment, and subsequently experienced as a form of harm.
>
> (Fileborn, 2013: 11)

Prior experience of the forms of sexual violence given particular legitimacy through law forms a key context through which participants made sense of each new encounter with intrusion. Women who openly acknowledged the links between their experiences with rape and other intrusive practices along the continuum anchored their understandings of the connections in a shared felt fear. This was not the fear of crime referred to in much of the literature on women, fear and public space, but an explicit fear of men. Across accounts, participants referred to intrusive men as 'them', 'they', demonstrating the ubiquity of experiencing intrusions in public space and the men practicing them.[5] The operations of this connective fear is described by Viola, a victim-survivor of rape and childhood sexual abuse, as non-linear, impacted on not only by an individual's own experiences, but more widely by the experiences socially prescribed as within her field of possibilities.

> It works together doesn't it? You have an experience and then you make sense of that in light of the wider messages given out. So you see it in a certain light and that might maybe make you more fearful when something else (happens), which then maybe makes you more likely to experience something in a certain way to make sense of it again.
>
> (Viola)

This meaning and impact of men's stranger intrusion is reminiscent of the shift in thinking around intimate partner violence given by Evan Stark (2009), supporting a move away from an episodic approach towards a model of experienced 'living' reality marked as continuous and cumulative. Viola's suggestion that, in attempting to make sense of men's intrusive practices, women both read new experiences through old experiences and revisit the meanings placed on intrusions occurring historically, is supported by many of the women in this project identifying as victim-survivors. Kirsten, a victim-survivor of both intimate partner violence and rape within that relationship, expands Viola's framing to include the impact of the present, speaking of how men's stranger intrusions were experienced whilst she was also coping with violence from her intimate partner, including rape.

> It makes it more intense I think, it makes you feel more humiliated because you've got that boyfriend and then this happens on top of that. It just makes you feel even worse.
>
> (Kirsten)

Both Anna and Alice describe a change in the living experience of intrusive practices along the continuum after their experiences of rape and sexual assault.

> There's a voice that's like this could get really nasty now because once you've seen that side of it … if you ask what's changed from before then, from my early twenties to now, that's what's changed, I have a fear now that I didn't have before, because I didn't know how nasty they could get.
>
> (Anna)

> Before my assault if someone said 'you look nice, that's a nice skirt, you've got a nice body', which I don't necessarily find negative because a compliment is a compliment is a compliment and at the end of the day at the time I didn't find any threat in that. But after that, those men start to mean something different, those comments start to mean something different and those comments start to mean something that I can't control.
>
> (Alice)

Here there is a difference to the feeling expressed by Katie at having been raped by a stranger in public space where, having had the 'worst thing' happen, other forms of men's intrusion lost their impact. For Kirsten, raped by a partner, Anna, raped by a new acquaintance, and Alice who was sexually assaulted by a man working in a takeaway shop, the threat of stranger rape is heightened through experiencing criminal forms of intrusion from other known and unknown men. Bec recognised a similar transformation in the ways she experienced routine interruptions after an unknown man attempted to rape her.

> [Before] I think it was more like annoyed. Like, oh can you just go away you're annoying me, if they're annoying me. Or I would just ignore them.

Yeah. But now there's fear. And then I get angry that I'm so scared....
Angry at them. At them making me feel like I can't feel the way I used to
feel, just like free and confident and independent and safe.

(Bec)

Unlike Katie, who experienced an increase in feelings of safety in public space
after her rape, Bec experienced extremely high levels of fear and anxiety for
many months afterwards born of the feeling that she avoided it *this time*. For
Kirsten, Anna, Alice and Bec, the potentiality was still there and if anything, it
felt even closer.

The reshaping of the meaning of men's intrusion after an experience of rape
is similarly felt by Shelley after successfully fighting off an unknown man who
grabbed her at night when she was walking home, repeatedly punching her in the
face. For Shelley, as seen in Viola's earlier claim that 'it works together', practices across the continuum are experienced in relation to each other. It is not
solely that the attempted rape impacts on Shelley's sense-making of other intrusive practices, but also that these other practices impact on her process of understanding the attempted rape, something Shelley refers to as 'constant reminders'.

I think they're all linked, this is why it's harder to get over things because
you just get constant reminders. So the first thing happens and then every
time something else happens it just links it all back. It depends on the situation and what happens but you sort of get the same feeling of being
threatened.

(Shelley)

Key then across the experiential continuum of men's intrusion is an understanding of female embodiment as a conduit connecting different practices of men's
intrusion. In the literature, though external and internal contextual factors are
considered in several studies (Esacove, 1998; Fairchild, 2010; Katz, Hannon &
Whitten, 1996), women's histories of men's violence and intrusion are unacknowledged. This suggests another reason for revisiting the 'street harassment'
framing – to explore how conceptually useful it is to separate this from other
forms of violence against women and girls when those too can be experienced in
public space (for example rape or stalking).[6]

For women in this study who acknowledged for themselves a position of
victim-survivor, experiences of criminal forms of intrusion formed a central
internal contextual factor in perceptions of intrusion – a factor that works to both
connect and confirm experiences of other forms of men's intrusive practices. For
participants who did not speak of experiences of criminal forms of men's violence, there was still often a connection recounted where particular practices of
intrusion are read through the possibility of escalation to other practices of men's
violence, most often to rape. This connection forms a bodily disposition that can
be usefully conceptualised using the existential-phenomenological concept of a
fundamental 'attunement' towards the world. There are difficulties in translating

Heidegger's (1996) concept of 'attunement' as the German, *befindlichkeit*, includes both how one feels (*sich befinden*) and also the core of the word (*sich finden*) meaning to find oneself.[7] Attunement then, in its phenomenological sense, is both the moods and feelings that 'tune' us into the world, and that through which our *thrownness* in the world, and the ability for things to come close to and affect us, is revealed. Heidegger conducts a detailed exploration of fear as a mode of attunement in *Being and Time* that, though outside the scope of our study here, offers possibilities for a philosophical exploration of women's fear of rape and the fear of crime paradox that has yet to be used in the literature. Instead of a paradox, claims of women's higher fear of crime may be the very reason why they are less likely to be victimised – having developed through this attunement a range of embodied responses and strategies to minimise that ever-present potential.[8] The concept of attunement will be developed over the following chapter to explore participants' attitudes towards their embodiment, their 'being-in-the-world', and how this is revealed in relation to men's stranger intrusions. In particular, it begins by going back – returning to women's earliest experiences of men's stranger intrusions to begin understanding the consequences of men's intrusive practices for women's developing sense of a bodily-self.

Notes

1 For the purposes of examining men's stranger intrusions, rapes committed by men known to the participant are not included in here, though they are recorded later in the chapter. The definition of rape in the United Kingdom is drawn from the Sexual Offences Act 2003 and is limited to penile penetration of vagina, anus or mouth without a reasonable belief in consent.
2 Direct quote: Mariag.
3 The initial conversation with Katie was lost as the phone which I was using as a recorder was stolen from our table in a café by an unknown man. Interestingly for the study, the criminal encounter began with a routine intrusion; the man leant into the window of the café, said 'excuse me sweetheart' and then, when we both looked up, stole the phone and ran.
4 Direct quote: Viola.
5 As noted in Chapter 2, the exceptions here were where the ethnicity of the man or the context of the intrusion (such as a holiday) rendered the man in some way memorable.
6 This is not an argument against (or for) the usefulness of separating practices for legislative and policy action and reform. I am suggesting that our frame for prevention, intervention and support may be falsely drawn if we are creating stark divisions between, for example, 'street harassment' and 'rape' – divisions which are evidently different to the ways in which they are experienced as overlapping and interconnected.
7 For a deeper examination of the difficulties see King (2001).
8 Across disciplines, writers refer to the phenomenological difference in women's experiences of intrusion in public as related to the threat of victimisation. Some agree with the 'crime paradox' (Gordon & Riger, 1989; Rosewarne, 2005), where research has consistently found that women fear violence in public spaces more than men yet their risk of victimisation by strangers, at least as measured by crime statistics, is far lower (Ferraro, 1996; Harris & Miller, 2000; Warr, 1984, 1985, 1990). Others recognise that the experiences measured in crime statistics may not represent the amount of violence women experience in their everyday lives, suggesting that women's higher fear of victimisation may stem from their daily experiences of 'minor victimisations', a

term suggesting reliance on a hierarchy of harm (Fairchild & Rudman, 2008; Harris & Miller, 2000; Macmillan, Nierobisz & Welsh, 2000). Madriz (1997: 43) suggests that studies which do find women have a higher fear of crime than men are tainted by the fact that 'women, by virtue of their socialization, are more open to admitting their fears'. In this way, the fear of crime paradox can be critiqued as failing to acknowledge the ways in which men's definitions of what is criminal become enshrined in law, and thus the claim that men experience more crime in public space misses the frequency of 'non criminal' intrusions that women experience (or those women experience but do not report) which may in fact form a central part of perceptions of susceptibility to crime. In addition, for Betsy Stanko (1993a, 1993b, 1995) and Michael Smith (1988) the fear of crime paradox fails to capture women's living and lived experiences of physical and sexual violence. Stanko argues that conventional criminology tends to look at street crime and not crimes happening behind closed doors with known perpetrators, thereby undermining the detection of crimes of violence against women. Here is where the notion of attunement could be developed, exploring a suggestion that women may be uniquely attuned, through their situation and the meanings attached to it, to the possibility of men's violence and intrusion.

References

Bartky, S. L. (1990) *Femininity and Domination*, Routledge.

Beauvoir, S. d. (1976) *The Ethics of Ambiguity*, Frechtman, B. (transl.), Citadel Press.

Beauvoir, S. d. (2011) *The Second Sex*, Borde, C. & Malovany-Chevallier, S. (transl.), Vintage.

Bowman, C. (1993) 'Street Harassment and the Informal Ghettoization of Women', *Harvard Law Review*, 106 (3), pp. 517–580.

Coy, M. (2009) 'This Body Which is Not Mine: The Notion of the Habit Body, Prostitution and (Dis)Embodiment', *Feminist Theory*, 10 (1), pp. 61–75.

Esacove, A. W. (1998) 'A Diminishing of the Self: Women's Experiences of Unwanted Sexual Attention', *Health Care for Women International*, 19 (3), pp. 181–192.

Fairchild, K. (2010) 'Context Effects on Women's Perceptions of Stranger Harassment', *Sexuality and Culture*, pp. 191–216.

Fairchild, K., & Rudman, L. A. (2008) 'Everyday Stranger Harassment and Women's Objectification', *Social Justice Research*, 21 (3), pp. 338–357.

Ferraro, K. F. (1996) 'Women's Fear of Victimization: Shadow of Sexual Assault?', *Social Forces*, 75 (2), pp. 667–690.

Fileborn, B. (2013) *Conceptual Understandings and Prevalence of Sexual Harassment and Street Harassment*, Australian Institute of Family Studies, www.aifs.gov.au/acssa/pubs/sheets/rs6/rs6.pdf [accessed 18 November 2013].

Gordon, M. T., & Riger, S. (1989) *The Female Fear: The Social Cost of Rape*, University of Illinois Press.

Harris, M. B., & Miller, K. C. (2000) 'Gender and Perceptions of Danger', *Sex Roles*, 43, pp. 843–863.

Heidegger, M. (1996) *Being and Time*, Stambaugh, J. (transl.), State University of New York Press.

Jeffner, S. (2000) *Different Space for Action: The Everyday Meaning of Young People's Perception of Rape*. Paper at ESS Faculty Seminar, University of North London, London, May, 2000.

Katz, R. C., Hannon, R., & Whitten, L. (1996) 'Effects of Gender and Situation on the Perception of Sexual Harassment', *Sex Roles*, 34 (1–2), pp. 35–42.

Kelly, L. (1988) *Surviving Sexual Violence*, Polity Press.

Kelly, L., & Radford, J. (1990). ' "Nothing Really Happened": The Invalidation of Women's Experiences of Sexual Violence', *Critical Social Policy*, 10 (30), pp. 39–53.

King, M. (2001) *A Guide to Heidegger's Being and Time*, SUNY Press, pp. 55–58.

Macmillan, R., Nierobisz, A., & Welsh, S. (2000) 'Experiencing the Streets: Harassment and Perceptions of Safety Among Women', *Journal of Research in Crime and Delinquency*, 37 (3), pp. 306–322.

Madriz, E. (1997). *Nothing Bad Happens to Good Girls: Fear of Crime in Women's Lives*, University of California Press.

McNeil, S. (1987) 'Flashing: Its Effect on Women', in Hanmer, J., & Maynard, M. (eds), *Women, Violence and Social Control*, Macmillan, pp. 93–109.

Rosewarne, L. (2005) 'The Men's Gallery: Outdoor Advertising and Public Space: Gender, Fear, and Feminism', *Women's Studies International Forum*, 28 (1), pp. 67–78.

Smith, M. J. (1988) 'Women's Fear of Violent Crime: An Exploratory Test of a Feminist Hypothesis', *Journal of Family Violence*, 3, pp. 29–38.

Stanko, E. (1993a) 'Ordinary Fear: Women, Violence, and Personal Safety', in Bart, P. B., & Moran, E. G. (eds), *Violence Against Women: The Bloody Footprints* (Vol. 1). Sage, pp. 155–164.

Stanko, E. (1993b) 'The Case of Fearful Women: Gender, Personal Safety and Fear of Crime', *Women and Criminal Justice*, 4, pp. 117–135.

Stanko, E. (1995) 'Women, Crime, and Fear', *Annals of the American Academy of Political and Social Science*, 539, pp. 46–58.

Stark, E. (2009) 'Rethinking Coercive Control', *Violence Against Women*, 15 (12), pp. 1509–1525.

Walklate, S. L. (2013) *Victimology: The Victim and the Criminal Justice Process*, Routledge.

Warr, M. (1984) 'Fear of Victimization: Why are Women and the Elderly More Afraid?' *Social Science Quarterly*, 65, pp. 681–702.

Warr, M. (1985) 'Fear of Rape among Urban Women', *Social Problems*, 32 (3), pp. 238–250.

Warr, M. (1990) 'Dangerous Situations: Social Context and Fear of Victimization', *Social Forces*, 68 (3), pp. 891–907.

Young, I. M. (2005) *On Female Body Experience: 'Throwing Like a Girl' and Other Essays*, Oxford University Press.

He was just behind the hedging
just looking at the girl's backs,
furiously wanking away.

I just kind of like glare at them.
He was looking at me and he goes oh, what's your name?
I'm always very polite, I'm very polite.
One of them kicked my foot, not in a hard way, just to get my attention.
I try to tone everything down a bit, I don't want to stand out.

This guy just walked next to me on my way home
and that night I had to actually take a really roundabout route
and make sure I was always on a main road
and that I wasn't actually heading home.

Men would go in and masturbate and be asking for clothes
I'm not looking at anybody, not engaging.
This guy called me fat out of a car window.
I probably would avoid, like cross the road.
The man tried to touch me on the boobs.
You don't smile back you just look back in complete terror.

This guy came up behind me and said oh my god
you're so beautiful,
is it okay if I walk behind you and touch myself?

And I looked at him and he waved.
In general I tend to ignore and flee.
He essentially had his cock out and basically ejaculated all over the lawn.
I don't engage at all.
They were looking, very very lecherous looking.
I'll take the long way around.
He just kind of started looking and like talking really loudly
about some girl that they knew and how big her tits were
and it was like yeah yeah her tits
are really big
while looking at me.
Then these guys kind of circled us, they made a circle around us.
I don't think there's any way to react other than to not react.
This man turned around and just had this huge erection.
So I just cross the road.
A guy was trying to rape me in the ladies toilets.
I just look straight ahead.
There was a whole row of guys who were standing down this wall
and as you walked past they just leaned and grabbed
whatever part of you
that they could.

He said he'd been watching me.
I always sit quite close to the driver.
He just bit my lip and carried on walking.
You always try to find the blame with yourself.
He was just trying to get really physically close just leaning.
I can block people out.
This car pulled up and had two guys in it
and the entire time the light was red
they just sat there staring at me and making comments.
A boy I sat next to put his hand on my leg and started rubbing it.
I have my keys in my pocket.
This guy was like excuse me, you've got a really nice figure.
I don't really look back.
And he just stood across the road taking pictures.
I avoid eye contact with men definitely.
He was just staring at me and when I got up to move carriage he got up
and loitered around the middle of that carriage.
He tried to kiss me.
He didn't have a proper hold of me but he tried to steer me into the house.
My coping strategy is that I move.
One of them shouted something along the lines of I'll fuck the shit out of you
I'll take flat shoes with me.
He was like have I been good? And I said yeah. And he goes tell me I've been good.
Normally I get really angry about it.

He was like,
I'd like to do things to you,
don't worry you won't have to pay for the cab ride.

6   It's all part of growing up

Beauvoir begins her analysis of women's living experience in the second volume of *The Second Sex* by detailing the formative years of a woman's life, from childhood through sexual initiation and adulthood. The impacts of experiencing the continuum of men's intrusive practices are acknowledged during these sections,[1] though Beauvoir spends little time unpicking men's practices in relation to women's situation. Such an absence is particularly notable given Beauvoir's recognition of men's role in casting woman as the inessential Other, and also in her explicit recognition of the impact of the experience of men's intrusion on women's emerging sense of a bodily-self. Adolescence, however, is singled out as having a particular place in the establishment of women's situation; an awareness of our body image for example, popularly understood as the way we feel about our outward appearance, is a key part of what for Beauvoir, signifies part of the transition from childhood, that is the girl 'becoming aware of her body' (Beauvoir, 2011: 351). Alongside this, participants almost unanimously reported that they were more likely to experience intrusion as a young woman. To investigate how the experience of men's intrusion is a constitutive part of women's situation then, we need to examine these early experiences. Our question here is what are the consequences of men's intrusive practices for women's developing sense of a bodily-self – what forms of bodily know-how emerge? We can explore this through drawing on Beauvoirian theory of situation to explore the experiences of participants both before and during their adolescence, alongside Merleau-Ponty's insights of habituated embodiments; the 'habit body'.

Written in the body

Like Beauvoir, June Larkin, Carla Rice and Vanessa Russell (1996) also located the pervasiveness of men's intrusion in public as an integral part of 'normal' female development. Larkin suggests later that harassing words and gestures 'are slowly absorbed into girls developing sense of self and become an essential part of who they see themselves to be' (Larkin, 1997: 121). This can be seen in many of the responses from participants in this study, such as Jeannine who uses the mechanisms of normalisation as an explanation for why, almost 20 years later, she can remember her first encounter with intrusion at 13.

I think that's why I probably remember the first time so well because it was like this horrible thing that happened to me and I have something to say about it but from then on, slowly over time, it's become more and more normal, just part of life, your daily routine as my mum said to me. She knew. Yeah, shitty, you're a female, this is going to happen.

(Jeannine)

In her study of women's embodiment as a gendered habitus, Ruyters (2012) suggests that women begin learning about what she terms their 'vulnerable embodiment' in adolescence when they receive warnings about the need for precautionary behaviours, and are exposed to adult fears about potential dangers. Analysing participant accounts in this study suggests that what is going on in women's adolescence is more than this; that the living experience of the female bodily-self is not only one of external warnings but also internal experiential knowledge of female embodiment as a site of unsafety. For participants, it was not the adult fears about potential danger that were embedded so much as the normalisation, minimisation and outright dismissal adults made of participants' own fears based on early experiences of men's intrusion.

Four-fifths of women (80 per cent, $n=40$) explicitly recalled experiencing men's stranger intrusion in public space before the age of 18, with the majority of these able to clearly remember the entire context of these encounters. As seen in the discussion of flashing in the previous chapter, for many these early experiences had particular impact in that, as stated by Theodora 'quite a lot of the time it's the first time you've ever seen a penis or the first time you've ever been groped'. Sophie, Josina and Mariag, all in the context of teenage or pre-teen experiences of men's public masturbation, describe such an impact.

When I was about, I must have been about 12, I went swimming with another female friend and we went into a big cubicle changing room and I remember this guy just got talking to us through the cubicle next door and before I knew it he'd stuck something under, there was a gap under the bottom of the cubicle, so basically this guy had stuck his penis through the bottom of the cubicle and was wanking. And we didn't know what it was but I remember thinking 'what is that?' So that was my first experience of a penis which is probably not the most healthy experience a person could have.

(Sophie)

I get less attention now than when I was 13, 14. When I was much, much younger that's when I was flashed. It hasn't happened for years ... in a park with a friend aged 11, that's when I remember it happening for the first time. A guy was wanking in the bushes, me and my friend were picking off blackberries. But we didn't know what masturbation was. I mean maybe I knew but I didn't know that's what he was doing, I just thought he was taking a piss for a really long time.

(Josina)

What would usually happen is [the flasher's penis] would be covered and he'd appear innocuous but then at one point you might look over … because obviously he's doing it to catch your eye, so then either he'd move whatever was over it, the coat or whatever. Your first reaction, I often think of it as a visual reaction, it's like 'what's that?' Or, 'that wasn't there before, what is that? Oh! It's your dick'. Also if you're that age you might not have seen any, I know for example a lot of kids see porn now, but we didn't see any porn, maybe once as a teenager, never seen my dad's, probably never actually seen one, so the first couple of times you see one you're like, 'what is that?'

(Mariag)

The living experience for participants of these intrusive men marked a particular point in women's development where the social meanings of sexual difference became embodied. Beauvoir describes the ways in which: '[f]or girls and boys, the body is first the radiation of a subjectivity, the instrument that brings about the comprehension of the world: they apprehend the universe through their eyes and hands, and not through their sexual parts' (Beauvoir, 2011: 293). The experience of men's stranger intrusions for participants in this research marked a point whereby the body moved from being experienced as the radiation of a subjectivity, wholly ours and wholly us, to the experience of *having* a body; Beauvoir's 'body-object'. This is evident in Jeannine's account of being whistled at as a 13-year-old on her paper route: 'it's the first time I think you realise I'm not a guy, and men have one up on you' (Jeannine). For Jeannine, it is not just that she experiences her embodiment as a body-object through men's intrusion, but that it is experienced as a *female* body-object. Here, women's situation under patriarchy begins to enter into the living experience of our embodiment, an ambiguous entanglement that is difficult to capture through the dualism of biological sex and social gender. Identifying men's intrusion as grounded in her 'femaleness', Jeannine, like many other participants, turned to the women around her to check her understandings.

I can very clearly remember the first time that a guy said something to me on the street, very clearly. I had a paper route and I was about 13 or 14 and this man was catcalling me from down the street and I completely, it's so vivid in my mind what happened. And I remember going home, talking to my mom, being very upset about it and she was like, 'this is life'.

(Jeannine)

The message she received was common across women's accounts: that of men's intrusion as ordinary. Bea recalls a similar response from her mother, 'I remember as a kid men whistling at me and stuff and my mum just laughed it off and said "stupid man."' Both mothers here are referring here to the mundanity of men's intrusion in women's lives. Such reactions, however, play key role in what is for Beauvoir 'how woman is taught to assume her condition, how she experiences this, what universe she finds herself enclosed in, and what escape mechanisms are permitted her' (Beauvoir, 2011: 289). The lesson here is that part of the situation of a woman's body is that this body can be acted on by men – that men's intrusion is embedded in women's embodiment. Drawing from Frantz Fanon (2008) this learning is not so much internalised as *epidermalised*, written in the body.

Similar messages are seen in accounts from Jacqueline and Carolyn, the latter given in a follow-up conversation as Carolyn reflected on what made her first experience of men's intrusion in public stand out so powerfully.

> [W]hen I was 15, I was walking up to my boyfriend's house and this man exposed himself to me, quite close as well, and I didn't really know what he was doing. And the police weren't called because, well I'm not sure why they weren't called, my mum said 'it's all part of growing up'.
>
> (Jacqueline)

> My first experience of street harassment was traumatic, I remember thinking that I must be a 'woman' now and then must have subconsciously adapted my behaviour. It was also around the same time that my mum gave me a pink rape alarm. Suddenly the outside world didn't seem so safe. It is just awful when you think about it that you can get pink rape alarms marketed at young women, and I don't blame my mum for buying me it she was just trying to make sure I was safe. But that just shows the extent to which feeling unsafe in public has been normalised and passes from one generation to the next.
>
> (Carolyn)

This generational knowledge, passed down from women to girls (or from men to boys) is conceptualised by Maria Garner (2016) as a gendered heritage, resonant with Beauvoir's claim that women are 'heirs to a weighty past' (Beauvoir, 2011: 289). For both Jacqueline and Carolyn, this inherited mode of being-in-the-world (Heidegger, 1996) includes the continuum of men's intrusive practices as ordinary and women's bodies as its source. Even in accounts of intrusion before adolescence, participants spoke of learning that men's intrusion is part of the living experience of being a woman, either explicitly from adult women who told them to ignore or implicitly from the lack of response. A powerful example of this comes from Cathy recalling being sexually abused as a nine-year-old girl on a public bus by an unknown man. Travelling on a long bus journey, Cathy and her 13-year-old brother both wanted window seats.

> [S]o what we did was sat at the back of the bus and pretty soon after we set off this man came on the bus and sat next to me. And he molested me on the bus on the back seat. And my feeling about it is that for me now I'm almost not even sure if it happened or what happened but the fear was so huge and afterwards when we got there it wasn't like 'oh we got there', it was 'my

brother didn't help me and everyone on the bus didn't help me, they just ignored it'. So there was a lot of confusion … on the bus they didn't even turn around. At one point I began to weep and nothing happened … I had this feeling it was like 'why isn't anybody helping me?' I was really in distress and nothing happened. And so that's why I think sometimes it's like did anything happen, I just don't know.

(Cathy)

Cathy's response to the lack of anyone reacting, even as an adult, is to doubt whether the encounter happened at all. This invalidation of women's reality is seen across accounts, both early experiences and those in adulthood, leaving women with a sense that they are unable to confirm their own sense of encounters as abusive. New Mum experiences the same kind of uncertainty when recalling her experience of being raped as a teenager.

And you have to say to yourself, I have to say to myself, did I make this up? Was it that I had sex and then regretted it but then actually no I said no, I said stop. You know I did do that, I did do that.

(New Mum)

These early lessons have particular importance given that practices of intrusion were rarely experienced solely as episodic for participants, but that over time became experienced in relation to each other, a model of continuous, cumulative, living reality. Here the connections between episodes of intrusion operate on another layer: not only are they experienced in relation to each other, they are also lived as irrevocably enmeshed in the body. In this way, the episodic *becomes* embodied.[2]

Such a framing is embedded in Beauvoir's concept of 'situation'; the total context grounding our freedom and agency, and that through which, and in which, we understand the world and ourselves. In the words of Beauvoir, what is happening is that the meaning given to these practices 'settles into her body, it becomes the most concrete reality' (Beauvoir, 2011: 352). This is part of the meaning behind Beauvoir's claim that the body forms a situation itself. To understand the impacts of this on how women enacted their embodied selfhood it helps to examine further participants' early experiences of intrusion both before and during their adolescence.

'It happens before you even know what it is':[3] childhood intrusion

Just over a third (36 per cent, $n = 18$) of participants recalled an experience of intrusion at 12 or younger, with four of these recounting experiences of intrusion from known males, both adults and, mostly, from amongst their male primary school peers. In *The Second Sex*, Beauvoir describes what she terms the 'puberty crisis', a key point in the development of our living body.

The crisis begins much earlier for girls than for boys and it brings about far greater changes. The little girl approaches it with worry and displeasure. As her breasts and body hair develop, a feeling is born that sometimes changes into pride, but begins as shame…. Of course, from birth to puberty the little girl grew up, but she never felt growth; day after day, her body was present like an exact finished thing; now she is 'developing': the very word horrifies her … in the blossoming of her breasts the little girl feels the ambiguity of the word 'living'.

(Beauvoir, 2011: 331)

Here Beauvoir is not making a biological or essentialist argument; rather it is the *situation* (both the socio-historical and the material) that evokes this crisis. Many participants in their earliest accounts of men's intrusion expressed the ambiguity that Beauvoir finds tied to the developing female body (where her embodiment begins to be experienced as both the vehicle for her freedom and the source of her oppression) as a feeling of bewilderment.

I was in primary school, we had a fancy dress party and typical me everything was a last minute rush and we couldn't find a costume and I hadn't told anyone about it so it was the old bin bag liner kind of thing. So bin bag liner went to the school, it was dark on the way back and it must have looked to someone going past like I was wearing a mini leather skirt or something and I must have been seven. And someone wound the window down and went 'wahay!' And I remember thinking, 'what's that? Like what is that? I don't understand what that is?'

(Claire)

I can remember from 12 or even earlier, at primary school, I remember people in vans shouting stuff out. And obviously you don't understand it at that age and you put different meanings on it as you grow up.

(Bea)

The confusion found in the accounts of Claire and Bea is reminiscent of women's experiences of experiencing men's public masturbation before having seen a penis. These early intrusions occurred before women had developed experiential knowledge of men's intrusive practices as connected. Recalling the discussion of Heidegger's concept of *geworfenheit* or 'thrownness', where we are thrown without knowledge or choice into a world where we are already in a particular situation, is useful here. Thrown into a situation where our living body, which initially was experienced as ourselves acting through, is now experienced from the outside as acted on and through by men, our embodiment begins to be experienced as a site of tension and anxiety. For Beauvoir, our body starts to escape us.

The little girl feels that her body is escaping her, that it is no longer the clear expression of her individuality; it becomes foreign to her; and at the same moment, she is grasped by others as a thing: on the street, eyes follow her, her body is subject to comments; she would like to become invisible; she is afraid of becoming flesh and afraid to show her flesh.

(Beauvoir, 2011: 332)

The process of 'becoming flesh' is the process of coming to experience one's *female* embodiment; a process whereby our living body begins to mark both the source and limit to our freedom. Clare drew connections between her early experiences of men's intrusion, and those of attempting to perform femininity.

Well I was trying to think for today, I was trying to think when it started, when I was growing up as a teenager ... thinking when I was almost 12 I went to a party and I put some high heeled shoes on and some ankle socks on, I never felt comfortable. And I distinctly remember trying to walk, it would have started about 10, 11, 12, trying to walk as a female. And going from tomboy to trying to walk as a female, and putting higher shoes on, putting my mother's winkle pickers ... thinking 'how do you walk like a lady? How do you walk around wearing a skirt?' So first of all I think it started me feeling, having gone from a tomboy, to then suddenly feeling the physical restriction of feminine clothes.

(Clare)

Palpable here is the way in which Clare's experience of her body is one of it becoming 'not her', forming instead a particular situation, marked by restriction and discomfort. In linking this purposive becoming to her early experiences of men's intrusion, Clare highlights the ambiguity embedded – but often over-looked – in Beauvoir's famous statement of the category 'woman' as a state of becoming, not a moment at birth. Clare is not speaking here of a voluntarist account of gender, though she is describing a deliberate choice in taking up and 'claiming' the femaleness of her body through bodily practices of femininity. This choice, for Clare, is also grounded in her body as a situation. As a survivor of childhood sexual abuse, Clare's agency here can be seen as arising out of a situation where her body has been experienced as the source of men's intrusion. Feeling bodily restrictions and discomfort, or, more so, actively taking up prac-tices resulting in this, helps Clare enact a mode of embodiment where the body is experienced as distanced from the self – a thing to be restricted, adjusted, con-trolled. No longer is the self exposed through its 'vulnerable embodiment', rather the embodied self is protected through adopting a mode of alienation towards the unsafe body.

'I didn't feel like I tried at all and I still got it':[4] adolescent intrusion

Almost two thirds (62 per cent, $n=31$) of participants described experiences of intrusion during adolescence. Some participants reconciled the confusion common in pre-teen accounts during this period, through employing a dominant narrative of men's intrusion as complimentary, as described by Becky and Mariag.

> Definitely going to school, and I find that even more disconcerting now in hindsight, that I used to go to a school where you had a to walk a bit through town to get to the sports grounds, and cars used to beep at us all the time and we were obviously at school, we were in uniform ... I think probably when you're 11 or 12 you're not sure what to make of it and you probably think it's a compliment.
>
> (Becky)

> [T]he thing is when you go to your mum or Aunties or mates and they say to you, and those people say 'oh it's flattering love, it's a good thing'. And you think, depends who you are, but you might be a bit conflicted then, because you think 'it didn't feel that way but apparently that's what it means'.
>
> (Mariag)

This reconciliation, even where it conflicted with women's experiential reality, allowed for a feeling of reclamation in respect to an agency situated in their female embodiment. Marly and Mia described how they experienced an embodied capacity through evoking a reaction from men based on their appearance.

> I think I was 17 at the time, 16 or 17, and I went with my friend who is equally as tall as me, we're both 180, and was some wearing short skirts or something like that and we just got whistled at constantly and I think at that time it was the first time I'd found it happening to me and it was great, amazing, like 'oh my god', came to [city] one day and got someone totally flirting with me on the beach and I was like 'wow, amazing', and I felt really positive about it then.... Just being the first time it happened. An awakening of being reacted to as a sexual being.
>
> (Marly)

> [I]t was this time of being 15 or 16 and being underage in pubs ... and you would be wearing the skimpiest dress and really enjoying being, probably looking awful but at the time thinking you looked sexy, and all these slightly loser-ish guys who were 36 in the pub, and you would think it was really cool. And I actually really liked that and I think personally it's really good for girls to go through that, to test your boundaries of being an object. Ok I don't agree with this whole idea of it being a power but testing that whole relational thing, and figuring it out and getting something between the leers and inappropriate comments and guys hitting on you and trying to figure it out.
>
> (Mia)

The embodiment enacted here is one whereby the capacity of the bodily-self is lived through the body image and an agency is experienced in taking up one's own body as an object. This agency is not expressed by the body as being the self *in* action, acting on others and the world, but rather through a mode of embodiment where the body is distanced from the self, lived as a body-object to be acted on. The body image becomes that through which women live the abilities of their bodily-self, a modality of embodiment marked by *using* one's body instead of *being* one's body (see Budgeon, 2003; Carman, 1999).

Such a framing connects to Beauvoir's descriptions of how women learn to resign themselves to the position of inessential Other.

> [W])ith some resistance, the girl consents to her femininity ... she discovers the power in it; vanity is soon mixed with the shame that her flesh inspires. That hand that moves her, that glance that excites her, they are an appeal, an invitation; her body seems endowed with magic virtues; it is a treasure, a weapon; she is proud of it.
>
> (Beauvoir, 2011: 360)

It is the key phrase 'with some resistance' that underlies the difficulties in claiming such agency as the expression of an ontological freedom. There is an agency here but it is a situated agency, expressed within the whole context of a situation. This situation is marked by tension – diminishing women's subjectivity alongside experiencing female embodiment as the source of men's intrusion. A dilemma exists then, between living one's embodiment as a body-subject, where that body (and thus the self) is a site of discomfort and unsafety, and enacting a mode of embodiment whereby the body is taken up as a body-object. For participants such as Marly and Mia, a sense of self was asserted through adopting this latter modality of embodiment – performing the practices of femininity and understanding men's intrusion as a result of this. Such a framework, however, can be disrupted through continued contradiction between the narrative of men's intrusion as complimentary and particular experiences of intrusion, as Abbey and Rosie describe.

> I was wearing like some ratty old jeans and a t-shirt with like a rubber duck on it or something like that. It was just like the most ridiculous outfit, it was too big for me, it didn't fit me right, and I was walking on this bridge and a guy honked at me, and I just thought that was the weirdest thing because I was hot and I was sweaty and I was alone and I was wearing just nothing, like nothing exciting at all and I just couldn't understand why he thought I looked attractive at that point, because that's what I assumed it was, it was 'you look hot today', that sort of thing ... that was the first point at which I just didn't get why I got it at that point. Because I assumed that I had to look good in order to get it basically, I didn't feel like I tried at all and I still got it.
>
> (Abbey)

I used to like it as well ... it actually is quite a boost to confidence, because I suppose when you're 16 and you're going to college, you know you dress, you want to dress as nicely as possible because you're showing off your fashion ... after sixth form I stopped caring so much about dressing really fashionably or whatever and trying to like look nice all the time but the beeping of the vans still happened so it was like, 'ok now they don't think that I'm attractive, they are just beeping at me'.

(Rosie)

Meg was also confused when she experienced men's intrusion without believing her external appearance 'deserved' it.

I think I was about 12 or 13, and you know when you're 12 or 13 you're not looking your best, you're making your presentation mistakes, and my friends and I were in this little seaside town, just been to the beach, weren't actually in bikinis or anything I think, trying to remember what we were wearing, I think it was Easter so it wouldn't have been hot. I think we were in like jeans and hoodies or whatever.... And we were walking down here and a car with a guy in it just kind of came onto the pavement and he said something to us, I can't remember what it was, we were all like, 'oh my God! What is he doing?' And we carried on walking and he started reversing.... And it was just really creepy because we were like, 'why did you come up on the pavement? What were you doing? Why did you reverse?'

(Meg)

The ensuing disorientation, where men's intrusion is experienced as complimentary but not connected to a positive self-evaluation, is also found where intrusion had been experienced as frightening but is framed by others as apparently ordinary. Uncovering such contradictions occurred for many participants during adolescence. Bec was 16 years old when a taxi driver asked her to exchange sex for her cab fare.

He started asking me things like 'do you have a boyfriend? Have you ever had sex?' And I was like [high pitch laughing] 'oh'. And then he said 'I'd like to do things to you, don't worry you won't have to pay for the cab ride and I'll give you a little bit of money and you wouldn't have to do anything'.

(Bec)

Bec managed to force him to stop the car and leave her on the side of the road, after which she flagged down another cab and made her way home. She did not tell her parents 'because I did feel, oh maybe I had done something wrong', but on talking to a neighbour, Bec reported the intrusion to the police.

When I went to report it the police were just, oh I remember I said to the policeman, 'maybe you could help me, in the future if something like this happens to me Mr. Police officer what should I do?' And he went, 'I don't know, hit him over the head with your shoe?' And I said 'I was wearing rubber shoes'. And he said, 'oh well I don't know then'. Like, wow. I feel like a valued member of our community right now. How helpful. It was just like, 'oh well you're a woman, I don't really give a crap'.

(Bec)

Having made sense of the intrusion as her fault, Bec receives validation that it is criminal, only to have the police reframe it as ordinary.

This confusion between what is ordinary, what is complimentary and what is dangerous was further complicated for many participants in adolescence through experiencing the escalation of men's intrusion. Returning to Marly, this escalation started to jostle against her previous feelings of an embodied agency through her body 'causing' men to intrude.

But then I started school and I started going out more with friends and then I was in University for a year, so that was between 17, 18 up to 21 I think. And in that time I changed radically how I felt about that kind of attention because I had things that I remembered, I had someone wanking on the underground.... And things like I was at a party and I left by myself and I had to walk through tunnels that I didn't know very well and this guy came up behind me and said 'oh my god you're so beautiful, is it okay if I walk behind you and touch myself?'

(Marly)

Here, enacting an embodiment which distances the body from the self is reified in the discovery that this alienated body – 'ours' but not 'us' – is now not even our own to act on. This is also seen in Hannah's account of the first intrusion she can remember. Walking home from work as a teenager, Hannah had a car with two 20-year-old men pull alongside her and ask for directions. The man in the passenger seat told her she was pretty.

And then he said, what was it he said next? I can't remember exactly but ultimately he said, 'give us a blowjob'. And then made a lewd gesture. His friend who was driving the car obviously didn't realise that he was going to say this because he got a bit uncomfortable and wanted to drive off. And I just went, again, just, 'no'. And he went, 'why not?' And I just said, 'I don't even know you' and his friend at that point obviously just thought, 'that's it, I'm driving off' and just started driving off, but that was probably the first time that I'd ever had anything like that said to me ... [I was] shocked. I had absolutely no idea why anyone would say that to somebody. And like I say because it was my first experience of that I just couldn't believe that someone had just said it to me. So I guess it was mostly shock but also humiliation because even though nobody would have heard that conversation it was just humiliating to be singled out like that ... I just didn't understand their motives. I didn't understand why they would want to say something like that to someone like me, just walking home.

(Hannah)

Hannah's account, and her confusion, supports Beauvoir's claims of the female body as a site of ambiguity. This man's initial statement of Hannah being 'pretty' is understood as arising from how she has acted on her body, something within her control and an expression of her freedom. Following this, his rapid escalation to asking for oral sex leads to a feeling of humiliation through the contradictory discovery for Hannah that she is not in control of when, how and *how much* men will act on her body. Her female embodiment is experienced as both the source of her freedom and the source of its constraint.

'I didn't walk home that way again':[5] developing a habit body

In an attempt to reclaim a sense of control over the alienated body, women spoke of beginning, during their adolescence, to develop strategies for being in a public space that would limit men's intrusion. Key here is that for most participants this was not marked by embodied practices that expanded out into the world but rather through restriction. In describing their early experiences, most participants acknowledged a conscious adaption of behaviour, movement and bodily posture, recalling women's attempts to alter their expression to counter calls to cheer up. Delilah's first experience illustrates the ways in which intrusions combine, moving from a verbal intrusion through to following, and how 'nothing really happened' hides the ways in which the unremarkable 'something' that did happen was a change to the way women experienced the freedom and capacity of their bodily-self. Delilah was followed off a bus at 16 on her way home from an exercise class, altering her route so as to ensure she wasn't being followed home and eventually stopping outside a busy hospital and telling the man that if he didn't leave she would scream. For Delilah this experience resulted in limiting her freedom.

> I completely stopped going to that exercise class actually because it was at that time of night. I just thought I'd rather go earlier, go straight after school. Which is a shame because it was such a good class, but I just thought I don't want to have to run into him again or anyone else who might want to follow me.

(Delilah)

Similarly, for both Sophia and Carolyn the first experiences of men's stranger intrusion that they could remember resulted in explicit adaptations of their behaviour – adaptations that, like Delilah, decreased their 'space for action' (Jeffner, 2000) through restricting their freedom of movement.

When I was about 11 or 12 we had a high school that was quite nearby so I was allowed to walk home from school, it was probably about a 15-minute walk, but on the way there'd be construction crews I had to pass. And almost every single day without fail I'd get a wolf-whistle, I'd get a comment, I'd get a 'oi' or something, they were trying to interact with me, and I was a 13-year-old girl. I was uncomfortable and I just tried to follow my route. But then it started changing and I started realising that ok right if I pass by that group of men they call me so I have to cross the street now and I have to walk on the other side of the street.

(Sophia)

I remember the first time it happened to me when I was walking home from school. I was wearing a skirt and I didn't normally wear a skirt and some guy just wound down his window and started shouting at me. And I think he poked his tongue out … I just felt really demeaned. And like I didn't want to wear my skirt again … it certainly made me aware of what I was wearing out. And actually I didn't walk home that, I walked home the main road that day because I wanted to get something from the petrol station, I didn't walk home that way again. I walked home through the park instead, not on the road because I didn't want to get that. It made me change my walk home from school, that's how much it affected me.

(Carolyn)

For all three women here, these adaptations were spoken about in a similar way to Lisa's account in the previous chapter, of changing her route home; as expected and as necessary.

The level of strategising and planning that women undertake in responding to, avoiding and/or coping with men's violence, such as the imposition of limits, has been conceptualised by Liz Kelly as 'safety work'.[6] 'Safety work' is seen as similar to the 'emotional labour' described by Arlie Hochschild (1983), whereby the work of managing one's emotions is embedded in one's profession, with the ability to regulate one's emotions habitually becoming itself a form of economic capital. Such work, repeated over time, becomes habitual and through this a form of hidden labour, absorbed into the body. This is the meaning behind Merleau-Ponty's claim that habitual bodily practices express 'our power of dilating our being-in-the-world' (2002: 166): bringing together self, body and world in that inextricable entanglement described by Heidegger (1996), through forming a pre-reflective intentional arc projected towards an anticipated world. Here, the nature of the body image is elucidated as a system that is both 'open on to the world and correlative with it' (Merleau-Ponty, 2002: 166). These habitualised modes of embodiment developed in response to men's intrusion, however, were marked by Young's (2005) 'inhibited intentionality' and a strategic alienation from, rather than enmeshment in, body and world. Experiences of men's intrusion both before and during adolescence led to modalities of habitual embodiment whereby women's projected intentional arc included within it the possibility of intrusion. Some participants were able to explicitly connect this projection, and the bodily practices enacted to prevent its realisation, to particular encounters with intrusive men lived as just part of growing up. Theodora's experience of having a man sit next to her and masturbate whilst she was on a bus for example, affects the way she occupies public space over a decade later.

> I was sitting on the bus, on the inside seat which is something I quickly learnt never to do if I can find another seat available ... I don't do it anymore. Oh no, I would never now get onto a bus and sit by the window. I do that really annoying thing which everyone hates where I sit on the edge even though there's a seat right there and then if someone comes to sit next to me I'll stand up and let them sit in, even in particular if it's a guy. Actually not even in particular if it's a guy. If it's someone who's bigger than me, I'll let them go inside because then I figure at least I can get away.
>
> (Theodora)

Similarly, Cathy's pre-pubescent experience with an abusive man on a public bus, discussed earlier, resulted in an embodied anxiety leading to her avoiding public transport until early adulthood.

> I was terrified getting on the bus so what I did was if I'd see a lady on her own, I'd wait for the bus to start moving and I'd get a place but as soon as it started moving and I saw someone appropriate to sit next to I'd go sit next to them, so the bus was moving and then this old biddy would be like 'what the hell are you doing?' So I felt guilty about that, bothering a person who wouldn't have minded a seat on their own, and then it was just years and years and years of on public transport being terrified.
>
> (Cathy)

Merleau-Ponty's claim that 'it is the body which "catches" (*kapiert*) and "comprehends" movement' (Merleau-Ponty, 2002: 165) suggests that part of what is revealed in exploring women's bodily practices in public spaces is an embodied knowledge of men's intrusion. Using this notion, it is possible to explore in detail how women described the impact of men's intrusive practices as resulting in particular embodiments in public space. As seen in the accounts of Theodora and Cathy, early experiences of men's intrusion inform an adaptation of the ways women are embodied in public space. No longer is the body lived through as an authentic expression of the self (our living body), nor is the world an open field for our intentions (our being-in-the-world); rather an embodiment is enacted where both body and world are held at a distance – habitually acted on, restricted and adjusted in order to create a sense of safety. Many of the conscious strategies employed by participants to maintain this feeling of protection, through avoiding or preventing men's intrusion, were similar to those previously noted in the literature.[7] The methodological frame of this study, however, also gave insight – through the notebooks – of women's hidden habitual bodily responses.

Such responses demonstrate how men's intrusion underlies particular modalities of female embodiment. The following chapter will explore how these can be understood through adapting Merleau-Ponty's concept of the habit body, drawing on his conceptualisation of the bodily-self where: '(c)onsciousness is in the first place not a matter of "I think" but of "I can"' (2002: 159).

Notes

1 See for example Chapter 2, *The Girl*: 'If they wander the streets, they are stared at, accosted. I know some girls, far from shy, who get no enjoyment strolling through Paris alone because, incessantly bothered, they are incessantly on their guard: all their pleasure is ruined' (Beauvoir, 2011: 358).
2 'Become' is used purposefully here, in its Beauvoirian sense of a project, both freely chosen and situated.
3 Direct quote: Bea
4 Direct quote: Abbey
5 Direct quote: Carolyn
6 See Liz Kelly's explication of this concept in the Foreword.
7 Carol Brooks Gardner (1995) for example outlined seven strategies of women's responses to men's intrusion that involve the body: invoking an absent protector; ignoring, blocking and repressing: the pretence that 'nothing is happening' to provide defence or to screen or mask their own reactions (including, for example, the use of sunglasses, business-like walks); staged compliance; answering back, acting back; redefining an already redefined situation; scening and flaunting: acting up by acting out; and finally official and informal complaints. She found that: 'the most common restrictive behaviours women said they regularly engaged in related to being "on guard" while in public, particularly when they are alone' (1995: 113). Similarly, Esther Madriz's (1997) study of women's fear of crime based in interviews from Black, Latino and White women living in New York City revealed bodily strategies including: self isolation; hardening the target; strategies of disguise; looking for guardians; ignoring or denying fears; carrying protection; and fighting back including accessing police protection.

References

Beauvoir, S. d. (2011) *The Second Sex*, Borde, C., & Malovany-Chevallier, S. (transl.), Vintage.
Budgeon, S. (2003) 'Identity as an Embodied Event', *Body & Society*, 9 (1), pp. 35–55.
Carman, T. (1999) 'The Body in Husserl and Merleau-Ponty', *Philosophical Topics*, 27 (2), pp. 205–226.
Fanon, F. (2008) *Black Skin, White Masks*, Philcox, R. (transl.), Grove Press.
Gardner, C. B. (1995) *Passing By: Gender and Public Harassment*, University of California Press.
Garner, M. (2016) *Conflicts, Contradictions and Commitments: Men Speak about the Sexualisation of Culture*, Doctoral Thesis, London Metropolitan University.
Heidegger, M. (1996) *Being and Time*, Stambaugh, J. (transl.), State University of New York Press.
Hochschild, A. R. (1983) *The Managed Heart: Commercialization of Human Feeling*, University of California Press.
Jeffner, S. (2000) *Different Space for Action: The Everyday Meaning of Young People's*

Perception of Rape. Paper at ESS Faculty Seminar, University of North London, London, May, 2000.

Larkin, J. (1997) 'Sexual Terrorism on the Street: The Moulding of Young Women into Subordination', in Thomas, A. M., & Kitzinger, C. (eds), *Sexual Harassment: Contemporary Feminist Perspectives*, Open University Press, pp. 115–130.

Larkin, J., Rice, C., & Russell, V. (1996) 'Slipping Through the Cracks: Sexual Harassment, Eating Problems, and the Problem of Embodiment', *Eating Disorders*, 4 (1), pp. 5–26.

Madriz, E. (1997). *Nothing Bad Happens to Good Girls: Fear of Crime in Women's Lives*, University of California Press.

Merleau-Ponty, M. (2002) *Phenomenology of Perception*, Smith, C. (transl.), Routledge.

Ruyters, M. (2012) *Vulnerable Bodies and Gendered Habitus: The Prospects for Transforming Exercise*, Doctoral Thesis, RMIT University.

Young, I. M. (2005) *On Female Body Experience: 'Throwing Like a Girl' and Other Essays*, Oxford University Press.

This guy had stuck his penis through the bottom of the cubicle and was wanking.
I try not to look at people.
He took a photo of my cleavage.
I pretend to phone someone, or I look in my bag.
Just a guy standing in the bushes exposing himself and wanking.
I'll always look to see when the last bus is.
One of them past me by the door and said ooo lovely.
I avoid eye contact.
I block it out.

This guy came up behind me and grabbed me between my legs,
like properly grabbed me.
He was trying to rape me.
And this guy just took his pants off.
I tend not to respond.
He did the whole look me up and down thing and said I think Ti Amo?
I don't really go on the top deck of the bus at night.
He said something like hi how are you doing.
I find myself calling someone quite a bit.
He was following me, clearly following me between train carriages.
I never make eye contact, I just look straight ahead where I'm going.

This really creepy man walking really close behind me
and pretty much breathing down my neck
and whispering things.
Never talk to a man.
He raped me.
I will get a taxi for that walk.
He did a u-turn to try to pick me up. In a semi-trailer.
Basically if I just walk with my eyes closed and my earphones on it'll be fine.
And one of them just said hi as I walked past.
I consider what I wear more.
He just started talking to me and he wouldn't leave me alone
and he wouldn't let me walk past.
He said give us a blow job.

A group of guys one of them pinched my bum when I was going up the stairs.
I wear a lot of black, I feel vulnerable when I wear too much colour.
This guy at the next table looked over and said hey sweet lips!
I walk in the middle of the road a little bit because then no one can jump out.
And then he said, so how do you guys relate to each other, I mean sexual relations.
I'll stop dead and get my phone out.
I had in the street a group of guys try to stop me and be like hey
you should totally come back to ours.
He tried to grab my ass.

Slag.

He was following us, he carried on like a whole block.
I'll have my phone in my pocket rather than in my handbag.
He turned around and went, do you know that you're beautiful?
I wear my iPod all the time.
This guy came up to me said hey, hey sexy.
I always apologise, always.
Two men walking behind me talking about my behind to each other
obviously in a very loud voice so I would hear.

He molested me on the bus on the back seat.

He said hey you know what girl, I like the way you look.
I look at the floor. I never make eye contact with anybody.
And then he was like oh you're such a frigid cunt.
I just listen to my music.
He was staring at me, drunkenly staring at me.
I have to fight the urge to cover up so people don't look at me.

They shouted something at me, can't remember exactly what the words were
but it was something like your ass or something about that.
A guy was wanking in the bushes.

This guy came past and said alright love.
I can deal with it now. I always have a comeback for everything.
He was just like oh hey how are you, do you want to come with me?
I'll take my phone out or pretend to be doing things.
He was eyeing me up and down and sort of shuffling closer step by step to me.

I start to become really conscious of how I'm walking
and what I'm wearing
and how I'm looking.

So he sat on the corner of the chair
and again, legs akimbo, whipped it out, had a go.
A guy in a doorway tried to slide his hands down me.
Obviously I'll be looking away.
He wasn't looking at my face he was looking at the rest of me.
I'll call people or pretend that I'm calling people.
He told me that I looked tired.
Stop, check your phone, tie your shoe lace,
He was like get in the car,

                                                  I want to, I want to.

He used to corner me so I couldn't get out from my desk.

7 Embodying intrusion

For Merleau-Ponty, the bodily-self as 'I can' is grounded in a bodily knowledge not always accessible to conscious awareness, yet revealed in part through an exploration of our habits. Beginning with an acknowledgment that our living body is: 'not an object for an "I think," it is a grouping of lived-through meanings which moves towards its equilibrium' (2002: 177), exploring the habit bodies of women in public space helps reveal some of the pre-reflective ways they experienced their being-in-the-world. The notebooks asked participants not only to be aware of the times and spaces where men did intrude but also to record their experiences of anticipation – moments where intrusion was expected even when it was not borne out. The notebooks revealed two important points of disjuncture with what participants had claimed in the initial conversations, which combined reveal the impact of men's intrusion on women's embodiment. The first, disparity in projected impact, demonstrated how participants were unaware of the levels to which they were restricting their freedom in response to the possibility and actuality of men's stranger intrusions in public. The second, disparity in projected frequency, was more surprising, with most of the women participating initially believing intrusion happened more often than was evidenced when they began recording it. To help make sense of this we need to move to an exploration of women's habitual modes of embodiment, marked by an external awareness on the environment and an external perspective on the bodily-self.

'It's never really made me augment the way I live':[1] projected impact

For some participants, the very act of reflecting on the way men respond to them in public in the initial conversations raised awareness of how many of the embodied practices they employed in public space operated pre-reflectively. Hannah reflected on the ways in which her experience of being propositioned from the car at 16 was absorbed into the ways she lived her embodiment in public space. In describing the impacts of the experience, Hannah suggested that it was difficult to directly connect impacts to episodes: '[I]t's like you've tried to rationalise it in your head, you've gone through the process and then it's just filed away in your brain somewhere. Only for you to discover years later that it happened' (Hannah). The ways in which the incorporation of men's intrusion into women's embodiment operated both on a conscious and unconscious level was described by Viola.

> I guess the difficult bit about it is that it's so ingrained in everything you do that a lot of the time you aren't really aware that you're doing it. So there might be times when you're very aware because you have to go somewhere that's a bit unsafe or do something that you're a bit uncomfortable with in public space but then on a day to day basis you do it as well without even thinking.
>
> (Viola)

Both Hannah and Viola are articulating here how many participants incorporated bodily strategies to resist, avoid or manage men's intrusion into their very being-in-the-world with the result that the work they were doing became hidden, embodied to the point of naturalisation. This becomes particularly evident in an account given by Claire where, within the space of the initial conversation, she realised how an episode of a men's stranger intrusion had worked to alter her behaviour in such a way that the episode itself had been buried and the change in her behaviour was subsequently framed in terms of her spontaneous choice. After talking about how she used to walk through a city centre park at three in the morning after a night out, something she would no longer do, Claire claimed nothing had happened to make her change her behaviour.

> I really don't know what it was that changed, there was no incident or anything like that. I think it was just slowly thinking I need to change my behaviours; I don't remember a determining factor where it was like 'right that's it now' or anything that happened to a friend or anything like that. I think it's just, I don't know.
>
> (Claire)

Later in the conversation however, Claire remembered that in fact there was a particular incident that altered her behaviour, that what she experienced as a free choice to act was situated within a context of men's intrusion.

> Actually thinking about it after saying nothing happened actually something did happen where I was walking through [the park] at about 10.30 and it was dark and I was aware that someone was walking kind of at the same pace but slightly behind me. And there was a road crossing so I stopped and he stopped and he asked me what time it was and I said 'I don't know, I haven't got the time' because I was aware that if I looked down he could have done something, so I just said 'no, no I don't have the time sorry'. And then just as I was about to set off again and the road was clear he kept asking, 'excuse me, excuse me, excuse me' and I thought, 'no I'm not having this, because he's already asked me the one question, there can't be

anything more pressing than this' and I just kept going. And I think just as he started to follow me a car came and it meant that he couldn't follow me so I went even quicker down the road. And there was something in that that made me think this is really silly, there's no one around and it's pitch black and it's so badly lit that I can't keep walking through here. So I'd stick to the main road.

(Claire)

Merleau-Ponty's (2002) conceptualisation of the habit body, combined with the findings presented already about early encounters with men's intrusion, helps to address this mechanism of forgetting as a form of self-defence. For Merleau-Ponty, habitual practices are greater than the sum of their parts. An analogy of his framework is suggested by Nick Crossley (2001): when we learn as a child to withdraw our hands from a hot object we do not thereby learn to retract our hands from hot objects; we learn not to touch hot objects in the first place. What is acquired through habituation is not solely a direct mechanical response to a particular practical situation, as seen in Merleau-Ponty's example of a typist who 'incorporates the key-bank space into his bodily space' (Merleau-Ponty, 2002: 167), but also an embodied principle of responding to similar situations. For Merleau-Ponty 'the subject does not weld together individual movements and individual stimuli but acquires the power to respond with a certain type of solution to situations of a certain general form' (2002: 164). This is the meaning behind Gail Weiss' (2010) claim that habit enables us to inhabit our world: enabling the unfamiliar to be transformed into the familiar so that we can orientate ourselves quickly within experientially similar contexts. Habit is thus not simply about the fact that we employ routine behaviours in our daily lives; it represents how the bodily-self takes up and takes on meanings – how we make 'the' world, 'our' world. Exploring habit in this way helps us understand the processes informing the embodiment of men's intrusion: the general principle of 'walking through a park at night is unsafe' is taken in as a form of bodily knowledge. This builds on Ann Cahill's (2001) argument that the threat of rape plays a central role in shaping distinctly feminine bodies, finding that it is not solely feminine bodily comportment which is in part constructed here, but also our habitual ways of being in, and making sense of, our world. It is also not only the threat of rape which plays this role, but the culmination of messages received as part of growing up that men's intrusion is inevitable and women's bodies are the source. The ways in which, in this sense, habit operated as a form of self-protection was identified by Cathrin, who raised a concern that participating in the notebook process may undo the ways in which forgetting operates as a form of coping.

[M]y worry about partaking in the study was that I would become more conscious of [men's stranger intrusion] and it would affect me. Because these coping mechanisms, conscious or unconscious, they're working so I don't get angry anymore or, not much. I don't want to say not at all but I don't get as angry as I used to, where it would just stick with me and really hurt and I just don't want to feel like that now.

(Cathrin)

There is a tension here, in that there are both benefits (identified by Cathrin) and limitations (identified by Claire) in the burying of particular episodes that forms a key part of the process of habituation. The benefits are that through habituating a particular mode of embodiment in response to the possibility of men's intrusion, experiences of intrusion no longer have the impact they did during adolescence. By including the possibility of men's intrusion into a projected intentional arc, we thus include it into our being-in-the-world. The disorientation and confusion seen in women's early encounters, resulting from our *geworfenheit* or 'thrownness' (Heidegger, 1996), is mostly evaded. It is only different or unexpected forms of intrusion (or of intrusive men) that are experienced as having an impact, with the rest lived as ordinary and expected. The limitations of embodying intrusion, conversely, are seen in how it can construct women's 'safety work' as an act of choice, minimising or hiding the impact of men's practices. Reviewing Claire's account, it is evident how the ways in which the embodied principle acquired through habituation (a principle that restricts her freedom of movement), is reconfigured as being in fact an expression *of* her freedom – in this case Claire's freely made decision, developed over time, to slowly change her behaviours.

This reframing is most acutely seen in an account given by Jacqueline in her notebook. Two men who work in Jacqueline's building repeatedly stared at and commented on her when she used the downstairs café. Jacqueline was married to an abusive man who had strangled her to the point where she was hospitalised for several months. It is in relation to her ex-husband's violence that Jacqueline experiences the intrusion from the two unknown men, claiming '[i]t would take more than this to take away my hard won freedom – so now I choose to eat in my office' (Jacqueline). Jacqueline's freedom here, as Claire's agency above, is situated by the continuum of men's intrusive practices. Jacqueline is not free to eat in her work café without being observed, but as this is less constraining than living with a dangerous man – limiting her 'space for action' (Jeffner, 2000) but not her entire 'life space' (Lundgren, 2009) – this limitation is experienced as an expression of freedom in that it is self-imposed. That the continuum of men's intrusion is a context situating freedom and agency, however, is hidden through the process of habituation.

'The other forty-nine':[2] projected frequency

Another key finding in terms of habituation was the disparity in projected frequency noted earlier. For almost 90 per cent ($n=26$) of the woman participating in the notebook process, the experience of men's intrusion during the period of recording was significantly less than anticipated. In her follow-up meeting, Charlie spoke about how she found the notebook process 'initially difficult as oddly it seemed the incidences of street harassment seemed much fewer than usual'. This was also reported by Lisa: '[i]n typical fashion, nothing happened to me after I was given the book'. Experiencing a similar disjuncture between projected and experienced instances of intrusion during the notebook process, Sophia linked the disparity to the impact of her earlier encounters with men's intrusion.

> [A]ctually, when I focused on it, unpleasant and unwanted attention came a lot less often then I first made it out to be. I'm not really sure exactly why either, but I think what might have had an impact is that I started getting uninvited attention when I was so young that it has had a lasting impression and instilled a weariness in me. I dwell on any experience I have had, making it feel like it happens all the time when in actual fact it was a handful of specific moments which led to this discomfort. When I think about it, this experience has made me more aware that actually, overall, I don't get half as much unwanted attention as I thought.
>
> (Sophia)

Alice spoke in the initial conversation about how she 'can't leave the house without feeling constantly like I'm being bombarded by all these men'. Revisiting this sentiment after completing her notebook, Alice also noted a distinct change.

> I think it was a feeling that didn't actually manifest as much as I thought it would. I feel scared and aware of myself and wary of men but whether, does that come to fruition? Not really to the same extent. Certainly not on a level I would describe as bombardment ... but it feels like that because the threat level is technically, the threat is always there.
>
> (Alice)

Gail reported after participating in the notebook stage: 'that the frequency may not be once a week, it's nearer one in every fifty journeys for me. But that's enough to change my attitude, perception and behaviour on the other forty-nine'. This illustrates the power of the embodied principle, demonstrating that what is learnt through habituation is not simply a mechanical response to stimulus. Claire, who had mentioned in her initial conversation that her experience of being in public space was weighed down by 'something about always knowing who's around you and how you're behaving and being alert and a constant feeling of being observed', had a similar revelation after participating in the notebook process.

> I thought in a way this is just going to make me really aware of everything and I'm going to end up filling a notebook with stuff and then I carried on with my business and didn't really pick up on much stuff ... I think it's the feeling. I don't think you're constantly observed but I think it's the feeling that you are. There's that awareness in how you position yourself. There's definitely a feeling there that someone could be watching me.
>
> (Claire)

Abbey, after stating in our initial conversation that she would 'notice at least one or two people staring everyday', also found this was not something borne out when she had her research notebook to record intrusions.

> I think it was interesting that I don't get as many comments or as much staring as I thought I was getting because I think I maybe even said when we first talked that it would be weird if a day went by without this kind of interaction happening, but actually it doesn't happen every single day, or I might get some looks but nothing that would make me adapt my behaviour, that only happens every couple of days. So I definitely noticed that.... It feels like it's happening every day because I'm always preparing myself for it to happen.
>
> (Abbey)

Alice, Gail, Claire and Abbey link the disparity they experienced in projected frequency with the continuum of men's intrusive practices as a context situating their freedom and action. What is evident is the anticipation; that the possibility of men's intrusion is itself a living reality, even in the physical absence of an intrusive man. Where Merleau-Ponty's (2002) 'habit body' enables us to project into an anticipated world, a fissure was found here between anticipation of men's intrusion and its actualisation. As in the earlier discussion of the impact of the gaze (see Chapter 5) Sartre's ontology of the body can also be useful here, particularly in how, as outlined by Dermot Moran, for Sartre: 'I experience how the other sees me, even in the physical absence of the other' (Moran, 2011: 14). Sartre's insights can be developed further for this project through using Merleau-Ponty's notion of the process of habituation based on acquiring a general principle. It may be, returning to Claire's account given earlier, that the principle she embodied was not (or was not only) that 'walking through a park at night is unsafe' or that 'unknown men will intrude'. These lessons combine with what was taken in as part of growing up, namely that such intrusion is ordinary, her body is the source, and the ways she enacts her embodiment can be used as a barrier. This takes a particular toll on the experience of being *in* the bodily-self as the continual work of anticipating the responses of an unknown other results in a perpetually disrupted interior world, similar to that seen in the discussion of calls to 'cheer up'. In addition to this, participants described two ways in which externality in public space was privileged, first in holding an external awareness (of environment and others) and second in maintaining an external perspective (on the bodily-self).

The right amount of panic: external awareness

Exploring participants' habitual bodily practices in public space revealed how these two interlinked yet individually powerful mechanisms intersected to encourage a particular modality of embodiment. The first, external awareness, relates to what Coy (2009) terms experiential templates of risk. Here, conceptions of risk combine with a female fear (Gordon & Riger, 1989) of stranger perpetrated sexual violence, to encourage a habitual attitude towards the world – Heidegger's (1996) concept of 'attunement' – marked by vigilance; manifesting in the maintenance of an external awareness when occupying public space. The second mechanism, external perspective, differs from external awareness in being not a consciousness of the environment but rather a consciousness of one's own embodiment. 'Perspective' here is used in the sense of being 'a particular attitude towards or way of regarding something' ('Perspective', 2001), thus where external awareness can be seen as an attunement towards the world, external perspective is an attunement towards our embodiment. This works alongside, but is distinct from, Foucault's (1979) concept of 'panoptic surveillance', which has been usefully employed by feminists to theorise an internalisation for women of the gaze of men (Bartky, 1990; Bordo, 1989). External perspective does not refer only to a consciousness of how one's bodily-self is perceived by (male) others, though it can include this. It represents, rather, a bodily attitude reminiscent again of Fanon's (2008) epidermalisation; a mood lived through the body 'tuning' us into our being-in-the-world.

During the initial conversations, the conscious level of 'safety work' women conducted in public spaces was immediately apparent, with many participants easily able to give lists of strategies adopted in public space in response to the possibility and actuality of men's intrusive practices. One of the most commonly repeated strategies was focused on scanning public space and identifying points of safety, as seen in the accounts of Lucy and Ginger.

> I usually try to sit next to women, at least nearby women unless it's the middle of the day and I feel confident to not but say late at night and the carriage is empty and there's somebody sitting on one end of it, I'll make sure I'll sit at the other end, otherwise they might think there's any reason to talk to me. A lot of times it's unnecessary because they're probably just as tired as I am. But just to be on the safe side, I'll make sure that I'm not on the same one. Other times I've actually waited for the person to get on the train. And then at the last minute I actually haven't gotten on the train myself, because I thought that they were paying too much attention to me and it's safer if I just skip this train. I have actually changed trains in the middle, when I'm on the train and I know somebody's there who I would rather not be in the same carriage with, I get off in the station and I change for the next one that's coming. Even if it makes me late for something.
>
> (Ginger)

> I try not to look at people, like I look at them to see where they are and who they are but not look at them in the eye. I look straight ahead I think. And a lot of the time if I'm walking late at night I carry my keys between my hand so I can stab ... and try to stand quite big as though I'm tough and can handle myself. And don't really respond to people, if someone says something either, sometimes what I try to do is be quite polite but stop the interaction quickly, because I don't want to make them angry as well. So I've

got to be polite but not too polite that they want to continue talking to me. And walk very fast, look like I know what I'm doing ... sometimes I'll pretend to talk on the phone, if no one's awake or it's really late ... I would prefer to sit next to a woman than sit next to a man. And I'll stand up if there's nowhere to sit on my own a lot of the time. I don't really go on the top deck of the bus at night if I'm on my own, I stay downstairs. And I always make sure, it's really weird but if someone gets off at the same stop as me, I always think they're following me. So I try and stop or maybe that's when I pretend to phone someone, or I look in my bag so then, they'll go in front and can't follow me.

(Lucy)

What emerged here was the ways in which both women's strategies of resistance and strategies of coping called on them to maintain an external awareness in public spaces. This awareness was not only of unknown men, but also of points of safety such as other women, or points of unsafety such as particular contexts on public transport (on the top deck of a bus in the evening for example). These reference points are not set; they differ between women and can change for the same woman at different points, based on experiential histories. Clare spoke about the change she experienced after she was almost mugged by a girl gang.

[F]or a while after that when I walked down the road I'd be running away from women and I'd be looking for the men. And that was the bizarrest sensation ever. I'd be walking back from my flat and it'd be at night and I'd see some women and I'd see a man and I'd think, 'oh the man's just over there'. So the point of safety had changed which was the bizarrest thing ever.

(Clare)

While what represented safety for Ginger, Lucy and Clare differed, all were scanning their external environment to find these points. Evident across these accounts is the way in which when avoiding or minimising the possibility of men's stranger intrusion conflicted with women's freedom, priority is given to the former. For Ginger, she would prefer to be late than be in the same carriage as a man she has identified as possibly intrusive. For Lucy, she would hang back after disembarking from a bus rather than begin immediately to head to her destination. This constant scanning and adapting own movements in response to anticipated and experienced intrusion is seen in the account of Jane, a committed runner, who constructed a map of anticipated intrusion.

I figured it out, my route around [city] I planned through experience very carefully, like from coming back to going out I'd change it, there was this one road that coming back was always busy with deliveries because it was about 7.30, always go through the square because that's full of bankers and they're not going to say something. I used to go past [a nightclub] but then I learnt don't do that, that's bad, but if you go past [the gallery] and

[that] building it's ok. But then I had to change that because construction got up that street so that got bad. I had every street on my run planned out to avoid it as much as possible. I knew which roads. Now I just get on a treadmill and watch television. No more following. No more grabbing.

(Jane)

For Jane, paying to run indoors became preferable to the possibility and reality of men's intrusion in public spaces. The context of such a decision is characterised by Kim Lane Schepple and Pauline Bart (1983) as a geography of fear and limitation, where in order to lessen the former, we may need to raise the latter. Again, as seen in the earlier accounts of Claire and Jacqueline, men's intrusion is seen as a key context situating women's freedom and agency.

Measuring the ways in which (or indeed if) a habituated external awareness in public spaces works to decrease the amount of intrusion women experience is difficult. Such embodiment will rarely be experienced as 'capable' in terms of acting as a barrier to men's intrusion as the vast majority of 'safety work' is pre-emptive. Sue Wise and Liz Stanley (1987) highlight this, claiming that: 'the amount that sexual harassment is thwarted is a social invisibility – we can't see that women have skillfully and successfully assessed and dealt with a complicated social situation because success here is an "absence" of a predicted outcome' (Wise & Stanley, 1987: 171). This 'absence', however, may be made visible in studies that show men are more likely to be victims of crime in public space – the 'crime paradox'. The paradox can be explored through the issue of what is counted; suggesting that such studies count 'crimes' men are more likely to experience in public space (such as physical fights), but fail to tap into experiences such as those considered here. There may be, however, an additional reading that affirms the power of women's modes of embodiment to act on (male) others.

If participants such as Jane, Clare, Lucy and Ginger have their awareness focused externally, identifying (on what is sometimes a pre-reflective level) points of safety at the same time as limiting their movements in spaces they identify as unsafe, then it may not be that men are more targeted to be victims of crime in public space. It may be that women are skilfully navigating public spaces, disrupting opportunities for victimisation by assessing the environment and individual men whilst attempting to predict their intentions and practices. This process was conceptualised by Katielou as the impossible task of evaluating the 'right amount of panic'.

I'm used to being, well, we're used to being, I suppose it's conflicting messages isn't it, it's take care of yourself and you're being a silly woman ... you have to do just the right amount of panicking don't you.

(Katielou)

In attempting to gauge what 'the right amount of panic' was in a given situation, participants relied on the interplay between their awareness of the external environment and on their pre-constructed templates of risk to conduct an escalation calculation. The operations of this calculation were mostly hidden, conducted often without conscious awareness and grounded in the possibility of intrusion, with women trying to pre-empt and thus prevent unknown men's behaviours. It was revealed, however, quite powerfully, when the projected escalation of a particular man (or group of men) was not borne out by their actions.

> I left a club late at night and I was just going to go home and find a taxi and I was sitting down and this guy was like 'are you alright?' And I said 'yeah I'm fine'. But thinking 'why are you asking me that? That's a bit dodgy, I'll carry on walking'. And then this other guy just came out of the shadows of a doorway and just grabbed me, was just holding onto me and I was like 'what are you doing?' I just didn't know what to do and was trying to be really indignant and going 'let go of me now' because I really didn't know how to react. But at that point I wasn't on edge I don't think so I feel like I should have been more ready, should have had my keys. And then I felt bad because he wouldn't let go of me, this really tall guy and the other guy who'd asked me if I was alright came running down the road and yelled 'let go of her now', so he let go of me and I ran away. But then I felt really bad because initially I'd thought the first guy was evil but he was actually just checking if I was ok.
>
> (Lucy)

> I was much younger, maybe 17, 18 and living back home in [city] I was again just walking home, I wasn't far from where I lived, and this was in the evening, maybe 10 or 11 o'clock at night and this car slowed down behind me and followed me for a little bit and then overtook me and stopped, and this guy got out so again I started shouting at him, 'what do you want? Get back in your car!' And he just looked at me, really taken aback, and just pointed at the cigarette machine next to where I was standing, like I'm just trying to get some fags. Which is obviously super embarrassing.
>
> (Viola)

The accounts of both Lucy and Viola show the impossibility of 'the right amount of panic'; a Catch-22 where '[y]ou don't really know till something happens and then if nothing happens then it's automatically too much panic' (Katielou). Josina describes her anger at being judged for actions understood by a male stranger as motivated by laziness rather than fear.

> I guess risk perception is different from actually, like times when I actually thought I was in a really risky situation and I had no idea, and there are times when I'm being cautious and I'm not. One time I got on this bus and I sat down, and it was two stops later and I pressed the bell to get off, and the guy next to me, who I was sitting next to, he laughed and I looked at him like, not like 'please tell me what's on your mind' but like 'what the fuck? What's wrong with you?' And then he said 'oh I'm sorry it's just quite

funny that you, why did you bother getting on the bus it was only two stops?' And I was getting off the bus but I wanted to say something so I said 'look you're not a woman travelling on your own in the middle of the night. You've got no idea'. And he apologised, he was clearly just a bit cocky … I just thought you know I'm thinking so much in detail about how to get home safely on my own and you're judging me, you've got no idea.

(Josina)

The catch-22 of 'the right amount of panic' combines with what was seen in the previous chapter where, during the process of growing up, participants had learnt to doubt their own sense making of men's intrusion. The result is that the times where participants did successfully manage intrusive situations are discounted. This was evident in how, contrary to suggestions in the literature, many participants in this study mentioned feeling relatively safe most of the time in public spaces, such as Theodora.

I actually personally feel quite safe. The area where I live it's not, people say it's a bad area but I've never felt unsafe walking around it. Maybe that's because that's where I grew up. But I've always felt quite safe to be honest. I mean I tend to, yeah, as a general rule I feel quite safe … I've never felt like I couldn't walk home alone if I've needed to or wanted to.

(Theodora)

Such descriptions appear as the unproblematic reflections of an embodied agent, however, Theodora then goes on to describe the range of restrictions she has taken into her habit body to create and maintain this feeling of safety.

[S]top, check your phone, tie your shoe lace, anything like that. Always in a doorway though if you're tying your shoelace, don't get on the ground. Never. I would never, if I can, if I want someone to get past me I try to get my back to a wall. If you sort of stop and stand with your back to a wall and look at them I never want to do that because I think it might cause a confrontation but if you stand and sort of kneel down to tie your shoelace or something like that then it's a reason to stop if you see what I mean.

(Theodora)

It is here that the limits of the dominant narratives available to speak of men's intrusion in public spaces, being a binary of either pleasurable compliment (sexual) or frightening threat (harassment) hide the impacts on women's freedom. The most common outcome, as seen in Theodora's account above, was to habituate a limited freedom but reconfigure this as an expression of agency through forgetting its founding situation; the continuum of men's intrusive practices.

'Don't be in your body, watch your body':[3] external perspective

Throughout the research process, participants spoke about not only being aware of who is looking, but of how you look to them; an external perspective on the bodily-self and the adoption of specific bodily traits to limit or prevent intrusion. Beauvoir outlined a similar process during women's adolescence, which she termed 'erotic transcendence'.

> She becomes an object; and she grasps herself as object; she is surprised to discover this new aspect of her being: it seems to her that she has been doubled; instead of coinciding exactly with her self, here she is existing *outside* of her self.
>
> (Beauvoir, 2011: 360, emphasis in original)

Key here is this notion of being doubled, representing an ambiguous embodiment. The awareness of our bodily-self is not located internally, in an experience of the body as capacity and expression, but externally in the body image. The body is not lived *as* the self, instead the self is experienced as distinct from and yet tied to the body; a body that both is and is not herself. Here female embodiment is lived as split and contradictory; an experiential tension also found in Lilliana Del Busso and Paula Reavey's (2011) account of young women's embodied experiences in everyday life. The body is our living body still 'ours' in terms of being singled out, but it is not lived as the original locus of our intentionality – it is not lived as 'us'. In addition, given what has been seen previously in this chapter, this ambiguity itself is doubled in that, through men's intrusion, women learn their female embodiment is not only the source of their freedom, but also the source of its constraint.

The impacts of this awareness of the body from outside, a bodily-self consciousness, have already been seen in the discussion of the gaze. Exploring the role of the external perspective in the habitualised embodiments of participants expands the finding that public space represented for many women an experiential, though not always external, feeling of the gaze, in that women anticipated more intrusion than men actualised. It is not only the potentiality (and actuality) of the male gaze, but also the enactment of a modality of embodiment holding an external perspective towards the body that created Claire's initial feeling of constant observation.

The most common way that an external perspective was revealed in women's accounts was through identifying a division between safe and unsafe clothing. Sophie, Bea and Delilah described in detail the ways in which for them, appearance could be strategic.

> I used to wear, when I was about 17, 18, I used to go to clubs and wear short skirts and high heels and loads of make-up and all that stuff. And then I came to university in London when I was 18 and without being conscious I

think over that year my dress sense really changed, and I started like going out with all the freshers and that in my normal short skirts or whatever but I used to really hate the feeling of getting on the tube in a short skirt and the attention I would get whilst in those sort of clothes. And slowly and slowly, and I'm talking about 7 years ago now? I just stopped dressing like that, but instead of finding an alternative way of dressing that I was kind of comfortable with, I basically have been hiding myself for the last 6, 7 years, basically ever since I came to [city]. And I'm not, having come to that realisation, I'm not very happy about it.

(Sophie)

[I]t's mainly for me just that having to think about what you wear when you go out, that definitely, definitely changes. Like leopard print, definitely. Every time I wear it. It's weird. It definitely makes a big impact. I think maybe some people aren't aware of the impact it has on the choices they make every day but I think I am aware of it. Like if I'm going to get the night bus, it sounds so extreme, but I won't go out wearing a dress, I'll wear jeans just because it's safer and in the back of your mind you're probably thinking at least I can run away if I don't wear a skirt and high heels. It's ridiculous. But even, I walk to school at about 1 o clock every day and there's usually a few stragglers on the streets, people who aren't in work, and even at midday when it's not a particularly dangerous environment, I'm thinking, don't wear a low cut top, wear a scarf just in case you need to wrap it around. And it sounds so extreme but it's not something that's at the forefront of your mind, but it's always there.

(Bea)

I dress with scarves and things to just cover, take the focus away from (my breasts) ... also I now stay away from the colour red ever since I wore red one day and everyone just kept commenting, 'oh you with the tight red dress'. And I just thought it's not necessarily tight, it's knee length, it's got shoulders, it's not a provocative dress, but because it was *red* red and you should be a wallflower basically. So I steer clear of red which is such a shame because I love it, so I wear hot pink or burgundy, things that are similar to red but I always think a bit, ooo, think twice about wearing red. Yeah. I never really think that much about it but it does affect the way you carry yourself.

(Delilah)

For each woman here, a safety discourse combined with how the body was lived. An experiential template of risk thus moved from being a mapping of the external environment to a mapping of the body as seen from outside. This reveals how part of the general principle learnt through habituation is that women's body is itself a risk, what for Susie Orbach is 'the kind of foreboding women have always carried in relation to their bodies' (Orbach, 1978: 12). The ways in which participants framed the process of identifying, through early encounters, men's intrusion as grounded in their female embodiment, is evident in the ways in which this external perspective often saw markers of femininity as unsafe. For Sophie, Bea and Delilah above, this meant adjusting their clothing to ensure nothing would reveal too much of their breasts or their legs. For Louise and Gail, this resulted in an embodied practice of safety based on hiding the 'woman' signifier of their long hair.

> I have a hat for when I get cold but I'll tuck my hair into my hat because I know long blonde hair tends to attract attention. If it's raining I'll get my umbrella and have it as a stick just in case I get threatened. Sometimes I take a key and I have the sharp part in between my fingers just in case someone attacks me.
>
> (Louise)

> I'd tie my hair up for some reason, I'd think if I tied my hair up and scowled I just wouldn't look like anyone someone would want to talk to ... I'd just try to look like I didn't want anyone to talk to me. I think it's quite easy to disappear.
>
> (Gail)

Gail's additional strategy of what Goffman (1990) describes as 'impression management' or what Esther Madriz (1997) termed 'hardening the target', conceptualised by many participants employing this strategy as 'bitch face, where I look unapproachable' (Luella), reveals the contradictory modalities discussed by Young (2005). For Young (2005) this is based in how women are frequently put in the position of experiencing their bodily-self as both object and subject, with the mechanisms of objectification recognising our subjectivity at the same time as diminishing it. There are more contradictions revealed here, however, in that – similar to the impossible task of deciphering 'the right amount of panic' – women spoke of the difficulty in adjusting their bodily strategies in such a way as to meet often opposing means for the same end; to deflect men's intrusion. Participants thus attempted to balance: the need to look tough or unapproachable with the desire to not be told to cheer up; the necessity to be polite enough to not escalate an encounter but not so friendly as to be seen as encouraging the interaction; wanting to be evaluated as attractive enough to avoid insults on their appearance by men in public but not so attractive as to become a target; and wanting to disappear or be invisible at the same time as wanting to be seen and experiencing discomfort in wanting this. These strategies were encapsulated by Claire as 'don't get an A star get a B'. Recalling Beauvoir's ambiguity, the positions of subject and object are thus experienced by women as parallel and simultaneous, leading to an embodiment marked by contradiction, tension and unease. The contradictions of femininity become apparent, a balancing act lived through our embodiment.

> [Y]ou're being attractive but not too attractive. Risqué but not too risqué. Wear a skirt but preferably one you can run in. Don't go down that alleyway,

don't put your headphones in. I wouldn't dare walk down the street with headphones on. So yeah I think you're constantly being vigilant. And I also think you're kind of looking to see who's looking at you. Without necessarily, intellectually wanting to do that. And there really is a tension between the two.

(Clare)

The external perspective is thus a modality of embodiment where the body is lived as both self and not self (Young, 2005). Maintaining an external perspective on the bodily-self in public space leads to an increased awareness of the body image and an experience of discomfort and unsafety in the materiality of the body.

I become really aware of my body I think, and I feel like, I feel bigger and more conspicuous … it's vulnerability in feeling consciousness and conspicuousness about my body, that's what I feel like. And that's what I mean about feeling like big … I feel like legs and hips, I feel like that part of me I feel much more conspicuous about.

(Rosalyn)

It is, it's that feeling of self-consciousness. You should be allowed to sit on a train at half seven in the morning and just be like, 'ahhhhhh', and not have to be thinking about anything that you don't want to. The problem is that the gaze can disturb your, it can penetrate you. As can a comment, all of this stuff can, but the gaze penetrates in a way that, it's really hard to express.

(Sophie)

You're being judged. You're an object. You just become massively aware of yourself and think oh God this is so uncomfortable. And it's just a relief if you get past them and they don't say anything.

(Shelley)

This bodily-self consciousness, Rosalyn's feeling of being 'hips and legs', Sophie's feeling of being penetrated, encourages a fleeing from the bodily-self. As seen in the earlier discussion of the gaze, and explicitly understood by Rosalyn above, there is a particular vulnerability that comes with the acknowledgement of ourselves as a body that can be seen, and that can be hurt. In gendering this vulnerability, Beauvoir suggests that for the category 'woman': 'her whole body is experienced as embarrassment' (Beauvoir, 2011: 356). Given that men's intrusion has encouraged a relationship to the body marked by tension and discomfort: 'her body is suspect to her, she scrutinises it with anxiety' (ibid.). There is thus an undercurrent of shame in the ways in which women spoke about the experience of living the materiality of their body, particularly in relation to its 'femaleness'. In order to manage vulnerability, anxiety and suspicion, many women adopted a mode of bodily alienation as strategy, holding their body at a distance and enabling a mode of embodiment that was experienced as keeping the self safe.

'I'd never really thought of my body as me':[4] bodily alienation

Using Beauvoir to conceptualise this mode of bodily alienation facilitates an exploration of the role of ambiguity in both women's embodiments and situated agency. The modalities of embodiment women enact are situated in, and through, men's intrusion. Men's intrusion stimulates bodily alienation: necessitating an external perspective on the embodied self, alongside maintaining an external awareness of others and the environment, and at the same time experiencing the uncertainty of one's ability to make sense of one's own experience. Here, however, women may actively choose to take up an alienated mode to their bodies, a mode of embodiment that over time becomes habituated, in order to maintain a sense of self as solid and safe. The strategy of bodily alienation *is* an active coping mechanism; however, it arises out of the particularities of a situation in which the routineness of men's intrusion has encouraged an ambiguous embodiment.

In this conceptualisation of bodily alienation as a form of coping borne out of women's situation, the differences between Beauvoir and Sartre are evident – highlighting again how Beauvoir's conceptualisation of the situated body-subject offers unique, and often untapped, insight for modern feminist questions. Mobilising Beauvoirian theory in this way in fact enables a critique of how Sartre posited women's bodily alienation as a conduct of bad faith. In *Being and Nothingness* (2007) Sartre gives two famous examples of bad faith: an example for men's bad faith using a young man 'playing at' being a waiter and, interestingly, an example for women given in relation to the practices of men. Sartre watches a young woman on a first date attempting to avoid a man's advances: he holds her hands in his and the woman leaves her hand there, 'neither consenting nor resisting' (Sartre, 2007: 79), without noticing. Sartre views this as the woman's attempt to flee from her freedom, alienating her body and through this delaying the moment when she must choose either to acknowledge and reject his advances, or accept them. Using this study as the point of departure, what in Sartre is an act of bad faith can be reconceptualised as an expression of her situated freedom. Sartre may be describing a moment experienced by the young woman as intrusive. Caught by the need to not escalate the man's behaviour by either encouraging or challenging his behaviour (what is seen by Sartre as consenting or resisting), and unable to physically remove the bodily-self, the young woman protects herself by enacting a mode of embodiment whereby she lives 'herself as *not being* her own body' (ibid.). This act of 'bad faith' becomes a type of resistance, seen in Beauvoir's claim that under patriarchy the woman 'is too divided internally to enter into combat with the world; she confines herself to escaping reality or to contesting it symbolically' (Beauvoir, 2011: 376). This way of understanding the woman's actions may have been missed by Sartre but would be familiar to many women, and was found throughout participant accounts. The poetic transcript woven between the chapters here demonstrates the frequency with which participants' strategic response to men's intrusion was to distance the self from the body and the world. The extract below demonstrates how this type of response fell mainly into three interlinked categories, a version of which is seen in the example given by Sartre: you're not here; I'm not here; and/or this is not happening – a process Viola termed creating 'the world you want to be in'.

> He said hey you know what girl, I like the way you look.
> I look at the floor. I never make eye contact with anybody.
> And then he was like oh you're such a frigid cunt.
> I just listen to my music.
> He was staring at me, drunkenly staring at me.
> I have to fight the urge to cover up so people don't look at me.
> They shouted something at me, can't remember exactly what the words were
> but it was something like your ass or something about that.
> A guy was wanking in the bushes.
> This guy came past and said alright love.
> I can deal with it now. I always have a comeback for everything.
> He was just like oh hey how are you, do you want to come with me?
> I'll take my phone out or pretend to be doing things.
> He was eyeing me up and down and sort of shuffling closer step by step to me.
> I start to become really conscious of how I'm walking
> and what I'm wearing
> and how I'm looking.
> So he sat on the corner of the chair
> and again, legs akimbo,
> whipped it out, had a go.

Rather than being seen as acts of bad faith then, the ways participants spoke about resolving the paradox of living the bodily-self as subject and object in a context of men's intrusion as ordinary, was through habitualising a particular relationship to their embodiment, where the body is held at a distance. There is a subtle difference here from notions of dissociation and disembodiment. Dissociation, linked to a psychological framework, suggests a detachment from the body and/or the self and/or the environment. The accounts of participants, however, show connection to all three – women are aware of the environment (including the intrusive man), aware of their embodied self in that environment, and making particular decisions situated by this awareness. Disembodiment is a closer, though slightly different concept, whereby the self is not experienced as embodied – this again has ties to a psychological framework where the neural and sensory mechanisms underlying the internal representations of the body, termed by Merleau-Ponty (2002) as the 'body schema', can be disrupted, leading to an experience of the self as outside of the body. Such a response to sexual violence is seen in Jan Jordan's (2008) account of the resistance strategies of the women raped in Auckland by Malcolm Rewa. The mental processes described by some of the women surviving Rewa's attacks provided a means of withholding something of themselves where '[h]e may have control of their bodies, however, he could not control their mind, their spirit' (Jordan, 2008: 549). Jordan links this to some of the processes enacted by women in prostitution (Jordan, 1991; McLeod, 1982), connecting to Maddy Coy's (2009) work with young women. Using Merleau-Ponty's (2002) 'habit body' alongside Bourdieu's (1998) concept of habitus, Coy (2009) reports a consequence of (dis)embodiment in women's narratives of living in local authority care as well as in selling sex. Developing Coy's (2009) findings in contexts of ordinary intrusions, the accounts of participants suggest a departure from the concept of disembodiment, where the self is experienced as outside of the body, towards the concept of bodily alienation: the experience of the body is not as the self, it is a thing, an object. Beauvoir's account of bodily alienation holds the ambiguity of our living body: experienced as an obscure alien thing, separate to the self in some way (Arp, 1995), at the same time as experienced *as* the self. The experience of men's intrusion is both the recognition of our subjectivity (there is, after all, no point 'objectifying' a box or a suitcase: an object cannot be made aware of its 'thingness') at the same time as a depletion of it – Tuerkheimer's 'curious paradox of being both object and subject' (1997: 186).

Applying a Beauvoirian framework to the operations of alienation thus allows for the ambiguity and contradictions of women's living experience under patriarchy: the experience of the body as both the self and not the self. As a concept, it can also extend to women's relationship with their environment in a way disembodiment and dissociation cannot. As seen in Viola's claim that: 'you need to find a version of the world you can be in'; alienation as strategy can extend to the environment, with women blocking out intrusion or pretending it isn't happening: rupturing the bodily-self's entanglement in the world and returning to that feeling of being water in a glass. Habitually enacting a mode of embodiment whereby the body and world is alienated has a self-protective element in that individual experiences no longer have the force they did in girlhood. As seen in Chapter 6, girlhood was when women first experienced the transition from the body, self and world as interdependent, to experiencing the body as a separate, and vulnerable, object, situated in rather than of the world. The findings of this study suggest that such processes are evoked by women every day and every night (Smith, 1987), developing out of experiences with ordinary, routine intrusion as part of growing up, and habituated into a mode of embodiment marked by alienation. Here, however, this transition is claimed for ourselves, alienating the body and the environment through an act of will, and through this helping to reassert the sense of embodied selfhood diminished through men's intrusion. This is where the ways in which Beauvoir conceptualises sex and gender as enmeshed in a living body, rather than the idea of a biological body existing outside of its social meaning, joins with her understanding of our embodied self as always in the mode of 'becoming', to open up the possibilities for bringing the body back. It is here that we will turn in conclusion – to the potential of restoring a modality of embodiment which is lived as a united bodily-self, and the implications this has for theory and practice.

Notes

1 Direct quote: Alice
2 Direct quote: Gail
3 Direct quote: Bea
4 Direct quote: Sophie

References

Arp, K. (1995) 'Beauvoir's Concept of Bodily Alienation', in Simons, M. A. (ed.), *Feminist Interpretations of Simone de Beauvoir*, The Pennsylvania State University Press, pp. 161–178.

Bartky, S. L. (1990) *Femininity and Domination*, Routledge.

Bordo, S. (1989) 'The Body and the Reproduction of Femininity: A Feminist Appropriation of Foucault', in Jaggar, A. M., & Bordo, S. (eds), *Gender/Body/Knowledge: Feminist Reconstructions of Being and Knowing*, Rutgers University Press, pp. 13–33.

Beauvoir, S. d. (2011) *The Second Sex*, Borde, C., & Malovany-Chevallier, S. (transl.), Vintage.

Bourdieu, P. (1998) *Practical Reason: On the Theory of Action*, Stanford University Press.

Cahill, A. J. (2001) *Rethinking Rape*, Cornell University Press.

Coy, M. (2009) 'This Body Which is Not Mine: The Notion of the Habit Body, Prostitution and (Dis)Embodiment', *Feminist Theory*, 10 (1), pp. 61–75.

Crossley, N. (2001) 'The Phenomenological Habitus and its Construction', *Theory and Society*, 30, pp. 81–120.

Del Busso, L., & Reavey, P. (2013) 'Moving Beyond the Surface: a Poststructuralist Phenomenology of Young Women's Embodied Experiences in Everyday Life', *Psychology & Sexuality*, 4 (1), pp. 46–61.

Fanon, F. (2008) *Black Skin, White Masks*, Philcox, R. (transl.), Grove Press.

Foucault, M. (1979) *Discipline and Punish: The Birth of the Prison.* Sheridan, A. (transl.), Vintage.

Goffman, E. (1990) *The Presentation of Self in Everyday Life*, Penguin.

Gordon, M. T., & Riger, S. (1989) *The Female Fear: The Social Cost of Rape*, University of Illinois Press.

Heidegger, M. (1996) *Being and Time*, Stambaugh, J. (transl.), State University of New York Press.

Jeffner, S. (2000) *Different Space for Action: The Everyday Meaning of Young People's Perception of Rape.* Paper at ESS Faculty Seminar, University of North London, London, May, 2000.

Jordan, J. (1991) *Working Girls: Women in the New Zealand Sex Industry Talk to Jan Jordan*, Penguin.

Jordan, J. (2008) *Serial Survivors: Women's Narratives of Surviving Rape*, Federation Press.

Madriz, E. (1997). *Nothing Bad Happens to Good Girls: Fear of Crime in Women's Lives*, University of California Press.

McLeod, E. (1982) *Working Women: Prostitution Now*, Croom Helm.

Merleau-Ponty, M. (2002) *Phenomenology of Perception*, Smith, C. (transl.), Routledge.

Moran, D. (2011) 'Sartre's Treatment of the Body in Being and Nothingness: The "Double Sensation"', in Boulé, J. P., & O'Donohoe, B. (eds), *Jean-Paul Sartre: Mind and Body, Word and Deed*, Cambridge Scholars Publishing, pp. 9–26.

Orbach, S. (1978) *Fat is a Feminist Issue: A Self-Help Guide for Compulsive Eaters*, Berkley-Paddington.

'Perspective' (2001) in Pearsall, J. (ed.), *The New Oxford English Dictionary*, Oxford University Press.

Sartre, J. P. (2007) *Being and Nothingness*, Routledge.

Schepple, K., & Bart, P. (1983) 'Through Women's Eyes: Defining Danger in the Wake of Sexual Assault', *Journal of Social Issues*, 39 (2), pp. 63–80.

Smith, D. E. (1987) *The Everyday World as Problematic: A Feminist Sociology*, University of Toronto Press.

Tuerkheimer, D. (1997) 'Street Harassment as Sexual Subordination: The Phenomenology of Gender-Specific Harm', *Wisconsin Women's Law Journal*, 12, pp. 167–206.

Weiss, G. (2010). 'Can an Old Dog Learn New Tricks? Habitual Horizons in James, Bourdieu, & Merleau-Ponty', in Weiss, G. (ed.), *Intertwinings: Interdisciplinary Encounters with Merleau-Ponty*, SUNY Press.

Wise, S., & Stanley, L. (1987) *Georgie Porgie: Sexual Harassment in Everyday Life*, Pandora Press.

Young, I. M. (2005) *On Female Body Experience: 'Throwing Like a Girl' and Other Essays*, Oxford University Press.

This guy

walked down the street and gave me the full up and down
and just went 'nice' as he walked past.

This guy

said, really loud so everybody heard, something like can I fuck you?
I will often look at the ground.

Somebody from the other side of the street just yelled, hey mamacita.
I'll always sit next to a woman.
In the end we started running and he came banging on our front door.
I have responded in the past with like fuck off you pervert.

This guy

was like oh my God, look at your profile, it's so beautiful
I just have to take a picture.

This guy

was like I think you brought the bongos.
You just walk faster.

This big fat guy

just staring at me the whole time.
I am looking down, I never look at people.
He literally just came up to me and undid my top button.
I'm not going to cross the road, I live on this side of the road.
He started spitting at me.
He is checking my suitcase to see if there is any contraband
or any items that shouldn't be allowed through,
and he's chatting me up.
And then tried to kiss me.

This guy

was like oh give us a chip love.
I'd wear tights and a longer skirt.
He started whispering into my ear you're so sexy I want to have sex with you.
I walk with my key in my hand and then like between my fingers.
I must have been 7. And someone wound the window down and went wahay!
My decisions about how I look are related to this sexual danger.

This guy

walking past me just stopped,
stared out at me,
and then carried on walking.

I had someone wanking on the underground.
You have to text everyone to say you got home.
They started following us home, being a bit more intimidating.
I just block them out.
He was looking in quite an overtly sexual way, like a dirty sexual look.
I'll get my umbrella and have it as a stick just in case I get threatened.

And this guy was like are you alright darling?
And kept putting his hand on mine.
He was like 'hey where are you going tonight?'

                                                                              Slut.

He just did this horrible thing with his tongue.
I'll take trousers in my bag.
The guy walked outside, across the street, to try to take a picture of me.
I will ignore them, always.
He went to get his coat ready, as if he was going to flash me.
Just stepped out and groped my boob.

You turn into the street look which side has more men
and choose the other one
and then call somebody.

This guy had kind of walked past and looked me up and down.
I'll just ignore it and feel quite annoyed.
They then sent me a text message saying you're fit and you know it.
And then kissed me on the lips.

He absolutely came after me.

And I think that was probably the first time, from that point onwards,
constantly scanning for people
who would do you harm.

He started talking about football and was like 'oh
so does your boyfriend like football then?'
Just as he started to follow me a car came.
And he kept trying to engage me in conversation.
And then he pulled down his pants.
He raped me.

My thing is always when I get on the bus or public transport
right where are you going to sit?
He basically won't piss off for quite a while.
A car with a guy in it just kind of came onto the pavement.
He stood in my way.
He just kind of grabbed me.
They kept eyeing us up and down.
I'd tie my hair up for some reason.

One guy started saying, not hitting on me,
but just saying oh beautiful, beautiful girl
and he was walking with his little boy,
and it was 7 o'clock in the morning.

This man was following me.
He was obviously following me.
All like are you alright ladies, do you know where you're going?
Sometimes I'll walk back through a very scary place
and text on my phone saying where I am if anything happened to me
so I can just press send.

This man exposed himself to me.
They literally did a U-Turn to drive next to me.
And a guy just came next to me and started talking to me.
I used to sit in an empty carriage because I thought great
there's no one around.

He sat next to me and started chatting.
This guy who I was waiting for a train
and ended up inviting me to wherever it was
in Africa he was from.
He went in for the kiss.

He got a coin and threw it at me.
I was pulled off my bike by this guy.
He just shouted after me.
These two boys in a car wolf whistled.

                                        This guy, this guy, this guy

8   Inhabiting ourselves

Taking a feminist phenomenological approach to women's experiences of men's violence illuminates how, far from the trivialisation it is often afforded, the possibility and reality of men's intrusion forms a fundamental factor in how women understand and enact their embodied selfhood. Participants in this study have shown how the continuum of men's intrusive practices plays a key, and often unacknowledged, role in women's experience of their embodiment as contradictory and ambiguous – leading to the enactment of a habitual modality of alienated embodiment, alienating both body and world. This underlines the need for further theoretical work, grounded in empirical research, focused on developing a deeper understanding of the inter-relation between women's embodiment and men's violence against women and girls. Building a feminist phenomenology of violence against women provides a useful frame to do this, helping move towards an understanding that seeks to articulate the ways in which both are lived. There are benefits here in further working with the concept of our living body to complicate the division of the body-object as sex and the socialised body as gender; to better represent the living experience of embodied selfhood where the social is written into the material. This experience of our living body, like that of our dying body, represents a process, not an event, and crucially a process can be disrupted. Speaking in an interview on the twenty-fifth anniversary of the publication of *The Second Sex*, Simone de Beauvoir pointed towards this claiming that '[i]f you can check your habits, make it so that it's "natural" to have counterhabits, that's a big step' (Gerassi, 1976). It is this notion of counterhabits that uncovers possibilities for intervention; a way to inhabit ourselves.

Policy and practice

Examining the ordinary experiences of the continuum of men's intrusive practices, how these experiences are captured and given meaning through women's habitual modalities of embodiment, and what this then reveals of women's situated self, has implications across policy, research and activism on violence against women and girls. The finding that the possibility of men's stranger intrusion was lived as a reality for participants in public space suggests the importance of returning to the exploration of women's ordinary experiences of men's intrusion that was at the core of much early feminist work on violence against women and girls. In policy and legal frames, where experiences of intrusion in public space are acknowledged as important, it is still with a focus on criminal and criminalising behaviour – often with a view to increasing women's willingness to report intrusion to the police.[1] Reconnecting to the everyday highlights a benefit in bringing criminal and non-criminal practices back together when conceptualising messages around prevention or framing interventions for provision. For women in this study, men's intrusive practices were understood and experienced in relation to each other, as well as in relation to the living experience of the imminent potentiality of men's intrusion. Targeting intrusive practices (and intrusive men) as isolated or episodic is to miss how women and girls experience and make sense of them – in *relation* to each other. This opens up the possibility that campaigns that attempt, for example, to increase women's reporting of rape, would benefit from understanding how women experientially connect the continuum of men's intrusive practices, as the adjustments women make early in life in response to learning men's intrusion is ordinary has substantial implications for how women make sense of future experiences of sexual violence. Combined with this, such campaigns would be strengthened through drawing on Garner's (2016) work on gendered heritage to understand how, through learning that men's intrusion is interconnected and that its source lies in the female body, sexual violence comes to be lived as a women's inheritance – inevitable, unremarkable, given. Campaign messages would thus benefit from focusing on young women's experiences of ordinary forms of intrusion, aimed towards both young women and to older women through validating their historic experiences. Here the message is not solely about reporting such experiences, but about legitimating them as intrusions and reframing their source – from being located in the bodies of women and girls, to a grounding in the decisions of men and boys and how these are encouraged and endorsed by wider social structures. Such a shift in campaign messaging sits in tension with the dominant narratives available to understand men's stranger intrusion or 'street harassment', being threatening (and thus criminal so must be reported) or complimentary (and thus trivial so must be discounted), narratives that work to shape the stories that can be told both to others and to ourselves. These binary framings do not capture the complexities of women's habituated embodiments in public space, modalities of living our body that develop in response to early experiences and soon become embedded and naturalised. The shift then is part of a broader move towards a third framework for discussing the particular harms of men's stranger intrusion, and violence against women more broadly: freedom. The findings of this study have shown that women's freedom in relation to men's intrusion both relies on and is informed by the other two frameworks (criminal/trivial), as they are by it. The study has shown that intrusion impacts not solely on women's freedom of movement but, through drawing on the insights of existential-phenomenology, has revealed an impact on women's freedom to be in the self – the freedom to be embodied.

This opens up spaces in conceptual and theoretical work on violence against women. There is a need for further research to uncover more about the impact on and of women's freedom to be in the self. The focus for this study has been on the ordinary aspects of one form of men's intrusive practices, however there are unexplored possibilities in Beauvoir's concept of the situated bodily-self in relation to other forms across the continuum of men's violence and abuse. Both Eva Lundgren (1998) and Evan Stark (2009), for example, look at the impacts of men's intimate partner violence on women's ability to exercise their freedom, with Lundgren's discussion of the role of this violence in gendering the body particularly resonant with Beauvoir. This conceptualisation of the self as embodied freedom could extend feminist debates centred on conflicting accounts of women's agency and freedom, such as those on pornography and prostitution. The concept of 'situated agency' can be developed for these debates in relation to women's body forming a situation itself – one that both limits and expands our possibilities for action. In addition, a significant gap has been identified during the process of the research, from feminist phenomenological explorations of the body schema (Butler, 1990; Bartky, 1990; Weiss, 1999; Young, 2005) to perspectives in feminist psychology and psychoanalysis of the body image (Orbach, 2003, 2009; Griffin, 2012), in acknowledging the continuum of men's intrusive practices as an element in and through which women live their embodiment. Through men's intrusive practices women come to habitually live their body as a 'thing' to manipulate, control and regulate, rather than as an expression of their very beingness in the world. Here is where the terminology of intrusion assists in coming closer to the living experience and its impacts, intrusion not only onto but, crucially, into women's experience of their bodily-self. This has particular implications for theories of women's embodiment. Further research is needed to explore the connections between how women perceive our bodies (the body image), how we live our bodies (the body schema and habit body), and what this then means for our bodily-self, in relationship to the particular practices of men and a broader context of structural gender inequality. This also suggests that campaigning work on women's body image would benefit from engaging with women's experiences of violence against women, something recently begun in England (see GEO, 2014). A finding of this research has been that 'being' embodied for women is in tension with strategic responses to men's intrusion; women do not want to be their bodies if that embodiment is experienced as unsafe. There is thus a need to connect work being done to improve women's body image with feminist knowledge on men's violence and intrusion, alongside the need for a gendered understanding of both; where gender is understood as a living relation (McNay, 2004) and attention is turned to how the bodily practices of men have embodied consequences for women. The findings of this project, particularly some of the detail about how, where and in what ways men intrude on and into women's bodily selves, reveal a great need for more in-depth research with men about their practices – to explore the ordinary behaviours and experiences of men in relation to violence against women, as well as their habituated embodiments, where the structures of the gender order suggest these would most likely develop in relation to other men rather than to women.[2]

Habits of resistance

The research has also highlighted the need for an acknowledgment and reframing of the safety work women are incorporating into their daily being-in-the-world. In bringing to conscious awareness the connections between habituated modalities of living the body and our experiences of men's intrusion in our past, present and those we project forward, we can develop the understanding that modes can be changed; intervening on our habits to restore the bodily-self. This notion of restoration draws directly on the conceptualisation of Beauvoir and Merleau-Ponty where the body is a situation; it is not that 'the self' is posited in the body, and this body is then situated in the world – our bodies are ourselves, our very means of having a world at all. As has been seen, the continuum of men's intrusive practices encourages women to experience their bodies as a thing – distant and distinct from, rather than as a living manifestation of, their desires and intentions – however it may not be that a restoration uniting self, body and world, is desired or desirable in all contexts by all women. Consciousness-raising then plays a role here in providing an open space to interrogate how our modalities of embodiment arise from a situation of men's intrusion, rather than to further entrench a feeling of the body-for-others, often seen in well-meaning advice suggesting 'the right' response to intrusion. As argued by Fiona Wilson: '[w]hile harassment is always about power it is also about defiance. Women have learned self-protective behaviour and this should be recognized as a positive expression of their strength and resistance' (2000: 1092). Self-protective in this context includes the measures taken to protect the concept of oneself as a free subject (including the embodied habits of forgetting, minimising, denying), rather than solely the protection of the physical body often meant by the terms self-protection and self-defence.

There is thus space to reconceptualise women's bodily alienation into a strategy of resistance, where the agency underpinning such a strategy is acknowledged as situated. The ways in which participants spoke about embodied, experiential connections between and across the practices of men's intrusion highlights how their habit bodies were informed by both their own history of personal acts in particular situations as well as an awareness of the continuum of sexual violence as part of the collective 'legacy' of female embodiment. In such a context, distancing the body as a thing to be controlled and acted on rather than as our self, acting through, means the self is no longer exposed; the embodied self is protected through adopting a mode of alienation towards the unsafe body. This modality of embodiment includes our sense of being our bodies, and our sense of being *in* the world – with both of these impacting on the situation out of which our freedom arises. For this study, public space was focused on as a context; however, more work could be done building from the conceptual work here to explore women's bodily modes in 'private' spaces, to examine how they evolve and what modalities of embodiment are habituated. In addition to this, if, as Weiss (1999) claims, our bodily habits derive their significance from the situation out of which they have emerged and within which they are expressed, then exploring the differences and commonalities between women's bodily habits in response to men's practices also offers possibilities to illuminate differences and commonalities in the situation of women in given socio-historical locations. Further research on points of overlap and divergence amongst women's modalities of embodiment in relation to violence against women is needed. Accepting both the diversity and unity of women's experiences is central in attempts to inform and activate a movement for social change in that, as claimed by Rosi Braidotti (1993: 8) it 'seals a pact among women'. The pact here does not collapse differences, rather, if used correctly, it can become 'a foundation stone' allowing feminist standpoints to be articulated (Braidotti, 1993: 8).[3] Beauvoir's notion of 'situation' is useful for such a project, able to illuminate embodied and experiential differences between women, and provide a way of exploring the harms and impacts of men's practices onto and into women's bodily selves, without reducing female embodiment to an effect of men's behaviours and structural processes. Conceptualising the continuum of men's intrusive practices as a constitutive part of women's situation is not to flatten variations among women or to posit a single situation which all women share. Rather it is to acknowledge that men's intrusion is lived as part of the 'field of possibilities' (Butler, 1986: 45) of being a woman in public – a field within which our agency is situated. Both the practice and the possibility of men's stranger intrusion structure a material, experiential reality that is a formative part of women's situation, with templates of risk and safety work becoming embodied, naturalised and normalised.

There is an implication for 'street harassment' campaigns, including the growth in visibility through online forums – an implication that can also be applied to notions of feminist self-defence, to be discussed more fully below. Online activist platforms such as *Everyday Sexism* and *Hollaback!* are incredibly successful in giving women a space to talk about the intrusions they experience. However, for women who participated in the form of feminist consciousness-raising here, the level of their hidden labour was revealed in a way uncaptured in activism focusing on the experience of intrusion itself. This is due to the pre-emptive quality of most safety work – the finding that the possibility of men's intrusion is lived as an embodied reality for women. There is thus a tension between sharing women's stories in order to raise awareness and help combat the normalisation of men's intrusion in public space, and challenging the habitualised projection of frequency of men's intrusion in public space – a projection that may be leading some women to alienate their body and world in order to hold onto a sense of self. This tension is continued in self-defence programmes that focus on the body solely in terms of its role as a defence to men's intrusion, continuing the experience of the body as barrier – a stiffening against the aim to be enacted producing the 'inhibited intentionality' of Young – rather than reconceptualising to a mode of moving through the body. There is a need for work with women and girls to bring the experience of their embodiment as a capacity more regularly into awareness, beginning through this to reincorporate it into their everyday being. For Stevi Jackson, it is not enough to reveal the contexts whereby women's bodily-selves are acted on:

We need also to account for subjectivity and agency; for patterns of gendered interaction in everyday life as well as the institutional hierarchies within which they take place; the ways in which such interaction is endowed with, and shaped by, the meanings it has for participants; the micro levels at which power is deployed and resisted, as well as the macro level of systematic domination.

(Jackson, 2001: 286)

There is thus a need for dedicated projects to raise awareness of the safety work women are habitually practicing, rather than only focusing on the intrusion they are experiencing; a focus that inadvertently is reifying the position of women as acted on, not actors. The history of silence in women speaking about their safety work, about that constant negotiation of the right amount of panic, has meant that women's successful resistance can be discounted, even in feminist activism. The traditional frame used to explain the decline of men's stranger intrusions on women as they age is testament to this. Taught to locate the cause of men's intrusive practices in the externality or sexual value of their bodies, women often believe this generational change has to do with the aging body – no longer seen as 'in our prime', we are no longer treated as sexually desirable by unknown men. For some participants here there was a pleasure in this increasing invisibility, for some there was an unanticipated feeling of loss, but all located the source for the decline in their bodies as acted on, not in their embodied capacities, an acting through. This study however found that across the life course, women develop complex embodied strategies to limit the amount of intrusion they experienced – which may not be the same as the amount practiced – skills well honed, habituated and invisiblised. What if, as women age, *they* limit the intrusion they experience through the strategies they've embodied; what if our safety work is routinely successful and women are habitually intervening? We know such work does not, can not, always accomplish the ends it sets, and these are the only times currently counted. Developing projects to raise awareness of the range and extent of women's strategies for coping with, avoiding and resisting men's intrusions, strategies lived as forms of bodily know-how, may help us to reconnect with our embodied self as a capacity. They could also be used to challenge campaigns focused on giving women 'safety advice' for rape prevention, highlighting the many ways in which women already daily factor in safety work, and how much of this involves a restriction of freedom. Once our ordinary resistance is brought forward, we can reclaim an agency situated in our bodies. From here we can practice conscious intervention on any bodily habits we want to adjust.

Habits of restoration

The possibilities for changing the relationship to one's bodily-self, for those who want to claim an experience of the body as the self and the world as our own, thus lie in the possibilities of developing habits of restoration. Habituated practices have both positive and negative aspects, providing us with a sense of familiarity alongside reinforcing bodily practices that may no longer be useful or necessary (Weiss, 2010). Beauvoir's theory of the situated self in a constant mode of becoming, provides an opening for exploring how our relationship to our bodily-self can be consciously restored. The findings here have demonstrated that habitual modes of living the body generate particular practices, however it is also true that repeating practices over time, generates new habits and creates possibilities for restoring an embodiment where the body and world is acted through. Using Beauvoir's theory of ambiguity as underpinning women's situation, enables a conceptualisation of the living experience of men's intrusion that keeps the uneasy balance of the impacts of intrusion for women's embodiment alongside space for our situated freedom and agency. This means that we can hold both the ways men's intrusive practices may impact on women's embodiments, and also our abilities to act within and beyond this. Merleau-Ponty maintains the temporality of the embodied self and thus of our habits. As a grouping of lived-through meanings, the bodily-self as an 'I can' has the power of continuously modifying and renewing itself. The acquisition of habit demonstrates our power of absorbing new meanings, showing we have 'assimilated a fresh core of significance' (Merleau-Ponty, 2002: 169) and that we are exercising our body's abilities to continually discover more possibilities for meaning, expression, and exploration of our world. In adapting the concept of a gendered habitus to women's embodiment, Ruyters (2012) also argues that women can practice a new script for bodily comportment through conscious intervention on our bodily habits, supported by the work of McCaughey (1997) and Ann Cahill (2001). Such possibilities were only begun for this study, focusing on the first stage of raising awareness, however even here the possibilities of restoration were realised for some.

The process of identifying in conversation with another the embodied consequences of an early experience of men's intrusion led to Cathy evaluating her habitual mode of alienation in public spaces and the conscious decision to not only change this, but to make public the intrusion behind it.

> A few weeks after we met and I was on the train and this guy got on and he was standing there, looking at me, looking around and this other woman got on and sat next to him and she was patient with him. And I just, I was not in a happy mood that day and I saw him looking at me so I just looked back, not like don't mess with me but very neutral and he went to the woman 'you're nice, you're nice you are. But not her, look at her, she's not nice. She's not nice'. And I just went, 'you know what? I got molested at 9 years old, I got on a bus and everyone in this carriage they think it doesn't happen but it happens all the fucking time'. I just went ballistic and he was like (draws in breath) 'sorry I didn't know'. And everyone was like, 'oh!' And I was really shook up, I was really upset but I thought I'm not going to move, I'm going to hold my ground. I'd just basically said look at me, I was molested. I'm embarrassed now, I was so embarrassed but I just thought this

has to be done. I've done something right. I've just made it public ... it was an exorcism. But it wouldn't have happened if we hadn't of had our talk.

(Cathy)

Cathy firmly locates the change she experienced in how she was embodied in public space to her experience of participating in the research conversations – a process she claims as 'ours'.

Sophie, who reported in the previous chapter that she was unhappy with how she used her external appearance as a defence against men's intrusion, learned during the notebook process that how she was living her body was based on her habitual maintenance of external awareness, rather than solely on men's practices.

It's only happened one or two times the whole time and I've come to the realisation that actually people aren't looking at me. I'm looking at them. And that's been a massive thing because I was convinced everyone was staring at me ... and realising that has been really liberating it's like, right, I'm going to wear that top that I want to wear. And it's not like it's been a massive change, you can see I'm still in my black and baggy jeans combo, but at home in [city] I've definitely been rocking out some outfits that I've had and never worn. I bought this amazing dress when I was in Ghana. It's bright blue, tie-dyed, halterneck and it's just so cool and I would never wear it and now I wear it and I feel great in it, and there's other outfits too. I just feel ownership of my body and I feel a bit more at peace with it all having done this ... I feel excited.

(Sophie)

This marks an entry point for future work on recognising our habitual ways of being in the world and the possibilities for adopting different modes of embodiment or a relationship to the bodily-self whereby we can be embodied. For habit is not simply a mechanical response to external or internal stimulus but rather is a form of embodied and practical understanding, a bodily know-how which shapes the way we make sense of our environment and enables us to inhabit our world. We can use this process to our advantage and embody a different learning for ourselves and others, a learning of women's bodies as strong and capable. This adds to the growing dialogue seeking to reclaim feminist self-defence (see McCaughey, 1997; Cahill, 2009; Seith & Kelly, 2003). Where such work can be seen as sitting in tension with notions of victim-blaming, feminist self-defence is fundamental to peeling back the ways in which men's intrusive practices have created embodiments for women marked by an experience of alienation and limited capacity. For Ann Cahill (2009: 367) it is that '[f]eminist self-defense courses offer a different way of living one's body', a way of naturalising the 'counterhabits' of Beauvoir. There is a note of caution here, suggested by Nicola Gavey; heralding the importance of feminist self-defence is not new, in fact 'we could say it has been tried and faltered' (2009: 116). This study suggests possibilities for a reworked approach, focused on the acknowledgment of women's safety work. For some, like Sophie and Cathy, the recognition alone of their hidden labour may begin to change their habitual modes of embodiment. Once such modes are made conscious women can choose to intervene, and this is where a reframed feminist self-defence enters. The subtle shift suggested is from a defensive to an offensive starting position, an acting out and through for our own intentions rather than in response to the actions of others, and as such McCaughey's (1997) terminology of 'physical feminism' may be a better fit.[4] Situating such work in this way, could help expand the practice beyond its role in rape prevention to a place in campaigns on women's body image and mental well-being: encouraging women to experience their bodily capacities – capacities that express the self and extend out into the world – a campaign to help women live their embodied self in a habitual mode of 'I can'.

Inhabiting ourselves

This book has detailed how men's intrusion impacted on women's experience of their embodied selfhood, examining participants experiences of the continuum, alongside exploring the habituated, often pre-reflective modes of embodiment women described as adopting in public spaces. Where Beauvoir directly addressed such intrusion,[5] she held it as constituting a uniquely gendered 'weight'; a heaviness that, over time, may adopt the illusion of the ordinary. For Merleau-Ponty this is a process of bodily habituation that in turn informs perception, impacting on our experience of the present.

> I have made it my abode, that this past, though not a fate, has at least a specific weight and is not a set of events over there, at a distance from me, but the atmosphere of my present. The rationalist's dilemma: either the free act is possible, or it is not – either the event originates in me or is imposed on me from outside, does not apply to our relations with the world and with our past. Our freedom does not destroy our situation, but gears itself to it: as long as we are alive, our situation is open.
>
> (Merleau-Ponty, 2002: 514)

This, then, was the theoretical starting point: to investigate the weight of men's intrusion identified by Beauvoir alongside Merleau-Pontian theorisation of how the weight of the past is lived through our bodies. What was found was that men's intrusive practices changed women's emerging sense of a bodily-self both before and during their adolescence, impacting on their experience of their embodied selfhood. Examining these experiences, not as isolated episodes but rather in terms of the meanings participants placed on them in relation to other experiences of intrusion, revealed that experiential importance lay not solely in the content of these intrusions but in the ways in which women took them into and lived them through their embodiment. An ambiguous embodiment was revealed: with female embodiment experienced as both a source and constraint of woman's freedom. This modality of embodiment is reminiscent of Young's (2005) 'inhibited intentionality', where she found that girls experience a thrown ball as coming at them whereas boys will reach out to take the ball. It also corresponds to Eva Lundgren's (2009) concept of 'life space', whereby the motivations of men who are violent towards their partners are theorised as based in part in the desire to set limits on aspects of women's life space. Here, however, the limits were found to not be set by particular men, but by women – most often in adolescence – in response to a situation where men's intrusion is understood as routine and compulsory. Following this, notions of being embodied for women became inextricably connected to tension and discomfort. In an attempt to resolve this conflict, participants spoke about adopting an early relationship to the body where a sense of subjectivity is experienced through alienating the body and taking it up as an object to be acted on: a modality of embodiment marked by *using* one's body instead of *being* one's body.

In considering how to translate the framework behind this in a way that holds the complexity yet is readily understandable, the analogy employed by Sara Heinämaa of femininity as being like a musical theme may be useful. For Heinämaa femininity is 'not determined by its earlier performances but is living and evolving in the environment created by them' (Heinämaa, 1999: 124). This helps to capture some of what has been revealed of the living experience of 50 women's accounts of men's stranger intrusions, and the impacts for their bodily selves. Similar to the conception Milan Kundera (1999) makes of the novel, the continuum of men's intrusive practices can be conceptualised as a musical theme with variations running through the lives of women, a way we 'tune in' to our world. The motif is established for most women during adolescence, though some women in this study experienced rape and other forms of contact sexual abuse and men's intrusion in their early childhood, and some could not remember experiences of men's intrusive practices before their early adulthood. It is embedded through personal experiences, experiences of family and friends, wider experiences of other women reported in the media and cultural narratives of women's particular vulnerability to rape, and comes to be embodied – lived as part of women's bodily-self.

Our bodily-self thus is not wholly determined by its earlier realisations, but rather, like a melody, past experiences are experienced as habitual and familiar. This links to Merleau-Ponty's description of the body as comparable to a work of art, 'a nexus of living meanings' (Merleau-Ponty, 2002: 175). Freedom exists here but it is a situated freedom, bound by the situation of female embodiment and what that embodiment means. Uncovering our habituated embodiments, learning the tune we carry, is to recognise the weight of our past and its impact on our present. It is to reveal those actions we perform for a purpose, 'counted the most understandable' (Nietzsche, 2003: 89), but the least understood. Acknowledging this weight, both personally and collectively, is to create possibilities for letting it go.

[T]he future remains wide open … [t]he free woman is just being born.

(Beauvoir, 2011: 767)

Notes

1 Seen recently in London, England with the campaign 'Project Guardian' a joint initiative by the British Transport Police, Transport for London, Metropolitan Police and the City of London Police, launched in 2013.
2 For the beginnings of this see Bird, 1996; Quinn, 2002.
3 Simone de Beauvoir was aware of the ways in which feminist activism and research on men's violence could work to mobilise women across different situations and standpoints, pointing in her later years to its revolutionary potential. Interviewed in 1976 by Susan Brison, Beauvoir speaks of both the 'anti-rape' and the 'domestic violence' movements as potentially fulfilling the need of diverse feminisms to 'find issues all women can be interested in and, on that basis, make them understand that their problems are experienced by all women, not only them, and give them a sense of solidarity' (Brison, 2003: 197).
4 Though stressing the essential fundamental importance of the physicality and embodiment of change, the use of 'physical feminism' is not without its problems. The term may limit understanding of the depth and range of work contained in feminist self-defence programmes, including the ways in which such programmes seek psychological, emotional, attitudinal and social change, alongside teaching embodied habits of resistance and restoration. Claudia da Silva's work, continued by Richard Chipping at the London Centre for Personal Safety, is an excellent example here.

5   Even little things for example: the streets belong to everyone. But in fact, for a young woman, it doesn't matter if she's pretty or ugly, walking down the street can be an ordeal after 8 or 9 at night, or even during the day. Men will follow her, bother her, to such an extent that she'll prefer to go home. If you tell a man that he'll smile, act surprised, say 'I don't do that'.... He doesn't realise what a weight it is for a woman to always feel like she's in danger.

(Beauvoir, 1975)

References

Bartky, S. L. (1990) *Femininity and Domination*, Routledge.
Beauvoir, S. d. (1975) 'Pourquoi je suis féministe', Questionnaire. (J.-L. Servan-Schreiber, Interviewer) www.youtube.com/watch?v=W6hmVO7t_Bs [accessed 4 April 2011].
Bird, S. R. (1996) 'Welcome to the Men's Club: Homosociality and the Maintenance of Hegemonic Masculinity', *Gender & society*, 10 (2), pp. 120–132.
Braidotti, R. (1993) 'Embodiment, Sexual Difference, and the Nomadic Subject', *Hypatia*, 8 (1), pp. 1–13.
Brison, S. J. (2003) 'Beauvoir and Feminism: Interview and Reflections', in Card, C. (ed.), *The Cambridge Companion to Simone de Beauvoir*, Cambridge University Press, pp. 189–207.
Butler, J. (1986) 'Sex and Gender in Simone de Beauvoir's Second Sex', *Yale French Studies*, 72, pp. 35–49.
Butler, J. (1990) *Gender Trouble: Feminism and the Subversion of Identity*, Routledge.
Cahill, A. J. (2001) *Rethinking Rape*, Cornell University Press.
Garner, M. (2016) *Conflicts, Contradictions and Commitments: Men Speak about the Sexualisation of Culture*, Doctoral Thesis, London Metropolitan University.
Gavey, N. (2009) 'Fighting Rape', in Heberle, R. J., & Grace, V. (eds), *Theorizing Sexual Violence*, Routledge, pp. 96–124.
GEO (2014) *The Watched Body: Gender Roles, Body Image and Public Intrusions*, Government Equalities Office, www.gov.uk/government/publications/gender-stereotypes-academic-seminar-report [accessed 12 December 2015].

Gerassi, J. (1976) 'The Second Sex 25 Years Later: An Interview with Simone de Beau-voir', *Society* 13 (2), pp. 79–85, Blunden A. (ed.), www.marxists.org/reference/subject/ethics/de-beauvoir/1976/interview.htm [accessed 12 October 2012].

Griffin, M. (2012) 'Ruptured Feedback Loops: Body Image/Schema and Food Journaling Technologies', *Feminism & Psychology*, 22 (3), pp. 376–387.

Heinämaa, S. (1999) 'Simone de Beauvoir's Phenomenology of Sexual Difference', *Hypatia*, 14 (4), pp. 114–132.

Jackson, S. (2001) 'Why a Materialist Feminism is (Still) Possible—and Necessary', *Women's Studies International Forum*, 24 (3), pp. 283–293.

Kundera, M. (1999) *The Book of Laughter and Forgetting*, Harper Perennial Modern Classics

Lundgren, E. (1998) 'The Hand that Strikes and Comforts: Gender Construction and the Tension Between Body and Soul', in Dobash, R. E., & Dobash, R. P. (eds), *Rethinking Violence Against Women*, Sage, pp. 169–198.

Lundgren, E. (2009) 'Speech at the Arctic Women Conference: The Same Violence – or Absent Violence', Appendix 5 of Engman, E., & Hedberg, M. (eds), *Arctic Women Against Men's Violence*. Nordic Council of Ministers, pp. 53–60.

McCaughey, M. (1997) *Real Knockouts: The Physical Feminism of Women's Self-Defense*, NYU Press.

McNay, L. (2004) 'Agency and Experience: Gender as a Lived Relation', *The Sociological Review*, 52 (2), pp. 173–190.

Merleau-Ponty, M. (2002) *Phenomenology of Perception*, Smith, C. (transl.), Routledge.

Nietzsche, F. W. (2003) *Daybreak: Thoughts on the Prejudices of Morality*, Clark, M., & Leiter, B. (eds), Hollingdale, R. (transl.), Cambridge University Press.

Orbach, S. (2003) 'Part I: There is No Such Thing as a Body', *British Journal of Psycho-therapy*, 20 (1), pp. 3–16.

Orbach, S. (2009) *Bodies*, Profile.

Quinn, B. A. (2002) 'Sexual Harassment and Masculinity the Power and Meaning of "Girl Watching"', *Gender & Society*, 16 (3), pp. 386–402.

Ruyters, M. (2012) *Vulnerable Bodies and Gendered Habitus: The Prospects for Trans-forming Exercise*, Doctoral Thesis, RMIT University.

Seith, C., & Kelly, L. (2003) *Achievements Against the Grain: Self-Defence Training for Women and Girls in Europe*, Child and Woman Abuse Studies Unit, London Metro-politan University.

Stark, E. (2009) 'Rethinking Coercive Control', *Violence Against Women*, 15 (12), pp. 1509–1525.

Weiss, G. (1999) *Body Images: Embodiment as Intercorporeality*, Routledge.

Weiss, G. (2010). 'Can an Old Dog Learn New Tricks? Habitual Horizons in James, Bourdieu, and Merleau-Ponty', in Weiss, G. (ed.), *Intertwinings: Interdisciplinary Encounters with Merleau-Ponty*, SUNY Press.

Wilson, F. (2000) 'The Subjective Experience of Sexual Harassment: Cases of Students', *Human Relations*, 53 (8), pp. 1081–1097.

Young, I. M. (2005) *On Female Body Experience: 'Throwing Like a Girl' and Other Essays*, Oxford University Press.

Afterword

I had a nice chat once with this really sweet Turkish guy
who got on the bus at Shoreditch,
and we had a nice chat about his job as a Graphic Designer,
then he asked me to wake him up at Stockwell
and that was it.

You need to find a version of the world you can be in.

Index

Page numbers in *italics* denote tables, those in **bold** denote figures.